NEW YORK:

A Guide To Information And Reference Sources

by

Manuel D. Lopez

The Scarecrow Press, Inc.
Metuchen, N.J., & London
1980

Library of Congress Cataloging in Publication Data

Lopez, Manuel D
  New York, a guide to information and reference sources.

  Includes indexes.
  1. New York (State)--Bibliography. 2. New York
(City)--Bibliography. I. Title.
Z1317.L66 [F119]   016.9747   80-18634
ISBN 0-8108-1326-2

The

Tr
Wa

Au
Su

CONTENTS

PART I: NEW YORK STATE

iii

INTRODUCTION

For the individual investigating any aspect of New York State's cultural, economic, political, or social life, this classified, selective, annotated bibliography of over one thousand information and reference resources will, I hope, be useful. Foreign language materials, dissertations, and theses are excluded; entries are generally limited to books, serials, and government publications, with periodical articles representing less than one percent of the citations. Although not intended to be inclusive or comprehensive, the purpose is to provide access to the desired data. Consequently, the availability of the information source, if it has an index, bibliographies, or other reader aids, and the extent of the published literature on a topic were all factors in the decisions concerning inclusion.

This bibliography has two main sections: Part I, New York State; Part II, New York City, which are not mutually exclusive. Though New York City is not the state capital, it is a world city/center for many businesses, activities, and professions, and also incorporates many facets of our national life. Consequently, any consideration of a New York topic must consider aspects of state and city interaction. The division into two sections is a matter of reader convenience. However, there are a percentage of titles, inclusion of which in one category rather than another could provide the basis for endless debate. Admittedly, these decisions reflect the compiler's own view of the subject and as such remain his sole responsibility. The subject index, the cross-references, and detailed table of contents are designed to compensate for any resulting confusion.

Within the categories of the classified arrangement, the entries are cited according to the internal logic of the topics: from the general to the specific, the current to the retrospective, chronologically, or simply alphabetically by author. A brief note at the head of each category explains the arrangement.

Often within a category, due to limitations of space, only a restricted number of entries could be cited, thus indicating representative authors, types of organizations, or forms of publications. For example, in the category <u>Associations, Societies, Academies,</u> references were selected to illustrate the subject range of such New York organizations. Any attempt to list all New York associations and societies would require a separate publication.

The Author Index lists all corporate bodies and individuals who were creatively and/or intellectually responsible for the cited work. Those individuals that contributed prefaces, introductions, and "special features" are also included. The Subject Index expands and complements the topical arrangement of each section by providing access not only to the annotations but also to the content of the cited materials. The Subject Index is supplemented by an extensive system of cross-references.

Acknowledgments

It is with pleasure that I acknowledge my debt to Miss Anna May Lilly, University Library, State University of New York at Albany (another "Yorker" by choice), who without reservation shared with me her enthusiasm for and extensive knowledge of New York State, its people, history, and contributions to our national life. I am also indebted to all those anonymous interlibrary loan librarians throughout the country who so accurately and efficiently provided me with hundreds of volumes.

I am delighted to be able to publicly express my thanks to those individuals in the Interlibrary Loan unit of Lockwood Memorial Library, State University of New York at Buffalo, who with such good grace endured my handwriting and seemingly endless requests: Ms. Rebecca Kroll, unit head, and her staff, Ms. Colleen M. Hayes, Ms. Carol Ann Clemente, Ms. Mary Claire Burg, and Ms. Lillian Stanley.

Manuel D. Lopez
Buffalo, New York
May 1979

BIOGRAPHY
(retrospective arrangement)

1. Who's who in New York (City and State). 1st- 1904-
   New York: Who's who publications, 1904.
   Inclusion is based upon prominence and effectiveness in civil, commercial, economic, industrial,
   military, professional, and political affairs.

2. The Men of New York: a collection of biographies and
   portraits of citizens of the Empire State prominent in
   business, professional, social and political life during
   the last decade of the nineteenth century. Buffalo:
   G. E. Matthews, 1898. 2 v.
   Vol. 1: Biographies of those living in the western
   section of the state. Vol. 2: Biographies of those
   living in the rest of the state; arranged by sections:
   Manhattan, Eastern, Genesee, etc. Each volume has
   its own alphabetic index and volume two has a synop-
   tical index of the set. Brief data on each biographee.
   With few exceptions, all biographees were living in
   1896 and 1897.

3. Encyclopaedia of contemporary biography of New York.
   Illustrated. New York: Atlantic publishing and en-
   graving, 1875-1885. 6 v. Port.
   Inclusion was based upon success in one's chosen
   career, contributions made to the advancement of the
   state's welfare and "personal worthiness." Each has
   its own name index.

4. Biographical directory of the State of New York, 1900.
   New York: Biographical Directory Company, 1900.
   567 p.
   Brief sketches of some twelve thousand living (on
   January 1, 1900) business and professional men.

SEE ALSO 63, 72, 73, 75, 119, 295, 315, 348, 462, 465,
486, 522, 524, 638, 721, 841, 875.

BIBLIOGRAPHY
(general to specific)

5. Research and publications in New York State history.
New York (State).   Office of State History.   Albany,
1968/69- annual.
Previously printed in New York History for sixteen
years, this bibliography of books, articles and work
in progress has a classified arrangement: architecture
and the arts, biography, cities and town, counties,
New York City, economic life, education, government
and politics, military affairs, religion and churches,
Indians, statewide, and miscellaneous studies.   Ex-
cludes, with qualifications, genealogical publications,
juvenile literature, audio-visual aids, narrative of re-
cent events, reprints, etc.

6. Clum, Audna T.   New York in books; a bibliography for
junior and senior high schools.   Albany: University
of the State of New York, State Education Dept.
Bureau of Secondary Curriculum Development, 1960.
26 p.
Books, pamphlets, and government publications arranged in categories of Reference, History, Indians,
Government, Folklore, Biography and Fictional Biography, New York in Adult Fiction, Regional materials, Pamphlets and Periodicals; only a small percentage of the entries are annotated.

7. New York (State).   Division of Secondary Education.
New York in books, a bibliography for junior and
senior high schools.   Albany: University of the State
of New York Press, 1954.   16 p.
A selective list with brief annotations, primarily
for secondary school students; however, adults will
also find entertaining and informative items listed in
the New York in Adult Fiction, Reference and the New
York History sections.   Includes lists of New York
State periodicals and pamphlets.

SEE ALSO 329, 331, 506, 507.

Government Publications
(current to retrospective)

8. New York (State). State Library, Albany. A checklist
   of official publications of the State of New York. 1-
   Oct. 1947- monthly.
   Listed alphabetically by issuing agency, thus pro-
   viding something of a subject approach.
   Supplemented by:

   New York (State). State Library, Albany. A checklist
   of official publications of the State of New York: Author Index, Vol. 1-23, 1947-December, 1969. Albany: University of the State of New York, New York
   State Library, 1970.

   Dictionary catalog of official publications of the State
   of New York, Dec. 1973- September, 1976. Albany:
   University of the State of New York, New York State
   Library, 1977.

9. Moore, Kay K. A checklist and index for the University of the State of New York bulletins, numbers 255-
   1094, June 1902 to June 1936. Albany: University
   of the State of New York, 1938. 369 p. (University
   of the State of New York: bulletin, 1152).
   Lists the bulletins with full bibliographic information plus necessary descriptive notes. Authors, titles,
   subjects and personal names, indexes.

10. Hasse, Adelaide. Index of economic material in docu-
    ments of the state of the United States: New York,
    1789-1904. Prepared for the Department of Econom-
    ics and Sociology of the Carnegie Institute of Washing-
    ton. Washington: Carnegie Institution of Washington,
    1907. 553 p.
    Pt. 1: Citations to general sources of information,
    indexes, and other reference materials relating to
    New York State documents. Pt. 2: Alphabetic ar-
    rangements of topics limited to the contents of reports
    of legislative committees, administrative officers,
    special commissions, and the messages of governors.
    Citations under topic headings are chronological and
    have full bibliographic data. The term "economic"
    has been broadly defined concerning materials in-
    cluded in this reference work.

Manuscripts and Documents
(current to retrospective; general to specific)

11. New York. State Library, Albany. Manuscript and History Section. Official document book, New York State Freedom Train. Albany: New York State Freedom Train Commission, 1950. 72 p.

"... It shall be the duty of the commission to initiate ... the creation of a New York State freedom train to provide for the exhibition throughout the state of original documents, manuscripts and other historical materials preserved in the archives of the state library or in any other libraries or sources within or without the state, reflecting the traditions of library and freedom and the historical heritage of the people of the state...." (Session Laws of New York, 1948, Chapter 659)

The Freedom Train, six railroad cars painted gold and bright blue with the New York State seal on their sides (three cars for documents exhibits) was put into commission January 26, 1949. The documents (84) that were exhibited are reprinted here without comment and have only identifying dates and factual exposition delineating New York State's contribution to the evolution of American freedom.

12. Historical records survey. New York (State). Guide to depositories of manuscript collections in New York State (exclusive of New York City). Prepared by the Historical records survey, Division of community service programs, Work projects administration. Albany, 1941. 509 p. Index: 357-509.

Detailed descriptions of manuscript collections in 226 locations within New York State. These collections, located in the libraries of cities, towns, villages, colleges and universities, and those of historical societies, were conservatively estimated to contain over 10,000,000 pieces. Included are account books, diaries, journals, ledgers, records of businesses and organizations (Y.M.C.A.), land records, etc. Arrangement is by geographic location, then by institution.

13. New York (State). Secretary of state. Calendar of historical manuscripts in the office of the secretary of state, Albany, New York. Ed. by E. B. O'Callaghan. Albany: Weed, Parsons, 1865. 2 v.

Vol. 1 reprinted: Calendar of Dutch historical manuscripts in the Office of the Secretary of State, Albany,
New York, 1630-1664, by Edmund B. O'Callaghan.
Vol. 1: Calendar of Land Papers list the original
Dutch records for the period 1630 to 1664. Includes
the Register of the Provincial Secretary, Council Minutes, Correspondence, Ordinances, Fort Orange Records, Writs of Appeal, Curacao Papers, Delaware Papers, Patents and Deeds. Vol. 2: Calendar of Historical Manuscript for the period 1664 to the Revolution. Concerned with executive action, that of the
Governor and his council as reflected in Letters,
Claims, Petitions, etc.

14. Documents relative to the colonial history of the State
of New York. Albany: Weed, Parsons, 1853-1887.
15 v.
Vol. 1-10: Documents relating to the colonial history of the State of New York: procured in Holland,
England, and France (Vol. 1-2: Holland documents,
1856-58; Vol. 3-8: London documents, 1853-57; Vol.
9-10: Paris documents, 18-5-58). Vol. 11: General
index to Vol. 1-10. Vol. 12: Documents relating to
the history of the Dutch and Swedish settlements on
the Delaware River.... Vol. 13: Documents relating to the history and settlements of the towns along
the Hudson and Mohawk Rivers (except Albany) from
1630 to 1684. Vol. 14: Documents relating to the
history of the early colonial settlements principally
on Long Island. Vol. 15: New York State archives.
Documents are translated into English and chronologically arranged.

15. New York (Colony) Council. Minutes of the Executive
council of the province of New York.... Vol. 1- Ed.
by Victor Hugo Paltsits, state historian. Albany:
State of New York, 1910.
Covers the period 1668 to 1673. The annotations
of the Minutes are derived from original manuscripts
and engrossed records in State archives. Secondary
sources are also used to provide data concerning
individuals and incidents.

16. Van Laer, Arnold J. F., comp. New York historical
manuscripts: Dutch. Translated and annotated by
Arnold J. F. Van Laer. Edited with added indexes
by Kenneth Scott and Kenn Stryker-Rodda. Baltimore:

Genealogical Pub. Co.

Vol. 1: Register of the Provincial Secretary,
1638-1642. Vol. 2: Register of the Provincial Secretary, 1642-1647. Vol. 3: Register of the Provincial Secretary, 1648-1660. Vol. 4: Council minutes,
1638-1649.

The registers contain bonds, court depositions,
deeds, leases, and other legal documents. The Council Minutes record the activities of the executive,
legislative and judicial branches.

17. New York (State). Secretary of state. Calendar of
     historical manuscripts, relating to the war of the
     revolution, in the office of the Secretary of state,
     Albany, New York. Albany: Weed, Parson, 1868.
     2 v.

     The manuscripts were transferred in 1881 to the
     New York State Library. Papers placed before the
     New York Provincial Congress (1775-1793), including
     Credentials of Delegates; Lists of persons who signed
     or refused to sign; Petitions; Military Committee
     Proceedings; Military Returns; Letters; Muster Rolls,
     etc. Arranged chronologically.

18. Historical records survey. New York (City). Guide to
     manuscript depositories in New York City. Prepared
     by the Historical records survey. Division of profes-
     sional and service projects. Work projects adminis-
     tration. New York, 1941. 149 p.

     Provides access to manuscripts in sixty-eight de-
     positories: historical and patriotic societies, academ-
     ic institutions, museums, private and public libraries.

19. Historical records survey. New York (State). Inventory
     of the county archives of New York State (exclusive
     of the five counties of New York City). Prepared by
     the Historical records survey, Division of women's
     and professional projects. Work projects adminis-
     tration, no. 1- Albany: Historical records survey,
     1937-1940.

     Basically the same format used for each: histor-
     ical background of the county and historical data,
     descriptions of organization and function of county
     agencies whose records are listed. Entries include
     limiting dates, contents of individual series and the
     location of records. Each volume has its own index.
     No. 1: Albany. No. 2: Broome. No. 3: Cat-

taraugus.   No. 4: Chautauqua.   No. 5:   Chemung.
No. 51, pt. II: Allster.

20.   Breton, Arthur J.   A guide to the manuscript collections of the New York Historical Society.   Westport,
Conn.:   Greenwood Press, 1972.   875 p.   (2 v.)
  Provides access to the Society's collection which
includes diaries, account books, minutes, letters,
order books as well as manuscripts.   For the period
1804 to April 1970 the subject range of these documents covers such areas as art, Indians, Naval History, and urban life.   These items are arranged
chronologically and most entries are described briefly.
Name index and a chronological listing of entries.

21.   Fernow, B.   Calendar of wills on file and recorded in
the office of the Clerk of the Court of Appeals, of the
County Clerk at Albany and of the Secretary of State,
1626-1836.   Baltimore: Genealogical Pub. Co., 1967.
657 p.   Reprint of 1896 edition.   Index of persons:
p. 489-657.
  Alphabetic list of abstracts of wills; the key to the
location of the original includes the letter and number
of each file (in the office of the Clerk of the Court of
Appeals) with the date of execution and of proof.   The
introduction reviews the legal history of "wills" and
"testaments."

22.   Hershkowitz, L.   Wills of early New York Jews, 1704-
1799.   With a foreword by Isidore S. Meyer.   New
York: American Jewish Historical Society, 1967.
229 p.   Bibliography: p. 216-220.
  Forty-one wills are reproduced here with facsim-
iles of more than half of them.   Such documents provide valuable genealogical and historical information.
While highly personal, they also reflect economic activities, relationships within and between communities,
the structure of law, religious and cultural traditions
and provide some insight into the institutions of the
times.

Newspapers
(general to specific, then alphabetical by newspaper)

23.   Rutherfurd, L.   John Peter Zenger, his press, his
trial and bibliography of Zenger imprints, by Living-

ston Rutherfurd, also a reprint of the first edition of
the trial. New York: Johnson Reprint, 1968. 275 p.
Reprint of the 1904 edition.
   "Bibliography of the issues of the Zenger press,
1725-1751"; p. 133-169. "Bibliography of the Trial
of John Peter Zenger": p. 247-(255). "List of issues of the New York Weekly Journal with the libraries possessing same": p. (257)-267.
   A trial that resulted in an important change in
libel law, establishing the freedom of the press in
North America and marked a new era in democratic
government.

24. Knights, Peter R. The press association war of 1866-
     1867. Austin, Texas: Association for Education in
     Journalism, 1968. 57 p. (Journalism monographs,
     no. 6).
        In 1848, six New York daily newspapers combined
     their foreign news-gathering operations under the name
     of the New York Associated Press, to solve and share
     the problems of the costs of telegraphic news. In
     1851, the New York Times became a member. The
     Western Associated Press, a second telegraphic news
     agency, was founded in 1862. The conflicts within
     the NYAP and between it and the WAP and Western
     Union provide some interesting aspects of journal-
     istic history, ethics, and ingenuity.

25. Follett, F. History of the press in western New York
     from the beginning to the middle of the nineteenth
     century; with a preface by Wilberforce Eames. Har-
     rison, New York: Harbor Hill Books, 1973. 65 p.
     facsim. Reprint of Haearmen's historical series.
        Originally published as a result of an annual "fes-
     tival" of printers and editors that was held in Roch-
     ester in 1846. Information for the history was solicited
     but not all counties responded. This narrative is
     limited to the following counties (dates in parenthe-
     ses indicate earliest printing mentioned): Cattaraugus
     (1818), Cayuga (1798), Chautauqua (1817), Chemung
     (1822), Erie (1811), Genesee (1807), Livingston (1817),
     Monroe (1816), Niagara (1822), Orleans (1822), Ontario
     (1797), Seneca (1816), Steuben (1796), Tioga (1800),
     Wayne (1817), Wyoming (1828), Yates (1823).

26. Morris, L. R. A bibliography of newspapers in two
     New York State counties: installment one--newspapers

of Chautauqua County. Fredonia: State University of
New York, College at Fredonia, 1976. 28 p.
    Arranged alphabetically by title, each entry includes
bibliographic information and the extent of files available in the libraries in Western New York.

27. Wilensky, Y. A bibliography of newspapers in two New
     York State counties: installment two--newspapers of
     Cattaraugus County. Fredonia: State University of
     New York, College at Fredonia, 1976. 13 p.
         Arranged alphabetically by title, each entry includes
     bibliographic information and the extent of files avail-
     able in Western New York libraries.

28. Harriman, L. G. "The Buffalo Evening News" and its
     courageous leader, Edward H. Butler. New York:
     Newcomen Society in North America, 1955. 28 p.
         Assesses the impact of the paper as a reflection
     of the standards and philosophies of both Butler and
     his son, as publishers and editors. Use of radio and
     television in conjunction with the newspaper is only
     one of his contributions to journalism.

29. Metzker, I. A Bintel brief; sixty years of letters from
     the Lower East Side to the Jewish Daily Forward.
     Compiled, edited, and with an introd. Foreword and
     notes by Harry Golden. New York: Ballantine Books,
     1971. 216 p.
         These letters, seeking advice about personal prob-
     lems, unemployment, moral issues, politics, deserting
     husbands and starving children, chronicle (1906-1967)
     the process of adaption, assimilation, and American-
     ization of the Jewish community in New York City
     between 1906 and 1967.

30. Chapman, J. A. Tell it to Sweeney, the informal his-
     tory of the New York Daily News. 1st ed. Garden
     City, N.Y.: Doubleday, 1961. 288 p. Illus. Index:
     p. 281-288.
         Includes considerable information about the social
     and economic history of New York City.

31. Mallen, F. Sauce for the gander. White Plains, New
     York: Baldwin Books, 1954. 243 p.
         A history of the brief eight-year existence of the
     New York Evening Graphic, published by the colorful
     physical culturalist, Bernard Macfadden.

32.   Johnson, Curtiss S.   Politics and a belly-full; the jour-
      nalistic career of William Cullen Bryant, Civil War
      editor of the New York Evening Post.   Westport,
      Conn.:   Greenwood, c. 1962.   209 p.   Reprinted 1972.
      Bibliography: p. 191-192.
         While Bryant is perhaps best remembered as a poet,
      this biography centers around his fifty-two years as
      editor of the New York Evening Post and emphasizes
      his involvement in such local and national issues as:
      free trade, the United States Bank, creation of the
      Republican part, slavery, and the establishment of
      Central Park.

33.   Nevins, A.   The Evening Post; a century of journalism.
      New York: Russell & Russell, 1968.   590 p.
         The men associated with the New York Evening Post
      such as Alexander Hamilton and William Cullen Bryant;
      its principles such as opposition to slavery, moderate
      Reconstruction policies, resistence to excessive tar-
      iffs and economic and military imperialism and its
      reporting--honest, accurate, and literate--combined
      to create one of the great newspapers in America.
      For over a century it was a national influence; its his-
      tory is a record of local, state, and national affairs,
      public service, and political leadership, and the devel-
      opment of journalism.

34.   Seitz, D. C.   The James Gordon Bennetts, father and
      son, proprietors of the New York Herald.   Indiana-
      polis: Bobbs-Merrill, 1928.   405 p.   Illus.
         Essentially biographical, this is a chronicle of the
      paper's impact, force, and success during the eighty-
      three years of its ownership by a fascinating family
      dynasty.

35.   Berger, M.   The Story of the New York Times; the
      first 100 years, 1851-1951.   New York: Simon and
      Schuster, 1951.   589 p.   Reprinted 1970.
         A detailed narrative of the Times' development as
      a newspaper and its evolution into an institution.   Re-
      lates some of the outstanding stories and their circum-
      stances as reported by the Times and that newspaper's
      participation in national and world events.   Appendices
      list: Pulitzer Prizes won by the Times and its staff
      members; circulation and advertising figures of the
      Times for the period 1896-1950.

36. Davis, Elmer H. History of the New York Times,
     1851-1921. New York: The New York Times, 1921.
     434 p.
        The people, philosophies, and values that made the
     Times an institution and the role it played in the
     Civil War, national politics, New York City reforms,
     and World War I. Includes eighteen facsimile pages--
     outbreak of the Civil War, Battle of Gettysburg, sink-
     ing of the Lusitania, Titanic Disaster, etc.

37. Talese, G. The kingdom and the power. New York:
     World Pub. Co., 1969. 555 p. Ports. Index:
     p. 531-555.
        A staff writer for the New York Times for ten
     years, the author presents an insider's view of a
     powerful newspaper, the people who own it, shape it,
     manage it, write for it, and are influenced by it.

38. Brown, Ernest F. The story of the New York Times
     Book Review. New York: New York Times Book
     Review, 1969. 23 p.
        This essay, reviewing the growth, firsts, and in-
     novations of the "Book Review" also appears in the
     introduction to the separate reprint of the New York
     Times Book Review for the years 1896-1968. In-
     cludes an assessment of the contributions of various
     editors, the criteria of reviewing and reproductions
     of several "Book Review" front pages.

39. Suares, J., comp. Art of the Times. New York:
     Universe Books, 1973. 127 p.
        Cartoons and caricatures that have appeared on the
     Op-Ed pages of the Times--a feature created in 1970.
     Mostly full-page reproductions.

40. Crane, B. A century of financial advertising in the
     New York Times. New York: New York Times,
     1957. 128 p.
        The techniques and rules of advertising gradually
     utilized in the New York financial world. Lavish
     illustrations and reproductions. Indirectly, a history
     of the New York financial community.

41. Greeley, H. Association discussed; or the socialism of
     the Tribune examined, being a controversy between
     the New York Tribune and the Courier and the

Enquirer, by H. Greeley and H. J. Raymond. New
York: Harper & Bros., 1874. 83 p.
The topic of "Association" was debated within the
philosophical context of Fourier, Godwin, Brisbane,
the Roxbury community, and other advocates of similar orientation--twelve articles from each of the op-
posing viewpoints represented by the newspapers.

42.   Isely, Jetter A.   Horace Greeley and the Republican
       Party, 1853-1861, a study of the New York Tribune.
       Princeton: University Press, 1947. 368 p.   "Selec-
       tive bibliography": p. 341-356.
       An assessment of Greeley, his involvement with
       the Republican Party, the use he made of his news-
       paper concerning that political party's objectives,
       slavery, and the war.

43.   Fahrney, Ralph R.   Horace Greeley and the Tribune in
       the Civil War.   Cedar Rapids, Ia.:   The Torch Press,
       1936.   229 p.   Bibliography: p. (211)-219.
       Acknowledging the tremendous influence of the
       Tribune and the political power of Greeley, the author,
       seeking an assessment of the effect of the Tribune
       upon public opinion, chronicles Greeley's rise as an
       editor and traces the Tribune's policies regarding the
       events and controversies that finally resulted in the
       War.   The major portion of this history is devoted to
       the exploits of Greeley and Tribune during and up to
       the end of the Civil War.

44.   Baehr, Harry W.   The New York Tribune since the
       Civil War.   With a foreword by Royal Cortissoz.   New
       York: Octagon Books, 1972 (c. 1936).   420 p.   Bib-
       liography: p. 397-401.
       Based on printed sources, the files of the news-
       paper and "confidential information" provided by con-
       temporary newspapermen, this seventy-year history
       is limited to the Tribune's life as a modern newspaper
       (1865-1936)--its philosophy, values, reputation, and
       growth, with details of its involvements in various
       national and political issues.

45.   Sage, J.   Three to zero; the story of the birth and
       death of the World Journal Tribune.   Prepared for the
       American Newspaper Publishers Association.   New
       York, 1967.   82 p.
       A review of the factors that resulted in a $40-

million loss and the termination of a newspaper.
Good discussion of the New York City newspaper industry and the labor union activity within it; particularly the attitudes and traditions of Local 6 of ITU.

SEE ALSO 595, 689.

Periodicals
(alphabetical by journal)

46. Nobile, P. Intellectual skywriting; literary politics
     and The New York Review of Books. New York:
     Charterhouse, 1974. 312 p.
         The personalities, the politics, and the contro-
     versies that were an integral part of the first elev-
     en years of the New York Review of Books and its
     role as arbiter of the intellectual and elite.

47. Grant, J. Ross, the New Yorker, and me. New York:
     Reynal, 1968. 271 p.
         Ross's wife provides an insider's view of the cre-
     ation, development, and success of the New Yorker
     and all the people that made it happen.

48. Kramer, D. Ross and the New Yorker (1st ed.) Gar-
     den City, New York: Doubleday, 1951. 306 p.
         This biography, more than most, presents day-to-
     day information about the growth of the New Yorker,
     and the people who worked there.

49. Gill, D. Here at the New Yorker. 1st ed. New
     York: Random House, 1975. 406 p. Index: p. 398-
     406.
         Personal recollections of a staff writer presenting
     his tales of Harold Ross and William Shawn, his edi-
     torial successor, particularly when they were involved
     with such contributors as Charles Addams, Peter
     Arno, Thurber, John O'Hara, Capote, etc.

50. Thurber, J. The Years with Ross. With drawings by
     the author. Boston: Little, Brown, 1959. 310 p.
     Illus.
         Written by friend and New Yorker editor, this bio-
     graphy is not chronological and each of the chapters
     is a self-contained unit without a particularly infor-
     mative title--"A Dime a Dozen"; "Up popped

the Devil", etc.   Does provide an intimate view of a
complex man.

51.   Elson, Robert T.   Time, Inc.; the intimate history of
a publishing enterprise, 1923-1941.   Edited by Duncan
Norton-Taylor.   New York: Atheneum, 1968.   500 p.
Illus., facsim.
      Authorized history by Time personnel which was to
"be candid, truthful and to suppress nothing relevant
or essential," based upon interviews, company files,
personal correspondence, autobiographical notes and
other documents.   Volume 2 (1941-1966) has the title
The World of Time, Inc.

Union Lists
(general to specific)

52.   New York State union list of serials.   Prepared under
the direction of the New York State Library.   New
York: CCM Information Corp., 1970.   2 v.
      Includes periodicals, serials, almanacs, domestic
and foreign government periodicals, general trade
catalogs, house organs, conference and congresses'
proceedings, experimental and agricultural station
reports, newspapers, local interest publications and
non-commercial and societal administrative reports.
Cites only the holdings of the: American Museum of
Natural History Library, Engineering Societies Library, New York State Library, Research Libraries
of the New York Public Library, Libraries of the
State University of New York Centers at Albany,
Binghamton, Buffalo and Stony Brook, SUNY College
of Ceramics at Alfred, SUNY College of Forestry,
SUNY Upstate Medical Center, Teacher's College Library and the Union Theological Seminary Library.

53.   Union list of serials (in) in the libraries of the State
University of New York.   1st ed.; 1966-   (Syracuse)
annual.
      The fourth edition (1972) lists approximately
43,000 items, their locations and holdings in one or
more of the seventy-two campuses that comprise the
State University of New York (University Centers,
Colleges of arts and letters, Specialized colleges and
centers, Agricultural and technical colleges and Community colleges).

54. Severance, Frank H. "Contributions toward a bibliography of Buffalo and the periodical press of Buffalo,
1811-1915." Buffalo Historical Society. Publications
19 (1915): 177-312.
An essay quoting various primary sources, about
the early publishing history of Buffalo followed by a
list of newspapers with bibliographic information.
Portraits of some publishers are included.

Printing and Publishing
(general to specific, retrospective arrangement,
then alphabetical by publishing house)

55. Morgan, Charlotte E. The origin and history of the
New York Employing Printers' Association: the
evolution of a trade association. New York: Columbia
University, 1930. 139 p. (Columbia University.
Studies in History, economics and public law, no.
319).
Detailed history of printing and of the development
of various printer unions and associations from 1693
to 1929, that resulted in the New York Employing
Printers' Association. Includes the contributions of
Theodore Low DeVinne and Horace Greeley to the
movement.

56. Hamilton, Milton W. The country printer, New York
State, 1785-1830. 2d ed. With a new introduction
by Ralph Adams Brown. Port Washington, New York:
I.J. Friedman, 1964. 360 p. Bibliography: p. 319-
330.
Appendices: 1) "Printers, editors, and publishers
of country newspapers, New York, 1785-1830"; 2) "Statistical analysis of the country weekly"; 3) "Libel
suits vs country printers, 1798-1830."
An assessment of the role of the country printer
in New York's social history. Includes descriptions
of ink, press, paper, and type; the medieval guild
aspects of the printer's craft; and the business aspects, country printers' political involvements.

57. Severance, Frank H. "Contributions toward a bibliography of the Niagara region. Pamphlets and books
printed in Buffalo prior to 1850." Buffalo Historical
Society. Publications 6 (1903): 547-605.
About 300 items are cited and described. Excluded

are newspapers and periodicals with the exception of
the Mental Elevator.

58. McMurtrie, Douglas C. "Pamphlets and books printed
    in Buffalo prior to 1850; being a supplement to the
    list compiled by Dr. F. H. Severance and published
    in the Buffalo Historical Society Publications, volume
    VI, appendix A, 1903." Grosvenor Library. Bulletin.
    16 (1934): 107.
        Chronologically arranged, this is also a union list.
    Appendix: "Some titles with Imprints of Buffalo Pub-
    lishers but not printed in Buffalo."

59.   . "Additional Buffalo imprints, 1812-1849."
    Grosvenor Library. Bulletin 18 (1936): 69-
    91.
        Lists and provides locations of sixty-four titles
    including The French Convert, the earliest known book
    printed in Buffalo. Also describes a Buffalo edition
    of the New England Primer. Extensive bibliographic
    descriptions for each entry.

60.   . Checklist of eighteenth-century Albany im-
    prints. Albany: University of the State of New York,
    1939. 83 p. (University of the State of New York.
    Bulletin no. 1155; New York State Library, Bibliog-
    raphy Bulletin no. 80).
        A preliminary list and record of holdings of 280
    titles plus thirty-one titles of doubtful Albany origin.
    No imprints recorded for 1777 to 1781 inclusive.

61. Hill, William H. A brief history of the printing press
    in Washington, Saratoga and Warren Counties, State
    of New York; together with a check list of their publi-
    cations prior to 1825, and a selection of books relat-
    ing particularly to this vicinity. Fort Edward, New
    York, 1930. 117 p. Reprinted 1937.
        An essay for each county, with some biographical
    data, covering the publication of newspapers, journals,
    and books up to and including the first half of the 19th
    century. There is also a brief article on early paper
    mills in the region.

62. Johannsen, A. The House of Beadle and Adams and its
    dime and nickel novels; the story of a vanished liter-
    ature. With a foreword by John T. McIntyre. Nor-
    man, Oklahoma: University of Oklahoma, 1950-1962,
    3 v. Illus., ports.

Appendices: reprint lists, index of titles, principal
localities, Beadle author pseudonyms, lists of principal Beadle publications, lists of Beadle series.
A very thorough history of this famous publishing
house of the "dime novel" from its beginnings in
Cooperstown to its activities in Buffalo and New York
City. Bibliography of series, titles, libraries, etc.
and biographies of dime novel authors. Lavish illustrations and reproductions.

63. Crowell, Thomas Y. Thomas Young Crowell, 1836-
1915; a biographical sketch. New York: Crowell,
1954. 51 p. Illus., ports.
A very detailed biography with emphasis on the
publisher's series and the commercial successes of
the firm.

64. Dutton, E. P. & Company. Seventy-five years; or,
The joys and sorrows of publishing and selling books
at Duttons, from 1852 to 1927; compiled from a variety of original sources and lavishly illustrated with
prints and engravings depicting the growth of Duttons
during three-quarters of a century and showing views
of the establishments of their many correspondents
in foreign lands. New York, 1927. 120 p. Illus.
Very factual account of the processes of publishing
lightened with charming stories of customers and
other people in the "trade." Many photographs of
buildings, stores, printing shops, interiors of the
bookstores, and rare book rooms.

65. Exman, E. The House of Harper; one hundred and
fifty years of publishing. New York: Harper & Row,
1967. 326 p.
While this history covers the period 1817-1967, the
firm's early years are described briefly as they were
extensively presented in The Brothers Harper (1817-
1853) and later by J. Henry Harper in The House of
Harper. Writers and artists are only briefly mentioned, the focus is on the people who created Harper's, publisher of books and periodicals, and worked
to give it a prominent place in American publishing.
Reproductions of title pages, drawings, woodcuts, and
engravings greatly add to this book's informational
value.

66. Madison, Charles A. The owl among colophons: Henry

Holt as publisher and editor. New York: Holt, Rinehart and Winston, 1966. 197 p.

Based upon a forty-year association with the firm,
company files, and other documented sources, this
history, emphasizing the values and character of Henry
Holt--his high standards and appreciation of ideas--is
limited to the period up to 1928 with the exception of
the firm's association with Robert Frost between 1915
to 1962. Henry Holt's relationships with his "authors"
gave him great satisfaction--William James, Henry
Adams, and others. These friendships are presented
in some detail. A separate chapter is devoted to H.
Holt's own writings.

67. Healey, Robert C. A Catholic book chronicle; the story
of P. J. Kenedy & Sons, 1826-1951. New York:
Kenedy, 1951. 56 p.

The only surviving link to the pioneers and giants
of American Catholic book publishing, this history of
J. P. Kenedy & Sons (publisher of the Official Catholic Directory) is also a chronicle of Catholic publishers (primarily New York City) Irish Catholics and the
Catholic Church in America.

68. Portrait of a publisher, 1915-1965. With an introd. by
Paul A. Bennett. (A. A. Knopf). New York: The
Typophiles, 1965. 2 v.

Volume I contains AAK's writings and addresses,
selections from the 50th anniversary Borzoi quarterly
supplement of 1965 and an edited discussion with Eric
F. Goldman, on the NBC program, "Open Mind." Volume II is a compilation of recollections and appreci-
ations by colleagues and friends plus essays by publishing associates, contemporary authors, designers,
and historians. Also includes the Geoffrey Hellman
New Yorker Profile of 1948 and John Tehbel's inter-
view, "Publisher to an Era." Volume I also contains
a portfolio of photographs taken by A. A. Knopf (au-
thors/friends).

69. Burlingame, R. Endless frontiers: the story of McGraw-
Hill, 1st ed. New York: McGraw-Hill, 1959, 506 p.

This is a rather unusual "biography" as the author
does not focus upon the company but upon the technology that has created the modern world (1858-1958)
while the development of this publishing firm is chron-
icled as a means of reflecting these changes and

transitions; sometimes even when this publisher has
been an agent of change itself. A very interesting
chronology of events (1858-1958) parallels significant
world events and McGraw-Hill developments.

70. Recalling Peter: the life and times of Peter Beilenson
     and his Peter Pauper Press. New York: The
     Typophiles, 1964. 86 p. (Typophile chap books, 40).
     Recollections by friends and peers of this printer/
     publisher of attractive but economical books--an artist
     with type. A special section reproduces title pages
     and samples of text. There are two chronological
     checklists: 1) items printed for other publishers and
     individuals; 2) Peter Pauper Press and (B-BA) titles.

71. Reynolds, Quentin J. The fiction factory; or from Pulp
     Row to Quality Street; the story of 100 years of pub-
     lishing at Street & Smith. New York: Random House,
     1955. 283 p. Bibliography: p. 270-271.
     Publisher of magazines (Charm, Astounding Stories,
     Mademoiselle), comics (Doc Savage, Buffalo Bill),
     books in series (Boys Own Library, Little Classics),
     yearbooks and annuals (Love story annual, Sport story
     annual), paper back books (The Eagle Series, Magnet
     Library, Western Story Library), weekly publications
     (Rough Riders, Jesse James Stories), etc. This nar-
     rative introduces to readers the processes and policies
     of publishing, particularly the relationships with such
     authors as Jack London, Mary Roberts Rinehart, Theo-
     dore Dreiser, Mac Brand, and Edgar Wallace. Ex-
     tensive quotations, reproductions of title pages, maga-
     zine covers, documents, and other illustrative mate-
     rials.

72. Stern, Madeleine B. William Williams: pioneer printer
     of Utica, New York, 1787-1850. Charlottesville: Bib-
     liographical Society of the University of Virginia, 1951.
     22 p.
     Scholarly account of a combination publisher-news-
     paper owner-bookseller-printer on the New York fron-
     tier.

73. Lawler, John A. The H. W. Wilson Company; half a
     century of bibliographic publishing. Minneapolis: Uni-
     versity of Minnesota Press, 1950. 207 p.
     Both a company history and a biography of Halsey
     William Wilson, founder of the publishing firm that

produces the bibliographic tools, catalogues, and indexes (art index, agricultural index, bibliographic index, reader's guide to periodical literature, etc.) that librarians, scholars, students, and research rely on. The appendices include: a selected list of Wilson indexes, and a chronological listing (1900-1949) of the company's general publications.

SEE ALSO 156, 515.

Booksellers
(general to specific)

74. Booksellers' League, New York. The Booksellers' League. A history of its formation and ten years of its work. New York: The Booksellers' League, 1905. 244 p.
      A chronological record of the League's activities. Primarily extensively quoted speeches made by publishers, authors, printers, etc. at their "smokers." Includes the League's constitution and list of officers and members.

75. Rogers, William G. Wise men fish here; the story of Francis Steloff and the Gotham Book Mart (1st ed.). New York: Harcourt, Brace & World, 1965. 246 p.
      Biography of the founder and owner of The Gotham Book Mart. Presents a very unusual view of the modern literary world--one that emphasizes such authors as Dylan Thomas, Allen Tate, Christopher Morley, their associations (the Joyce Society), and the role of a very special bookseller.

LIBRARIES
(arranged by format: directories, bibliographies, histories, documents and histories of specific libraries)

76. New York. State Library. Albany. Division of Library Extension. A directory of college and university libraries in New York State. (1st) ed.; 1965.
      Cites officers of the college or university library director, the interlibrary loan librarian and the reference librarian. Includes statistical data--no. of volumes, no. of periodical subscriptions, budget, size of staff, publications. Appendix I lists institutions in

rank order by number of volumes.   Appendix II is a
statistical summary.

77. A directory of medical libraries in New York State.   1st
     ed.; 1967.   Albany.
        Alphabetically arranged by parent institution: full
     address, names of librarian, institution's administra-
     tor, statements of ILL policy, photocopy policy, ac-
     quisition statistics, subject specializations, number of
     staff, annual budgets.

78. A directory of library systems in New York State.
     Albany: University of the State of New York, State
     Education Department, Library Development, 1976.
     106 p.
        Formed by the combination of A directory of New
     York State public library systems and A directory of
     reference and research library resources systems in
     New York State.
        Arranged alphabetically by Reference and Resource
     library system followed by public library systems lo-
     cated within the R & R region.   State institution li-
     braries listed at end of regional groupings.   Entries
     for each library system provide: name of director,
     address of system, telephone and dataphone numbers,
     names of principal staff, numbers of members librar-
     ies, population and land area served.

79. New York.   State Library, Albany.   Division of Library
     Extension.   A directory of New York State public li-
     brary systems.   Albany, 1960.   (Title varies: 1960,
     Directory of Library systems in New York State;
     1961, Library systems in New York State).
        Alphabetical, listing name of director, address of
     system, telephone and dataphone numbers, principal
     staff, counties participating in the system, number
     of branch libraries, population served, and area
     served.

80. A directory of reference and research library resources
     systems in New York State.   1st ed.; 1967.   Albany.
        Arranged by 3 R's district, lists officers and
     trustees, the executive director of the system, then
     alphabetically those public, academic, and special li-
     braries that are members of the district system.   The
     8th edition (1974) contains appendices with fiscal in-
     formation and program activity of each district as well

as the population/counties served and the public library
systems coterminus with the 3 R's system.

81.   Long range plan for library service to the people of New
       York State (July 1, 1975-June 30, 1980) utilizing local,
       state and Federal resources.   Albany: State Education
       Dept., University of the State of New York, 1975.
       51 p.

82.   State University of New York Librarians Association.
       Publications Committee.   Directory of librarians of
       the State University of New York.   3rd ed.   1976.
       n.p.:   The Association, 1976.   53 p.   Index: p. (43-
       53).
          Arranged by type of institution (university centers,
       colleges, community colleges, contract schools) then
       alphabetically by librarian with their title or depart-
       ment noted.   The directory is published at irregular
       intervals.

83.   Lopez, Manuel D.   Bibliography of the history of librar-
       ies in New York State.   Tallahassee: Journal of Li-
       brary History, School of Library Science, Florida
       State University, 1971.   140 p.
          Includes primary and secondary sources, published
       and unpublished, in English or translation, from the
       earliest located citation up to and including 1967.   Ci-
       tations are to monographs, parts of monographs, ar-
       ticles, proceedings, pamphlets, and documents (fed-
       eral, state, and local) as well as theses, disserta-
       tions, reports and papers required for the Master's
       degree in Library Science.   Part 1:   Specific sections
       on colonial, public, school, special, college and uni-
       versity libraries.   Part 2:   Alphabetic arrangement
       by city and town, then by individual library.

84.   _____.   Bibliography of the history of libraries in
       New York State: supplement, 1968-1972.   Albany:
       University of the State of New York, State Education
       Dept., 1976.   83 p.   (Bibliography Bulletin--New
       York State Library: 85).
          Scope and arrangement is the same as the basic
       volume.

85.   Roseberry, Cecil R.   For the government and people
       of this State: a history of the New York State Li-
       brary.   Albany: New York State Library, 1970.   126 p.

Good coverage of the people, politicians, and librarians, in conjunction with rare, extensive, and unusual bibliographic acquisitions (Nicholas Marie Vattemare, first draft of the Emancipation Proclamation, gifts of Pope Gregory XVI) that created a national resource, a justifiable object of pride for New Yorkers and eventually an institution that became a pioneer in librarianship and in education.

86. New York State Library School Association. New York State Library School register, 1887-1926. James I. Wyer memorial ed. New York, 1959. 175 p. Ports.
Chronologically by class year, then alphabetically by individual; brief biographies, lists of publications, current employment, addresses, etc. Includes a brief history of the New York State Library School and the New York State Library School Association, Inc.

87. New York Library Association. Committee on Standards for Adult Services. Proposed standards for adult services in public libraries in New York State. Rev. Woodside, New York, 1969. 15 ℓ.
Presents criteria for: administration of adult services-selections policy, personnel evaluation; the Community Library-staffing needs, volunteers, physical facilities, collections for adults, audio-visual materials; Services-hours, circulation, reference, guidance, services to adults with special needs, group services; the Central Library-book collections, non-book collections; the System Center-services, materials.

88. Nelson Associates, Inc. Strengthening and coordinating reference and research library resources in New York State. A study of state-wide aspects of the proposed legislation based on the Report of the Commissioner's Committee on Reference and Research Library Resources. Prepared for New York State Education Dept. New York, 1963. 98 p.
A report specifically concerned with the activities of the "3 R's" program, the relationship of that project with other organizations, financial factors, the possible application of automatic data processing to the program and the identification of areas appropriate for establishment of regional systems.

89. New York. Public Library. History of the New York public library: Astor, Lenox and Tilden foundations, Harry Miller Lydenberg. New York, 1923. 643 p.

Comprehensive, thorough history (1848-1911) of the
various libraries that were eventually consolidated into
one great library system.   The extensive index is a
reflection of the scholarship of this effort.

90.   King, M. (Morrison).   Books and people; five decades
of New York's oldest library.   New York: Macmillan,
1954.   372 p.   Index: p. 339-372.
Emphasis upon people, manners, and mores of New
Yorkers and the literary styles of the first fifty years
of this century.

SEE ALSO 602, 603.

ASSOCIATIONS, SOCIETIES, ACADEMIES
(representative selection, alphabetically arranged)

91.   Cowdrey, Mary B.   American Academy of Fine Arts and
American Art-Union, 1816-1852.   With a history of the
American Academy by Theodore Sizer and a foreword
by James Thomas Flexner.   New York: New York Historical Society, 1953.   (Collections of the New York
Historical Society for the year 1943.   The John Watts
De Peyster publication fund series, 76).
Separate histories of the American Academy of the
Fine Arts and the American Art-Union with details of
membership, officers, organization, etc.   Has annotated lists of the bulletins, catalogues, transactions of
the latter as well as art works distributed and tables
of the art works sold by artist, by purchaser, with
prices of the sale of the Art-Union holdings of 1852.

92.   American Chemical Society.   Western New York Section.
Fifty-year history and history of its precursors.   Buffalo, 1955.   83 p.
History includes chapters devoted to activities within the section, publications, awards, employment,
groups within the section, memberships, by-laws, ex-
ternal activities and relationships with other organizations, finances, and the final section is a fifty-year
tabulation of officers, program speakers and their
topics.

93.   Wisely, William H.   The American civil engineer, 1852-
1974:   the history, traditions, and development of the

American society of Civil Engineers, founded 1952.
New York: American Society of Civil Engineers, 1974.
464 p.
  Covers a period of 124 years, with considerable
detail, seeking to provide a documentary reference
source to the programs and activities of the ASCE.
Different aspects of the Society's activities are treated
separately. The appendices include: rolls of officers,
honorary members, presidents, awards, membership
statistics, code of ethics, historic engineering landmarks.

94. Wright, J. Geography in the making: the American
     Geographical Society, 1851-1951. Foreword by Richard
     Upjohn Light. New York: Published by the Society,
     1952. 437 p. Illus., ports, maps. Index: p. (419)-
     437.
       This account of the oldest geographical society in
     America includes both its development as an institution
     (guiding policies, constitution, staff, finances, collec-
     tions, awards, publications, etc.) and its impact and
     contributions to the country's social and intellectual
     life; consequently, it is also a history of modern geog-
     raphy and a contribution to the study of the sociology
     of institutions. Appendices include lists of: staff
     (1854-1951), governing boards (1851-1951) and publi-
     cations of the Society (1852-1951).

95. Scott, Charles S. "The Institute's first half century
     AIEE (American Institute of Electrical Engineers)."
     Electrical Engineering 53, no. 5, 1934, 645-670.
       Begins with the 1876 Centennial Exposition, the
     start of the Age of Electricity, the founding of the
     AIEE in 1884, its contributions to industry and the
     commonweal, and its response to its social, scientif-
     ic and economic environment. Covers relations with
     other engineering societies, lists papers presented.
     This anniversary issue includes other articles about
     the history, organization, and contributions of the
     Institute.

96. American Institute of Mining, Metallurgical, and Petro-
     leum Engineers. Centennial history of the American
     Institute of Mining, Metallurgical, and Petroleum En-
     gineers, 1871-1970. Prepared by A. B. Parsons,
     E. H. Robie, and J. B. Alford. New York, 1971.
     215 p.

Actually includes several histories: Joe B. Alford's
"History of the Institute: one hundred years of AIME,"
James B. Austin's "The Evolution of the Metallurgical
Society of AIME," and John Cameron Fox and John V.
Beall's "The History and Current Status of the Society
of Mining Engineers of AIME," and David L. Riley's
"History of the Society of Petroleum Engineers of
AIME." The format of each history is essentially the
same: origin, development, membership, officers,
awards, prizes, lecture series, publications, finances,
etc.

97. American Numismatic Society. The American Numismatic Society, 1858-1958, by Howard L. Adelson, staff
member. New York, 1958. 390 p. Illus.
    History of coin collecting in America and a group
of collectors that contributed to this interest both as
a hobby and as a scientific approach to historical
knowledge. Includes lists of officers and staff (1858-
1958), council of administration, governors, committees, award winners, and patrons.

98. Schleuning, H. W. "The First twenty years of the American Vacuum Society." Journal of Vacuum Science and
Technology, 10, no. 5 (Sept/Oct 1973), 833-842.
    Created in 1953, the Committee on Vacuum Tech-
niques, Inc. eventually (1957) became the American
Vacuum Society. The author was a charter member,
consequently, detailed information is presented concerning: the development of the Society, the symposia,
educational aspects, publications, awards and scholarships, as well as affiliations. Lists of officers included.

99. Landgren, Marchal E. Years of art: the story of the
Art student League of New York. New York: Robert
M. McBride, 1940. 267 p. Plates.
    A history of sixty-five years, 1875-1940, of at-
tempting to teach art and to raise the art-level of the
country. Contains a chronology, lists of presidents
and instructors, and plates of the work of seventy-two
artists associated with the League as members, students, or instructors.
    Updated by:

New York (City). Art Students' League. Art Students
League, centennial decade, 1968-1969. New York,

1969. 112 p. Illus. In 1875, dissatisfied students from the National Academy of Design formed the Art Students' League to teach and be taught. Separated entirely from the parent institution in 1877. List instructors for the years 1968/69, scholarships, classes, League presidents (1875-1968), selected artists associated with the League (1875-1968) with one page (text and reproductions/illustrations) of works by the instructors and exhibitors. Historical data pp. 89-90.

100. Revens, L. "The First Twenty-five Years." Communications of the ACM (Anniversary issue: ACM 1947-1972), 15, (1972), 485-490.

 Concise history of ACM (Association for Computing Machinery) with emphasis upon the last ten years. Covers meetings, types of members, awards, professional development, social responsibility and lists officers for years 1947-1972. The reader is referred in this anniversary issue to Eric A. Weiss's paper for a survey of the history of computing publications (p. 491-497). For a more detailed history particularly of the earlier years, see Franz L. Alt's "Fifteen Years of ACM" in Communications of the Association for Computing Machinery, V, no. 6 (June, 1962), pp. 300-307. Included chronology, lists of officers, regional divisions, and chapters of ACM, national meetings.

101. Martin, George W. Causes and conflicts; the centennial history of the Association of the Bar of the City of New York. Boston: Houghton, Mifflin, 1970. 436 p. Bibliography: 417-420.

 Well-researched, extensive details, this history should answer any question about the Association or the men who were members of it.

102. Buffalo Society of Natural Sciences. Seventy-five years: a history of the Buffalo Society of Natural Sciences, 1861-1936. Buffalo, New York, 1938. 204 p. (Buffalo Society of Natural Sciences. Bulletin, 18, 1938).

 Individual chapters by different authors on specific topics such as the collections (bird, geological, conchological, etc.), or some aspect of its educational services (adult programs, picture lending library). Includes a checklist of its scientific bulletin for the years 1861-1938 and its officers and trustees.

103.   Killefer, David H. <u>Six decades of the Chemists' Club.</u>
        New York: The Chemists' Club, 1957. 66 p.
        Very adequate history of the organization with
        many details of the club's past, the location of rooms,
        the meaning of its emblem, the development of the
        library, the circumstances of the acquisition of new
        quarters, etc. Indirectly provides a view of the
        scientific community from a very human vantage
        point.
        A related history is:

        Browne, Charles A. and Mary E. Weeks. <u>History of
        the American Chemical Society, seventy-five event-
        ful years.</u> Washington: American Chemical Society,
        1952. 526 p. Includes chronology, presidential
        addresses, biographical sketches of presidents, ap-
        pendices include editors of Chemical Society journal,
        officers. The Society started in 1876, in New York
        City.

104.   Civil War Round Table of New York. <u>Its history, pro-
        grams and members.</u> New York. 28 p.
        Includes constitution, by-laws, programs (1950-
        1957), officers, directors, committees, members.

105.   Engineering Foundation, New York. <u>Sixty years of
        service, 1914-1974 and annual report, 1973-1974.</u>
        New York: Engineering Foundation, 1975. 102 p.
        Brief biographical sketch of Mr. Swasey, founder
        of the Engineering Foundation, a concise history of
        the Engineering Foundation, a review of its activities
        (seed grants and support of research projects), the
        development of the Engineering Foundation Conferences.
        Also includes: officers and members (1914-1974),
        list of projects funded, chronology of Conference top-
        ics, selected Engineering Foundation publications,
        Engineering Foundation Conference publications, state-
        ment of grant policy, the rules of administration of
        the Engineering Foundation and its by-laws.

106.   Engineers Joint Council. <u>Organization and program.</u>
        New York, 1977/1978. 72 p. Index: p. 72.
        Members are thirty-six professional engineering
        societies; the Engineers Joint Council is the mech-
        anism by which the engineering profession attempts
        to attain common goals and solve common problems.
        Various programs, committees, and concerns are

described; there is a list of member societies, associate member societies (each with its logos) and corporate affiliates. The Council's organization is
charted with lists of directors, chairmen, and members of committees, as well as the committee's
charge. Included also are the Constitution and by-
laws, a history of EJC, and a bibliography of EJC
publications.

107. Levenstein, A. and W. Agar. Freedom's advocate, a
twenty-five year chronicle (by) ... in collaboration
with William Agar. New York: Viking, 1965. 304 p.
    A narrative history, covering 1939-1964, of the
policies, issues, and activities of Freedom House,
a voluntary organization of men and women seeking
to preserve the freedom of the individual within the
limits of personal responsibility.

108. Johnson, Robert U. Your hall of fame; being an account of the origin, establishment, and history of
this division of New York University, from 1900 to
1935, inclusive. New York: New York University,
1935. 194 p. Front., illus. Index: p. 188-
    The appendices contain the constitution, rules for
election, electors of 1935, the results of the seven
quinquenneal elections, 1900-1930, with winners
named and the names considered. Brief biographies
of those honored.

109. Whittemore, Laurens E. "The Institute of Radio Engi-
neers--Forty-five years of service." IRE. Proceedings. 95 (1975): 597-635.
    The Institute of Radio Engineers resulted from a
merger of two earlier associations in 1912. This
article includes its early explanation of the emblem
of the symbol of IRE, growth of membership, list
of chapters, development of publications, conventions,
awards, medal of honors, committees, photographs
of various buildings associated with IRE history.
Appendix I: "Previous publications of significance
relating to IRE history," p. 634-635.

110. Tweed, H. The Legal Aid Society, New York City,
1876-1951. New York, 1954. 122 p. Bibliography:
p. 111-122.
    The beginnings of legal aid and the Legal Aid
Society can be traced back to the German Society of

New York City that sought to prevent the exploitation
of German immigrants by protecting their legal rights.
The focus of this history is events, staff, and financial support.

111.   O'Neall, Thomas W. and J. Kastner.   "One hundred
        years of the Manhattan Chess Club." Chess Life and
        Review.   (1977): 644-646.
            Chronicle of the Club's various "homes," its cham-
        pions, the international and national tournaments and
        its associations with Fischer and Viktor Orchnoi.

112.   Walsh, James J.   History of the Medical Society of the
        State of New York.   In commemoration of the cen-
        tennial of the Medical Society of the State of New
        York, January, 1906.   New York: The Society, 1907.
        207 p.
            The emphasis is upon the laws and legislation
        affecting medical practices.   Includes essays devoted
        to the forerunners of the Medical Society, a list of
        19th-century fees, a discussion of the development
        of medical ethics, and an account of the reunion of
        the two state medical organizations.

113.   Clark, Eliot C.   History of the National Academy of
        Design, 1825-1953.   New York: Columbia University
        Press, 1954.   296 p.
            The Academy included in its membership the most
        prominent practitioners of the graphic arts, architec-
        ture, painting, and sculpture.   Appendices include:
        names of founders, presidents, lists of all members,
        fellows in perpetuity, fellows for life, and lists of
        prizes, scholarship donations.
            Supplemented by:

        Cummings, Thomas S.   Historic annals of the National
        Academy of Design.   New York: Kennedy Galleries,
        1969.   364 p.   A chronicle of this institution from
        1826 to 1865, including speeches, letters, programs,
        and other source documents.   Appendix: lists offi-
        cers from 1827 to 1865, exhibitions dates, receipts
        (1823-1863), numbers of students, rates charged
        (1823-1861).

114.   Bacon, Edgar S.   New York Academy of Dentistry; its
        first thirty-five years.   New York: New York Acad-
        emy of Dentistry, 1960.   257 p.

Begun in 1921, this history includes: the founding,
the organization, dental legislation, the war years.
The appendices list Academy programs, active fellows, allied fellows, etc.

115. Considine, Robert B. and Fred G. Jarvis. The first
      hundred years; a portrait of the NYAC. New York:
      Macmillan, 1969. 159 p. Illus., ports.
      The New York Athletic Club, started in 1868,
      brought to the rough and tumble 19th-century sporting
      contests the rule of the stopwatch, scales, and the
      tape measure, arbitrated the difference between ama-
      teur and professional and fostered fair play and
      sportsmanship. A narrative of the men and sporting
      events that combined to establish the NYAC as the
      standard bearer.

116. New York County Lawyer's Association. Yearbook, 1
      (1909)--annual.
      Lists officers from 1908 to the present, members
      of standing committees, joint and special committees,
      also lists members--active, associate, and life--and
      includes the by-laws, reports of the committees and
      a necrology.

117. "History of the New York Genealogical and Biographical
      Society." New York Genealogical and Biographical
      Society. Record, 60 (1939): 301-03.
      Lists of first officers (1869) and members, publi-
      cation of the "Bulletin" (1869), new members.

118. De La Chapelle, Clarence E. The New York Heart
      Association, origins and development 1915-1965. New
      York: New York Heart Association, 1966. 81 p.
      Ports.
      The New York Heart Association's success with
      its objectives (adequate clinical facilities for ambu-
      latory patients, clear criteria for diagnoses, uniform
      preparations of digitalis, definitions of the natural
      history of rheumatic and syphilitic heart disease) began
      to have national and international effects. Eventually
      the American Heart Association was established in
      1924. There is a chronology and lists of the pres-
      idents and directors of the New York Heart Asso-
      ciation.

119. Wall, Lillian B. Entre nous, an intimate portrait of
      Alexander J. Wall. New York: New York Histori-
      cal Society, 1949. 267 p. Ports.
          A biography of the Librarian/Director of the New
      York Historical Society and as such also constitutes
      a history of the Society during the first half of the
      20th century. Appendices lists: bibliography of
      published writings, lectures delivered, lectures and
      functions of the Society, congratulatory letters on
      appointment to Librarian, etc.

120. Vail, Robert W. G. Knickerbocker birthday; a sesqui-
      centennial history of the New York Historical Society,
      1804-1954. New York: New York Historical Society,
      1954. 547 p. Illus., ports, maps, facsims.
          Essays devoted to each of this institution's presi-
      dents constituting a gracious and detailed account of
      the Society's evolution and its contribution and indi-
      rectly is also a history of New York City and the
      United States. Additional descriptions of celebration
      dinners commemorating events, individuals, and
      honors given to the Society supplement the lists of
      the founders, officers, and trustees of the Society,
      the bibliography of the Society's publications, and
      the documents fundamental in the history of the Soci-
      ety's growth.

121. Bridges, W. Gathering of animals; an unconventional
      history of the New York Zoological Society. New
      York: Harper & Row, 1974. 518 p.
          A 75-year history (1896-1972?) of the Zoo and
      Aquarium that fostered conservation, education, and
      research concerning the world's wildlife. Includes
      details of the formation of the American Bison Soci-
      ety, founded in 1915 to save the bison from extinction.

122. Briggs, John L. "The PHS is 25 in 1976." Postal
      History Journal, 20 (1976): 2-6.
          Unusual history of the Postal History Society as
      it devotes itself to the clarification of some discrep-
      ancies and confusions regarding dates, definitions,
      etc.

123. Hays, Forbes B. Community leadership; the Regional
      Plan Association of New York. New York: Columbia
      University Press, 1965. 190 p. (Metropolitan poli-
      tics series, no. 3).

A study and history of the Regional Plan Association's role in metropolitan leadership with a focus
on policies, strategy, and organization.

124. Society of Iconophiles, New York. History of the So-
      ciety of Iconophiles of the City of New York:
      MDCCCXCV-MCMXXX and catalogue of its publica-
      tions with historical and biographical notes, etc.
      Compiled under the direction of Richard Hoe Law-
      rence, assisted by Harris D. Colt and I. N. Phelps
      Stokes. New York, 1930. 290 p. Illus., plates,
      ports.
          The Society's purpose was to issue a series of
      limited editions of engraved views of New York City,
      past and present, and portraits of important people
      associated with the City. First meeting, January 28,
      1895. This history includes the Society's activities
      up to 1930 and incorporates: a catalogue of the en-
      gravings, with reproductions and descriptions, issued
      by the Society; a catalogue of the books issued; a
      list of the books and engraving presented to the So-
      ciety and biographical and autobiographical notes
      about the artists that engraved plates for the Society.
      The index is unusual as it provides access to the
      subjects of ships, persons, buildings, streets, etc.
      that appear in the engravings.

125. Gable, John A. "The Theodore Roosevelt Association:
      a brief history." Theodore Roosevelt Association
      Newsletter. (1974): 5-8.
          Created in 1920 by admirers, associates, and
      friends of Theodore Roosevelt, its first director was
      Hermann Hagedorn, author, historian, and biographer.
      The Association restored and furnished the Theodore
      Roosevelt Birthplace (28 E. 20th St., NYC), created
      the Theodore Roosevelt Memorial Park (Oyster Bay),
      developed a scholarly library about Theodore Roose-
      velt, published an eight-volume collection of letters,
      and purchased and restored Sagamore Hill, the Theo-
      dore Roosevelt home from 1884-1919, which became
      a national shrine in 1955 and an Historic Site in
      1963. Good but brief history of the Association.

126. Irwin, William H. A History of the Union League Club
      of New York City (by) Will Irwin, Earl Chapin May
      (and) Joseph Hotchkiss. New York: Dodd, Mead,
      1952. 297 p.

Liberal, intellectual, and successful men, originally associated to correct and minimize some of
the evils of the Civil War, established an organization to provide socially responsible leadership and
to educate civic-minded leaders.

127. Chenery, William L. The University Club, yesterday
      and today. New York, 1955. 92 p. Illus.
      Reminds present members of the Club's past rec-
      ord and its present activities, contributions, and ac-
      complishments that have caused this organization to
      be known as "The Mother of University Clubs." In-
      teresting chapters on the library, wine cellar, Sir
      Winston Churchill's visit, admission of women, etc.

SEE ALSO 74, 134, 154, 155, 407, 444, 627, 855, 856, 867.

ARTS

Applied Arts
(alphabetical by craft or product)

Ceramics, Glass

128. Ketchum, William C. Early potters and potteries of
      New York State. New York: Funk & Wagnalls, 1970.
      278 p. Bibliography: p. 254-69.
      Emphasis upon craftsmen turning out utilitarian
      household wares for cooking, preserving, and serving
      food between 1650 and 1900. Excludes the potter
      who only made roof tiles or drain pipes; the "art"
      potter of the 19th century is not included.
      A specialized company history:

      Altman, V. The Book of Buffalo Pottery by Violet and
      Seymour Altman. New York: Crown, 1969. 192 p.
      A history of the Larkin Company and Buffalo Pottery
      (now Buffalo China, Inc.) with chapters on specific
      lines such as Deldare, Blue Willow, Gaudy Willow on
      forms such as fish, fowl, and deer sets, and on such
      products as commercial service, abino ware, histor-
      ical plates, etc. Extensive photographs.

129. Steuben Glass, Inc. The Story of Steuben glass. New
      York: Steuben Glass, 1945. 24 p.
      History and background of the firm that has given
      America first place in glassmaking.

129a. Koch, R. Louis C. Tiffany, rebel in glass. New
York: Crown, 1964. 246 p. Bibliography: p. 221-33.
Extensive and detailed assessment of the man and
his artistic contributions; more than a biography,
this is also a profile of an age. Lavish use of illustrations, reproductions, colored plates, etc.

Fashion

130. New York (City) Mayor's Committee for the Commemoration of the Golden Anniversary of the City of New York.
City of New York Golden Anniversary of Fashion, 1898-
1948. Official jubilee ed. New York, 1948. 1 v. Col.
plates.
History of New York as the center of fashion plus an
overview of the dress, coat, and suit industries, cos-
metics and other related businesses. Includes a series
of lithographs by Vertes about fashion world, a dress
chart for 1948, men's dress style of 1898, and a glos-
sary of clothing, textile, and fashion terms. The extensive advertisements, now, are historic documents in
themselves.

Furniture

131. Copley, Frank W. and W. H. Glover. The Story of
Kittinger furniture. Buffalo, 1957. 14 p. (Originally
published in the Niagara Frontier, 3 [1956]: 61-70).
History of predecessors and the evolution of this
famous firm as a creator and producer of fine furniture, Williamsburg reproductions and special order
items for the White House.

132. Albany (New York) Institute of History and Art. New
York furniture before 1840 in the collection of the
Albany Institute of History and Art. Albany, 1962.
63 p. (Cogswell Fund series. Publication no. 2).
The selections for this catalogue indicate the collection's quality and variety, not its extent. The
brief notes are concerned with the local background
of the individual items.

133. Meader, Robert F. W. Illustrated guide to Shaker furniture. New York: Dover, 1972. 128 p. Illus.
Intended to aid the collector and antique dealer in
the identification of Shaker furniture; extensive photographs of chairs, footstools, tables, desks, case
pieces, clocks, and stoves. Included is a reproduction

of an "Illustrated Catalogue and Price List of Shaker
Chairs, Manufactured by the Society of Shakers."
An additional Shaker study:

Andrews, Edward D. Religion in wood; a book of Shaker furniture by ... and Faith Andrews. Introd. by
Thomas Merton. Bloomington: Indiana University,
1966. 106 p. Illus. Bibliography: p. 105-06. The
emphasis is upon the spiritual forces that influenced
the craftsmanship. The furniture descriptions include
measurements, location, present ownership, and original use. A classic in the field of Shaker studies.

Numismatics, Coins

134. New York Numismatic Club. History of the New York Numismatic Club, 1908-1961. New York, 1961. 56 p.
Illus.
Includes the Club's origin, description of early
meetings, social/numismatic events, its publications,
influence upon U.S. coinage, collector protection,
A.N.A. conventions in New York City, local conventions and exhibits, meeting places, King of Italy medal, the Presidential medal series, and list of club
presidents with brief biographical notes.

Silver

134a. Darling Foundation of New York State Early American
Silversmiths and Silver, Eggertsville, New York.
New York State silversmiths. Eggertsville, New
York, 1964. 228 p. Bibliography: p. 197-200.
Alphabetic listing of New York State silversmiths
of the 18th and 19th centuries with reproductions of
their marks.
Examples of New York silversmithing are provided by:

Albany Institute of History and Art. Albany silver,
1652-1825; catalog of an exhibition of Albany silver,
1622-1825, March 15-May 1964. By Norman S. Rice,
curator. Foreword by Lawrence McKinney. Intro.
by Kathryn E. Buhler. Design by George Cole.
Photos by Helga Photo Studio. Albany, 1964. 81 p.
Bibliography: p. 78-81. Includes brief biographies
and notes about Albany silversmiths.

New York. Museum of the City of New York. New
York silversmiths of the seventeenth century.

Exhibition December 5, 1962-February, 1963. By V.
Isabelle Miller. New York, 1962. 1 v. (unpaged).
Includes the work of fourteen silversmiths.

Fine Arts

135. New York (State). State Council on the Arts. New York
     State Council on the Arts. Report. 1960-annual.
       Review of the activity of the Council's programs,
     recipients of grants, lists of Council members.

SEE ALSO 91, 99, 113, 546.

Architecture
(arranged geographically: capital area, western New York,
eastern New York, New York City, then unique styles/forms)

136. Roseberry, Cecil R. Capitol story, by Cecil R. Rose-
     berry with photographs by Arthur John Daley. Albany:
     State of New York, 1964. 128 p.
       Impressive in size, cost, and the reactions it gen-
     erates. The Capitol, due to its combination of archi-
     tectural styles (Romanesque, Italian Renaissance,
     French Renaissance, etc.) and the people associated
     with it, has been called many things--ugly, a mon-
     strosity, etc., but never dull. These factors and the
     personal and political aspects of its construction his-
     tory make it unique among state capitols. Actually,
     many people find this building attractive and this brief
     history with its numerous photographs of architectural
     details provides an explanation for this viewpoint.

137. Savell, Isabelle K. The Executive Mansion in Albany,
     an informal history, 1856-1960. Albany, 1960. 47
     p. Illus.
       History of the structure, its modifications. Inte-
     rior views. Biographical sketches of governors from
     S. J. Tilden (1875-1876) to N. A. Rockefeller (1959-
     1970).

138. Randall, John D. Buffalo and Western New York ar-
     chitecture and human values: a bi-centennial, archi-
     tectural compilation, with some notes about the spe-
     cial heritage of community-oriented human qualities
     of the makers of our great city and its architecture.
     Buffalo: Artcraft-Burow, 1976. 200 p.

Identifies buildings important architecturally and/
or historically, providing specific details for each
one.   Particularly useful for locating in Buffalo and
its environs the structures and contributions of Richard Upjohn, Frederick Law Olmsted, Henry Hobson
Richardson, George B. Post, Louis Sullivan, Eliel
Saarinen, R. A. Cram, Albert Kahn, Stanford White,
Daniel Burnham, and F. L. Wright.   Wealth of data
about building types, heights, fires, city plans, architects, construction, the building trades, etc.

139.   Conover, Jewel H.   Nineteenth-century houses in west-
       ern New York.   Photos by the author.   Albany: State
       University of New York, 1966.   161 p.   Illus., map.
       Bibliography: p. 159-61.
            Limited to Chautauqua County, there is a brief
       historical sketch of the economic, social, and geo-
       graphical context of the 19th-century domestic archi-
       tecture of the area.   A discussion of architectural
       styles is followed by annotated, almost full-page
       photographs of various homes, bandstands, summer
       houses, etc.   Arranged by geographic region within
       the county, and then by village and town.

140.   Reynolds, Helen W.   Dutch houses in the Hudson Valley
       before 1776.   With an introd. by Franklin D. Roo-
       sevelt.   Photography by Margaret De M. Brown.   New
       York: Dover, 1965.   467 p.   Illus., maps.   Reprint
       of the 1929 edition.
            Based upon a field survey conducted in 1925 and
       limited to four counties: Albany, Ulster, Westchester,
       and Dutchess; the criteria for inclusion of a building
       was that it provided a general and somewhat accurate
       idea of the average dwelling that existed along the pre-
       revolutionary Hudson River.   Nationality of ownership
       or builder was not first consideration.   A general
       section about the social/economic conditions of the
       area, architectural styles and materials, and the life
       of the early settlers preceded the geographic sections
       listing and describing the homes within the various
       counties.
            Additional sources:

       Bailey, Rosalie F.   Pre-revolutionary Dutch houses and
       families in nothern New Jersey and southern New York,
       by Rosalie Fellows Bailey, A. B.; with an introduction
       by Franklin D. Roosevelt; photography by Margaret

De M. Brown; Prepared under the auspices of the
Holland society of New York. New York: W. Mor-
row, 1936. 612 p. Reprinted: 1968. Bibliography:
p. 583-84. Companion volume to Dutch Houses in
the Hudson Valley before 1776; same format. Attempts to record the life and manners of early
"Dutch" settlers. Based upon a field survey; photographs were taken of each of the houses described.
Geographically arranged by county.

Reynolds, Helen Wilinson. Dutchess County doorways
and other examples of period-work in wood, 1730-
1830, with accounts of houses, places, and people.
Photography by Margaret De M. Brown. New York:
W. F. Payson, 1931. 205 p. Based upon a field
survey, land records, published records, and private
papers, the history of the house is presented and
the details of the home (windows, fireplaces, doors,
doorways, mantels, panelling, etc.) are described
and supplemented with 201 plates. Many of the
houses were also discussed, from another viewpoint,
in the author's Dutch Houses in the Hudson Valley
before 1776.

New York (State). Hudson River Valley Commission.
Historic resources of the Hudson; a preliminary inventory. Study prepared by Lewis C. Rubenstein,
staff historian. Tarrytown, New York, 1969. 96 p.
An inventory of 1,650 architecturally and historically
valuable resources, nationally, regionally, or in terms
of local interest, located within 300 square miles of
the Hudson River Valley. Map indicated and briefly
described with indices by county; cities, towns, and
villages; and historic sites.

141. Andrews, W. Architecture in New York; a photographic
history. New York: Atheneum, 1969. 188 p. Bibliography: p. 181-83.
    Arranged by architect, brief descriptive comments
with each photograph of the structure, interior, or
architectural detail. Chronological in sequence, beginning with the colonial period to Eero Saarinen
Associates.

142. Huxtable, Ada L. The Architecture of New York; a
history and guide. Garden City, New York: Anchor,
1964. 142 p. Illus. Bibliography: p. 133-35.

Limited to the buildings architecturally attractive
or historically significant on Manhattan, this volume,
the first of a proposed series, concentrates on the
Georgian style and the Greek Revival. Brief description, commentary, and history of each structure.
The author emphasizes the "cityscape," the character,
color, texture, and development of the city, that is
the sum of all of these factors.

143.   Wolfe, Gerard R.   New York, a guide to the metrop-
       olis: walking tours of architecture and history.   New
       York: University Press, 1975.   434 p.   Bibliography:
       p. 421-26.
           Twenty tours of two to five hours in length empha-
       sizing the many architectural styles in the city and
       the historical landmarks. The tours, in Manhattan,
       are arranged chronologically. A good street map
       with the tour route indicated supplements detailed
       walking directions. Descriptions of buildings are
       complemented by photographs and reproductions of
       the "period." Also includes tours in Brooklyn and
       Queens.

144.   Gayle, M.   Cast-iron architecture in New York: a
       photographic survey/text by Margot Gayle; photos by
       Edmund V. Gillon, Jr.   New York: Dover Publica-
       tions, 1974.   190 p.   Index of cast-iron buildings:
       183-85.
           Photographs of buildings and architectural details
       (fences, decorations, stairs, columns, etc.). Ar-
       ranged by street, each description includes the name
       of the architect, builder, or manufacturer, its use,
       history, and current status.

145.   Waite, John G.   Iron architecture in New York City;
       two studies in industrial archeology: The Edgar
       Laing stores (1849) (and) The Cooper Union (1853-
       59).   Albany: New York State Historic Trust, 1972.
       83 p.
           Brief history of cast iron architecture with photo-
       graphs and measured drawings of the Edgar Laing
       stores taken during their dismantling. Brief history
       of Cooper Union Institute with illustrations and meas-
       ured drawings.

146.   _____ .   A Compilation of historical and architectural
       data on the New York State Maritime Museum block

in New York City, by John E. Waite, Paul R. Huey
(and) Geoffrey M. Stein.   New York: New York Historic Trust, 1972.   1 v.   Bibliography: section V.
 The block (between John Street and Fulton Street
and between Front Street and South Street) in the
lower end of Manhattan Island has remained almost
intact and is representative of 19th-century American
commercial architecture.   This report includes photographs, schematic architectural drawings and spatial
analysis of present use supplemented by historical
data about the people who lived and worked in these
buildings.

147.   Malo, P.   Landmarks of Rochester and Monroe County:
a guide to neighborhoods and villages.   Photos. by
Hans Padelt and others.   Landmark Society of Western New York, sponsor.   Syracuse, New York: Syracuse University Press, 1974.   276 p.   (A York State
book).   Bibliography: p. 252-55.
 Geographically arranged with a tour format (maps
and detailed directions); some 111 structures were
selected as being representative of their time, and
the character of their locale.   Appendix I: "Chronological Listing of Monroe County Landmarks Mentioned in Text":   p. 231-36.   Appendix II: "Works
of Prominent Architects in Monroe County":   p. 237-
41.

148.   Lassiter, William L.   Shaker architecture; descriptions
with photographs and drawings of Shaker buildings at
Mount Lebanon, New York, Watervliet, New York
(and) West Pittsfield, Massachusetts.   Illustrated by
Constantine Kermes.   (1st ed.) New York: Vantage,
1966.   127 p.   Illus., plans.   Bibliography: p. 127.
 This volume contains a very extensive collection
of drawings, architectural plans, and photographs of
Shaker barns, dwellings, meeting houses, a school,
shops, and work rooms.

SEE ALSO 518, 519, 538, 569-575, 895.

Music--General
(current to retrospective,
general to specific)

149.   New York (State) University.   University at Buffalo.

Music Department and Music Library. Buffalo musicians, v. 1- 1976- annual.
     Lists faculty of music department, University lec-
turers, Creative associates, Slee professors, Edgard
Varèse Chair, Birge-Cary Chair, and Ziegele Chair.

150. Stoeckel, William C. Musicians directory, 1947-1953?
      Buffalo: Stoeckel Publishing, 1947.
      "Directory of non-union professional musicians
for Buffalo and suburbs--Buffalo and Niagara Frontier."
      Arranged by instrument, then alphabetically by
individual--name, address, telephone number. Also
lists drum corps, bands, choral groups, etc.

151. Music and dance in New York State. Sigmund Spaeth,
      editor-in-chief; William J. Perlman, Director and
      associate editor; (and) Joseph A. Bollew, assistant
      editor. 1952 ed. New York, Bureau of Musical
      Research (c. 1951). 435 p. Ports. "Personalities
      of Music and Dance," p. 159-385.
      This is a professional directory, also a section
about music and dance activities in New York City,
Buffalo, Syracuse, Auburn, Ithaca, Elmira, and
Schenectady.

152. Cron, Theodore O. and B. Goldblatt. Portrait of
      Carnegie Hall; a nostalgic portrait in pictures and
      words of America's greatest stage and the artists
      who performed there. New York: Macmillan, 1966.
      217 p. Illus., facsims, ports. "A Carnegie Discog-
      raphy," p. 207-08.
      Each chapter devoted to some aspect of the history
of the Hall or the history of an activity associated
with it: folk songs, dance, jazz, theatre, etc.

153. Aldrich, R. Concert life in New York, 1902-1923.
      New York: G. P. Putnam's Sons, 1941. 795 p.
      Originally written by the author for his column
in the New York Times. Chronologically arranged.

154. Erskine, J. The Philharmonic-Symphony Society of
      New York: its first hundred years. With programs
      of subscription concerts, 1917-1942. New York:
      Macmillan, 1943. 168 p.
      Concise, solid historical presentation limited to
the first sixty pages.

155.   Swift, Frederic F.   A history of the New York State
       School Music Association, 1932-1962.   Oneonta, New
       York, 1963.   247 p.
          Chronological in format, each chapter is devoted
       to some aspect of the Association's past or activity:
       festivals, conferences, leadership, constitutions,
       finances, the School Music News, other publications,
       etc.

156.   Howe, Mabel A.   Music publishers in New York City
       before 1850.   New York, 1917.   18 p.   Reprinted
       from the Bulletin of the New York Public Library,
       September, 1917.
          Alphabetic list of publishers, some engravers of
       music and some music stores; traced through the
       New York City directories prior to 1850.   Each
       change of address is noted by year.

Music--Opera
(alphabetical by opera company)

157.   Cone, John F.   Oscar Hammerstein's Manhattan Opera
       Company.   Norman: University of Oklahoma, 1966.
       399 p.   Bibliography: 371-85.
          While the Manhattan Opera Company only existed
       between 1906 and 1910, the author attempts to estab-
       lish and assess its importance by determining the
       status of opera prior to its founding, evaluate Hammer-
       stein's background in opera, review the criticisms
       of the productions, and create an accurate record of
       the performances.   He also delineates the relation-
       ship between the Met and Manhattan Opera Company.

158.   Merkling, F.   The golden horseshoe; the life and times
       of the Metropolitan Opera House, by the editors of
       Opera News....   Epilogue by Anthony A. Bliss.   New
       York: Viking, 1965.   319 p.   (A Studio book).
          The photographs, illustrations, diagrams, and
       plans dominate the text of this eighty-three-year his-
       tory--one that considers the financial, administrative,
       and social aspects of the Met as well as its artistic
       and cultural evolution....   Many close-ups of stars,
       opera scenes, and the backstage specialists that con-
       tribute so much to a successful performance.

159.   Kolodin, I.   The Metropolitan Opera, 1883-1966; a
       candid history.   (4th ed.)   New York: A. A. Knopf,
       1966.   762 p.

Chronicle in detail; supplemented with photographs
of individuals and stage scenes. Comment-critical,
historical, with lavish particulars. Unfortunately,
the famous section on the Diamond Horseshoe of the
1936 edition has not been retained entirely. Has
"The Metropolitan Repertory, 1883-1966"; p. 753-62.
Another view:

Seligman, P. Debuts and farewells; a two-decade photographic chronicle of the Metropolitan Opera. New
York, 1972. 180 p. Photographs of the Met, its
patrons and artists in a variety of moods, activities,
on stage, backstage, out front. Most are informal,
intimate. Good close-ups of stars.

160.   Carleno, A. The evils of music management: the
facts of life every singer, pianist, and musician
should know about opera and concert management:
an expose. New York: La Car, 1975. 298 p.
The Buffalo Nightingale, Ginetta La Bianca, is the
central figure and victim of this book about grand art
and low morals.

Music--Musical Theater
(alphabetical by title)

161.   Clarke, N. The mighty Hippodrome. South Brunswick,
New Jersey: A.S. Barnes, 1968. 144 p. Bibliography: p. 142.
The Hippodrome, a spectacle in itself, at the turn
of the century presented marvel after marvel of the
musical stage, contributing classics of that entertainment form. This history, social to a degree,
within the context of the showmen and characters of
Broadway, evaluates those productions in terms of
their contemporary values.

162.   Baral, R. Revue: a nostalgic reprise of the Great
Broadway period. Introd. by Abel Green. New York:
Fleet Publishing, 1962. 288 p.
The musical revues, particularly those of the
1920's and 1930's (Ziegfeld, George White, Earl
Carrol), are captured in text, personal comment,
and photographs. The appendix lists the shows, per-
formers, and numbers of performances from 1903 to
1945.

Music--Popular Music

163. Groia, P. They all sang on the corner; New York
      City's rhythm and blues vocal groups of the 1950s.
      (Rev.) Setauket, New York: Edmond Pub., 1974.
      147 p.
          Limited to male Negro groups who sang R & B
      music on the streets of New York City during the
      period 1947 to 1960. Some female singers have been
      included. A biographical, sociological, geographical,
      and chronological approach.

Music--Jazz
(chronological arrangement)

164. Shaw, A. The Street that never slept; New York's fa-
      bled 52nd Street. Foreword by Abel Green. New
      York: Coward, McCann & Geoghegan, 1971. 378 p.
          Essentially a history of jazz and music that was
      played from 1934 to 1950 on 52nd Street. Based on
      taped interviews, the author himself a part of The
      Street, presents his material in terms of the clubs
      that existed on the street during this period, the
      people who played/listened, performed, and were en-
      tertained there.

165. Marks, Edward B. They all sang, from Tony Pastor
      to Rudy Vallee, as told to Abbott J. Liebling. New
      York: Viking Press, 1935. 321 p. "Index of Names
      and Subjects": p. 313. "Index of Songs": p. 319.
          A song publisher's intimate recollections of the
      entertainment world between the turn of the century
      and the 1930's and the great and near great that peo-
      pled it. The appendices include outstanding songs
      of the period, famous names in minstrelsy and a
      list of "High and low life in old New York"--people
      and places.

Music--Radio

166. Dykema, Peter W. Women and radio music. New
      York: The Radio Institute of the Audible Arts, 1935.
      10 p. Bibliography: p. 7-8.
          The Radio Institute of Audible Arts, created by
      Philco Radio & Television Corp., had the objectives
      of cultivating a broader appreciation of the audible
      arts, the effective use of radio, and the public rec-
      ognition of the best in radio.

Museums
(general to specific)

167. Faison, Samson L. Art tours & detours in New York
      State; a handbook to more than seventy-five outstand-
      ing museums & historic landmarks in the Empire
      State outside New York City. New York: Random
      House, 1964. 303 p. Illus., maps.
         A survey of art on public view (seventy-eight mu-
      seums are listed) with some 408 items illustrated
      with critical comment; more than half are paintings,
      the rest include sculpture, prints, architecture, fur-
      niture, photography, etc. Nine geographic regions
      (excluded New York City) with alphabetic listing of
      museums by town or city. Entry includes descrip-
      tion of the institution, highlights of the collections,
      and comments on specific items. A supplementary
      list cites additional museums, historical societies,
      and other places of interest in each region.

168. New York (State). State Museum and Science Service.
      The New York State Museum; a short history. Al-
      bany, 1964. 31 p.
         A brief account of the oldest and largest of the
      state museums, its struggles, growth, and its im-
      pact upon the state and the nation.

169. Chapman, Allan D. Museum collections on Asia, Af-
      rica, Latin America, and the Soviet Union in New
      York State and their use in education. Prelim. ed.
      Albany: University of the State of New York, State
      Education Dept., 1964. 64 p.
         Lists thirty significant museum collections con-
      cerning non-Western countries: provides the address
      and description of the museum, its collections, edu-
      cational services available, and lists the museum's
      publications.

170. Herbert F. Johnson Museum of Art, Cornell Univer-
      sity, Ithaca, New York. Far Eastern art in upstate
      New York. Organized by Martie W. Young. Introd.
      by Martie W. Young. Ithaca, New York: Cornell
      University, 1977. 140 p. Bibliography: 136-39.
         Exhibition of 141 objects from seven upstate mu-
      seums includes hanging scrolls, vessels, porcelain,
      bronzes, sculpture, wood block prints, screens,
      jade, figures, etc. representing China and Japan.

Many of the selected items are from originally private collections that were later acquired by various institutions.

171/4. Everson Museum of Art of Syracuse and Onondaga County. Medieval art in upstate New York: (exhibition) Everson Museum of Art of Syracuse and Onondaga County; coordinated by Meredith Lillick; edited by Peg Weiss. Syracuse: Everson Museum, 1974. 130 p. Illus.
To create this exhibition a complete census of medieval art in upstate New York was taken (p. 123-29). This catalog of the exhibition includes photographs of each art work--manuscript, sculpture, statue, etc. that is discussed. Each description contains bibliographic references.

SEE ALSO 650-663.

Artists
(general to specific, then
alphabetically by artist)

175. Everson Museum of Art of Syracuse and Onondaga County. From Within; selected works by the artists/inmates of New York State Correctional Facility at Auburn (maximum security). (Exhibition held at) the National Collection of Fine Art, Smithsonian Institution, Washington, D.C. February 2--March 25, 1973. Washington, 1973. 35 p. Illus.
Catalogue of this exhibition includes the history of the Museum's prison art program and its results. Some of the artists' statements are in the form of poetry.

176. Baur, John Ireland H. Charles Burchfield (Research by Rosalind Irvine). New York: Published for the Whitney Museum of American Art by Macmillan, 1956. 86 p. 75 illus. Bibliography: p. (82)-85.
An expanded version of the catalogue of the 1956 Whitney Museum of American Art exhibition of Burchfield's paintings and drawings; the addition being new illustrations (black and white, colored reproductions, fifty-four plates), biographical and evaluative materials based upon the artist's own journal, correspondence, autobiographical notes, reviews, clippings, etc.

177.   Flexner, James T.   The World of Winslow Homer,
       1836-1910 by ... and the Editors of Time-Life Books.
       New York: Time, Inc., 1966. 190 p. Bibliography:
       p. 185.
            Biographical information and artistic development
       placed within the context of his artistic contemporar
       ies both American and foreign.   Line drawings, re-
       productions, and color plates are in lavish comple-
       ment to the text.

178.   Marsh, R.   The Sketchbooks of Reginald Marsh [Com-
       piled by] Edward Laning. Greenwich, Conn.: New
       York Graphic Society, 1973. 168 p. Illus.
            Famous for his pen and ink sketches, this artist's
       drawings, etchings, murals, paintings, and illustra-
       tions of New York City, Coney Island, the El, the
       Bowery, the waterfront, the burlesque theatre, and
       the people that are a part of those places, uniquely
       conveys an aspect of the vitality and energy of the
       City.

179.   Kallir, O.   Grandma Moses. New York: Abrams,
       1973.   357 p.   Illus., photos, col. plates.   "Selected
       bibliography: books written or illustrated by Grandma
       Moses," p. 341-42; "Index to the Works": p. 329-
       40; "Chronological list of exhibitions": p. 343-52.
            Very comprehensive but well organized presenta-
       tion of the artist's life and work.

180/4. Hassrick, Peter H.   Frederic Remington: paintings,
       drawings, and sculpture in the Amon Carter Museum
       and the Sid W. Richardson Foundation collections,
       foreword by Ruth Carter Johnson. New York: Abrams,
       1971. 218 p. Illus. Bibliography: 215-18.
            While his name for many is synonymous with the
       West, Remington was born in upper New York, edu-
       cated there and in New England.   This volume in-
       cludes his biography as well as ninety-six reproduc-
       tions and colored plates of his work, each with com-
       mentary and select bibliography.

Paintings
(chronological by period)

185.   Belknap, Waldron, P.   American colonial painting: ma-
       terials for a history. Cambridge, Mass.: Belknap
       of Harvard University Press, 1959. 377 p. Ports.,

coats of arms, facsims. Bibliography: p. 337-44;
"Catalogue of prints and paintings": p. 279-322.
This art history was "a combination of the critical and historical approach" which included genealogical techniques. A major portion of this book
is devoted to New York patrons and painters with
additional sections on New York limmers and painting in New York wills. Much genealogical material.

186. Flexner, James T. That Wilder image; the painting
of America's native school from Thomas Cole to
Winslow Homer. Boston: Little, Brown, 1962.
407 p. "Selected Bibliographies"; p. 375-94.
Places the Hudson River School in context as
well as other New York artists such as Remington
and Homer.

187/8. Howat, John K. The Hudson River and its painters.
Pref. by James Biddle. Foreword by Carl Carmer.
New York: Viking, 1972. 207 p. "Select Bibliography": p. 193-201.
Actually a history of the Hudson River School
with many fine colored plates of those artists' works
plus detailed maps of the Hudson Valley and colored
photographs of the areas represented in the paintings.
Relevant exhibitions:

Norton (R. W.) Art Gallery. The Hudson River
School: American landscape paintings from 1821 to
1907. A loan exhibition, October 14--November 25,
1973, the R. W. Norton Gallery, Shreveport, Loui-
siana. Shreveport, La., 1973. 106 p. Illus., col.
plates. Bibliography: p. 104-06. A catalogue of
the second largest exhibition of its kind in the 20th
century, 118 works by forty-seven artists of the
Hudson River School; limited to American views.
Biographical data is combined with critical evaluations of each artist.

New York. State University College, Geneseo. Fine
Arts Center. Hudson River School. (The inaugural
presentation of the Exhibition Gallery of the Arts
Center at the State University College of New York
at Geneseo, Feb. 27--Apr. 6, 1968). Geneseo,
1968. 200 p. Illus. Select Bibliography: p. 198-
99. Catalogue of the second major exhibition of
this school of art, forty-seven artists represented

by at least one painting; biographical data and
critical comment.

189. New York (State). State Council on the Arts. Art in
      New York State: the river, places, and people. An
      exhibition organized by the New York State Council
      on the Arts for the New York State pavilion at the
      New York World's Fair, 1964. Buffalo: Buffalo
      Fine Arts Academy, 1964. 1 v. Illus. (part col.),
      ports.
         The first two centuries of New York State art are
      represented by fifty paintings about the state by New
      York artists. All works were borrowed from New
      York collections. Brief notes include biographical
      and critical comments about the artists and their
      works.

190/5. Saarinen, A. (Bernstein). 5000 years of art in West-
      ern civilization by Aline B. Louchheim. With an
      introd. by Francis Henry Taylor and a foreword by
      Alfred M. Frankfurter. New York: Howell, Soskin,
      1946. 199 p. Illus.
         Chronologically arranged from "Early Civilizations"
      to "Our Own Time," the author, managing editor
      of Art News illustrates the flow of human endeavor
      and expression by works of art that are constantly
      on view in New York City.

SEE ALSO 609.

                     DESCRIPTION AND TRAVEL
                      (general to specific, then
                        alphabetical by area)

196. Fodor, E. Fodor's New York & New Jersey. Eugene
      Fodor, Stephen Birnbaum, Robert Fisher, editors;
      Thomas J. Fleming, introd.; Richard Joseph et al.,
      contributing editors. New York: D. McKay, 1974.
      442 p. Illus., maps. Index: p. 433-42.
         Format: general essays followed by sections on
      practical and general information (facts, figures, how
      to get around, seasonal events, parks, gardens, music,
      etc.).   The arrangement is from the general to spe-
      cific: New York-New Jersey area, New York City,
      Long Island, the Hudson Valley, the Catskills, Albany,
      and Saratoga, the Adirondacks, and the Thousand

Islands, Niagara Frontier, Western and Central New
York.   The introductory essays provide a historical/
cultural/literary/social orientation to the area followed by detailed information about hotels, motels, dining out, and "practical and general information about
special interests, features, expenses." Separate indexes for New York and New Jersey.

197.   Newberry, L.   One-day adventures by car; with full
       road directions for drives out of New York City.
       New York: Hastings House, c. 1971.   261 p.   Maps.
       Index: p. 248-64.
         Trips within 100-mile radius of the city are ar-
       ranged into eight areas--from New Jersey coast,
       southeastern New York, western Connecticut, Long
       Island, and Staten Island with longer trips to Penn-
       sylvania and Massachusetts.   Each entry includes
       distances, tolls, objectives of the trip (museums,
       festivals, parks, etc.), notes about seasonal activ-
       ities or exceptions, restaurants, and very detailed
       instructions for the driver.

198.   Flaste, R.   The New York Times guide to children's
       entertainment: in New York, New Jersey, and Con-
       necticut/by ..., with the assistance of Ellen Rodman
       and Dale Napolin Flaste.   New York: Quadrangle/
       New York Times Books, 1976.   226 p.
         Arranged by activity or theme, then divided into
       four geographic areas: New York City and vicinity,
       Upstate New York, New Jersey, and Connecticut.
       Topics include zoos, safaris, and real nature; Res-
       torations, recreation, preservations; Theme parks
       and amusement centers; Museums and exhibits; Plan-
       etarium, trains, boats, planes; Children's theatre,
       puppets, music, showplace, settlement houses; World
       of work, newspapers, legislature, stocks and com-
       modities; Restaurants, recreation, state parks, mis-
       cellaneous (bookstores, fish hatcheries, garden spots,
       skyscrapers).   Entries include travel directions,
       prices, times, and telephone numbers with brief de-
       scription of activity or items of interest.

199.   Sweet, Ellen B.   The 1776 guide for New York.   New
       York: Harper & Row, 1976.   248 p.   Illus., maps.
         Excursions (nineteen), with an American Revolution
       orientation, are arranged around four base cities (Al-
       bany, Buffalo, Syracuse, New York City).   Each

excursion includes a general historical narrative with
eyewitness accounts of the Revolutionary War, photographs of the high points of the tour-buildings, sites,
etc., each with its own historical description.   Detailed maps with information about fees, times, etc.
are useful.   Each excursion concludes with additional
recommendations concerning shopping possiblities,
cultural opportunities, restaurants.   Most of the trips
are one day; there is a separate section on tourist
information, transportation, campsites, public transportation.

200.   Writers' program.   New York.   New York, a guide to
the Empire State, compiled by workers of the Writers' program of the Work Projects Administration
in the State of New York ... Sponsored by New York
State historical association.   New York: Oxford University Press, 1940.   782 p.   Bibliography: p. 729-
39.
Topical essays, ranging from architecture to transportation, present a succinct historical overview up
to the 1930's.   Supplemented by profiles of cities and
special points of interest that include specifics about
public transportation, accommodations, radio stations,
theaters, annual events, and a narrative about the
historical, social, economic, and cultural aspects of
each locality.   The third section contains directions
for tours within the state, varying in length from ten
to over one hundred miles with explicit travelling ad-
vice and brief sketches of the towns and villages and
points of interest along the way.   While some of the
information is dated, this remains a valuable information guide.

Adirondacks

201.   White, William C.   Adirondack country.   Introd. by L.
Fred Ayvazian.   Afterword by Ruth M. White.   Drawings by Walter Richards.   New York: Knopf, 1967.
325 p.   Illus., maps.
A history with two themes: the ever-increasing
use of the area by vacationers and the problems that
threaten its beauty and future.   The afterword provides the observations and statistical data that char-
acterize the changes that occurred in the thirteen
years since the first edition.

Additional sources are:

White, William Chapman. Just about everything in the
    Adirondacks. Introd. by Alfred S. Dashiell. Blue
    Mountain Lake, New York: Adirondack Museum,
    1960. 101 p. Illus. Essays that originally appear-
    ed in "Topics of the Times" (New York Times), "Just
    About Everything" (Herald Tribune), and from Adiron-
    dack Country. Description of wildlife and human en-
    deavors around the village of Saranac Lake.

Hochschild, Harold K. Township thirty-four; a history,
    with digressions, of an Adirondack township in Ham-
    ilton County in the State of New York. New York,
    1952. 614 p. Illus., ports, maps. Bibliography:
    p. (569)-87. A great compendium of information
    about this section of the Adirondacks and its three
    lakes; a history from the earliest days up to the 20th
    century, including chapters on: mines, lumbering,
    stagecoaches, railroads, various families, literary
    visitors, garnet mines, and appendices that list just
    about everything--hotels, postmasters, steamboat
    crews, etc.

SEE ALSO 286-288.

Catskills

202. Burroughs, J. In the Catskills, selections from the
      writings of John Burroughs, with illustrations from
      photographs by Clifton Johnson. Boston and New
      York: Houghton Mifflin, 1910. 250 p. Front.,
      plates. Reprinted 1974.
      A well-known naturalist's essays of the nineteenth-
      century Catskills--the seasons, labors, wildlife, and
      rambles.

SEE ALSO 293, 294.

Champlain Valley

203. Cone, G. A selective bibliography of publications on
      the Champlain Valley. Plattsburgh, New York,
      1959. 144 p.

A comprehensive (covering 350 years) classified
and annotated bibliography that includes material on
Saratoga, Washington, Warren, Essex, and Clinton
counties. Selective, most of the entries are for
books, pamphlets, with some citations to articles
and newspapers. The main section (712 items) includes biographies, histories, almanacs, diaries and
journals, programs of public ceremonies, lists of
society or church members, pension rolls, cemetery
inscriptions, etc. For older and out-of-print titles
library locations are indicated. There are separate
sections for: atlases; bibliographies, guides to source
materials; manuscripts and source materials; fiction
and juvenile fiction.

Finger Lakes Region

204. O'Connor, L. A Finger Lakes odyssey. Lakemont,
     New York: North Country Books, 1975. 108 p.
          A collection of what were originally newspaper
     feature articles about Central New York. Arranged
     geographically and within each area provides inter-
     esting details and commentary about museums, bat-
     tlefields, wineries, gardens, wild life refuges, his-
     toric houses, parks, art, artists, and other unique
     features of the area. Many photographs.

Great Lakes

205. Ellis, William D. Land of the inland seas: the his-
     toric and beautiful Great Lakes country. Palo Alto,
     California: American West Pub., 1974. 285 p.
     Illus., maps. "Suggested Reading"; p. 279.
          Written by an award-winning author, this book with
     its lavish photographs, paintings, drawings, and maps
     (many of them in color) chronicles the development
     of the region from its earliest explorations to its
     growth as a great industrial/commercial heartland.
     New York State provides the shores of two of the
     inland seas.

206. Hatcher, Harlan H. A pictorial history of the Great
     Lakes by Harlan Hatcher and Erich A. Walter, as-
     sisted by Orin W. Kaye, Jr. New York: Crown,
     c. 1963. 344 p. Bibliography: p. 338.

A comprehensive view of the Lakes: geology, history, (explorers) ships, lake disasters, the shore cities, canal and locks, bridges, and the St. Lawrence Seaway are some of the topics presented.

207. Havighurst, W. The long ships passing, the story of the Great Lakes, Walter Havighurst, illustrated by John O'Hara Cosgrave II. New York: Macmillan, 1942. 291 p. Front., illus., map. Bibliography: p. 279-80.
   A history spanning a period from Jesuit explorers to the development of the St. Lawrence Seaway; a chronicle of Indian wars, lake disasters, commerce, visionaries, and shrewd businessmen, related chiefly in terms of individuals.

208/9. Hatcher, Harlan H. Lake Erie. Indianapolis; New York: Bobbs-Merrill, 1945. 416 p. (The American Lake series). "Bibliographical note": p. 357-63.
   A description of the lake and its human associations and the development of the two nations that border its shores and the role the lake has played in their growth.

SEE ALSO 445, 497.

Hudson River

210. Van Zandt, R., comp. Chronicles of the Hudson; three centuries of travelers' accounts. New Brunswick, New Jersey: Rutgers University Press, 1971. 369 p. Notes: p. 305-40.
   Historical authenticity was the basis for the inclusion of voyages or travels on or along the Hudson during a three hundred year period (1609-1905). Length of narrative was also an additional factor as an attempt was made to present the authentic experience of the journeys, not likely with brief accounts. Selections included are those from Robert Juet, Lafayette, and Henry James. The arrangement is basically chronological.

SEE ALSO 186, 187.

ECONOMICS AND BUSINESS

Directories

211. New York State industrial directory. 1963- New York:
      New York State industrial directory. Illus. Annual.
         Arranged in several sections: 1) alphabetically by
      firm name; 2) alphabetically by firm within county in
      the metropolitan New York City; 3) alphabetically by
      firm within county in upstate New York; 4) firms ar-
      ranged by product. Each entry includes address, tel-
      ephone number, number of employees, SIC number,
      product description, plant size and property size,
      names and titles of company officers, location of
      branch plants.

212. New York (State). Dept. of Commerce. Directory of
      industrial research laboratories in New York State.
      (5th ed.) Albany, 1972. 297 p. "Subject index of
      research activity": p. 243-97.
         Lists commercial, industrial, and academic lab-
      oratories. Alphabetical by firm or institution; entry
      includes address, name of executives, number of
      staff, activity, (research, testing) fields, and basis
      of assignments: internal only, external projects, fee
      basis, etc.

Business

213. Vernon, R. Metropolis 1985; an interpretation of the
      findings of the New York metropolitan region study.
      Cambridge, Mass.: Harvard University Press, 1960.
      252 p. (New York Metropolitan region study 9).
      Notes: p. (241)-44.
         A summary volume of a number of studies/reports
      produced for the Regional Plan Association that in-
      cludes projections of demographic and economic fac-
      tors to 1965, 1975, and 1985, which addresses itself
      to housing, labor, freight, economic growth, local
      government, and employment. The appendix contains
      tables of projections: population and employment.

214. New York (State). Office of Planning Coordination.
      New York State Appalachian development plan; a
      twenty-year plan for the fourteen counties of the New
      York Appalachian area. Albany, 1971. 89 p. Bib-
      liography: p. 77-78.

Combining the factors of the physical, social, and economic, this twenty-year plan was developed to provide a guide for state, local, and regional agencies. Stressing human and economic development, efficient and careful use of natural resources, the recommendations are based upon a 1990 population settlement pattern. Includes careful analysis of land use patterns.

215. Miller, N. The enterprise of a free people: aspects of economic development in New York during the canal period, 1792-1838. Ithaca, New York: Published for the American Historical Assn. by Cornell University Press, 1962. 293 p. Bibliography: p. 277-86.

Analysis of the methods and attitudes that New York State developed to encourage its economic growth. The construction of canals, the Erie and Champlain, is used to highlight those factors that were so influential in the realization of the State's economic resources: a new high in state direct intervention in the economy, the State entering the money market as a borrower, the canals invoking an unparalleled public response, and the Canal commissioners' management of the Canal fund and their policies' extensive impact upon the economy. The success of the canals confirmed New Yorkers in their pragmatism that accepted any combination of individual, corporate, or state effort to accomplish the public weal.

216. Harrington, Virginia D. The New York merchant on the eve of the revolution. New York, London: Columbia University Press, P.S. King & Son, Ltd., 1964, 1935. 389 p. (Studies in history, economics, and public law, ed. by the Faculty of political science of Columbia University). Bibliography: p. 369-81.

Emphasis is on the economic activities of colonial New York merchants the quarter century before the Revolution, compared and contrasted with the business communities on the Continent and Britain. The appendices: shipping data, imports and exports from New York to England, the West Indies, and comparative with Philadelphia, Boston, and Charleston.

SEE ALSO 526, 574, 598, 601.

Labor

Directories

217. New York (State). Dept. of Labor. Division of Re-
      search and Statistics. Directory of public employee
      organizations in New York. 1972- New York.
          Lists names and addresses of key officers, of
      national, state, and local organizations. Arranged
      into three sections: 1) National, international, and
      state; 2) Delegate organizations; 3) Local organiza-
      tions. These are each subdivided into seven geo-
      graphic areas.

Legal Aspects

218. Seidenberg, J. The labor injunction in New York City,
      1935-1950. Ithaca, New York: Cornell University,
      School of Industrial and Labor Relations, 1953.   171
      p. (Cornell studies in industrial and labor relations,
      no. 4). Bibliography: 163-67.
          Based upon court records, interviews with attor-
      neys, and use of legal secondary sources, this re-
      search chronicles the use of the injunction in New
      York City courts twelve years prior to the Taft-
      Hartley Act and in the first three years of its pas-
      sage.

SEE ALSO 223, 940.

Zoning Board

219. New York State Federation of Official Planning Organ-
      izations. Directory of planning and zoning boards,
      New York State, 1964/65. Albany: New York State
      Federation of Official Planning Organizations.
          Lists planning board chairmen and zoning board
      of appeals chairmen (with addresses) by city within
      county.

EDUCATION

History
(general to specific)

219a. New York (State). University. Education in New York
      State, 1784-1954; compiled and edited by Harlan Hoyt
      Horner. Albany: University of the State of New
      York, State Education Dept., 1954. 166 p. Illus.
         Historical overview of various levels of education,
      the role of the state, the function of the Regents, the
      development of public and private education, the edu-
      cation of children, special services and educational
      opportunities, vocational training, the education and
      up-grading of teachers.

220. New York (State). University. Division of Research.
      The New York State Education Department, 1900-
      1965. Albany, 1967. 63 p. Bibliography: p. 49.
         Since 1904, in New York State, all educational in-
      stitutions, private and public, elementary and sec-
      ondary, colleges, universities, libraries, and mu-
      seums have been included in one chartered institution
      and under the governance and control of the Regents
      of the University of the State of New York. Appen-
      dices list: the regents (1904-1966), commissioners
      of education (1904-1965); also a chronology and or-
      ganization charts.

221. Miller, George F. The academy system of the State
      of New York. New York: Arno Press & The New
      York Times, 1969. 181 p. (American education,
      its men, ideas, and institutions). Reprint of the
      1922 ed. Bibliography: p. 179-80.
         Considered to be one of the most successful sys-
      tems, this history (1787-1900) of New York acade-
      mies considers: their legal status, relationships to
      other types of schools, development and support,
      curriculum and methods, the education of common
      school teachers. Considerable comparative data.

Higher Education
(general to specific)

222.   Carmichael, Oliver C.   New York establishes a state
        university; a case study in the process of policy
        formulation.   Nashville: Vanderbilt University, 1955.
        414 p.
            Prefaced by chapters devoted to New York's her-
        itage in public education and the post-World War II
        higher education crisis, this is an analysis of the
        political origins of the legislation that created the
        State University of New York in 1948.   Examines
        such questions as who opposed/supported it, why,
        what were the public and private interest groups that
        were involved, what was their influence, etc.   Based
        upon unpublished reports, newspaper articles, and
        interviews.
            Related sources are:

        Milstein, Mike M.   Educational policy-making and the
        State legislature; the New York experience ... and
        Robert E. Jennings.   New York: Praeger, 1973.
        156 p.   (Praeger special studies in U.S. economic,
        social, and political issues).   Bibliography: p. 149-
        53.   Directed to the educational community, the fo-
        cus is on the interaction of interest groups, educa-
        tional governmental structures, the governor's office,
        and the state legislature in the process of educational
        policy making.

        New York (State).   State Library, Albany.   A guide to
        the papers of James E. Allen, Jr., President of the
        University of the State of New York and Commissioner
        of Education, 1955-1969.   Albany, 1970.   68 p.   "In
        summary, the Allen papers are a collection of doc-
        uments drawn from the files of the Commissioner's
        Office that relate most closely to James E. Allen, Jr.
        as a person and as New York's Commissioner of
        Education from 1955 to 1969."   Arranged in series,
        A-M: general files, organizational memberships,
        speeches, commissioner's engagements accepted, Com-
        missioner's engagements not accepted, Deputy Com-
        missioner's papers, notes of Regents meetings, con-
        gratulatory messages, news releases, Governor's
        office, copies of outgoing correspondence, important
        judicial decisions rendered.   Series are analyzed by
        box number.

223. Duryea, Edwin D. Collective bargaining, the State
      University and the State government in New York:
      report of survey and analysis of the impact of col-
      lective bargaining by academic and non-teaching pro-
      fessional personnel on the relationships between the
      State University and the State government by E. D.
      Duryea and Robert S. Fisk. Buffalo: Dept. of
      Higher Education, Faculty of Educational Studies,
      State University of New York at Buffalo, 1975.   51
      p. Bibliography: p. 51.
         This study is limited to the period from 1970,
      when collective bargaining became operative for the
      State University, to 1974, when the second contract
      agreement was made. In part, this report is also
      an examination of the increase in the use of legal
      prerogatives by the state to control and/or constrain
      the autonomy of public universities and colleges.

224. Brown, William P. Order and justice on the campus.
      Albany: School of Criminal Justice, State University
      of New York at Albany, 1971.   47 ℓ.
         Augmenting the limited literature on the subject
      with the experience of crime and violence on the
      campus of the State University of New York at Al-
      bany, the author focuses upon the formal security
      system, a hearing and review system used by uni-
      versity personnel in dealing with campus crime and
      disorder. He suggests that the problem and objec-
      tives of order maintenance and administrative leader-
      ship are related.

225. Bennis, Warren G. and Patricia W. Biederman. The
      leaning ivory tower. San Francisco: Jossey-Bass,
      1973.   145 p.
         The author, vice president for academic affairs
      at the State University of New York at Buffalo during
      the period described, profiles the crises of the
      "Berkeley of the East" in the late sixties. The ri-
      ots, the euphoria, the problems, and the innovations
      are incorporated into essentially three themes:
      search for new leadership, the expression and re-
      pression of dissidence within large organization and
      institutional large scale reform.

226. Dedman, W. Cherishing this heritage; the centennial
      history of the State University College at Brockport,
      New York. New York: Appleton-Century-Crofts,
      1969.   317 p. "Selected Bibliography": p. 302-06.

Spans a period of 136 years which highlights three
trends: a continuing reciprocal, mutually beneficial
relationship between the college and the community,
a chronicle of the very ordinary process of a 19th-
century academy eventually developing into an Arts
and Sciences college, typical of American higher education, and a very long history of loyal and sup-
portive faculty and graduates.

227.   Brush, Carey W.   In honor and good faith; a history
of the State University College at Oneonta, New York.
Oneonta, New York, 1965.   330 p.   Bibliography: p.
319-24.

The author had three objectives: 1) write a comprehensive history/reference book for future faculty
and students; 2) make a scholarly contribution to the
history of higher education; and 3) recreate an interesting story for alumni and friends of the college.
Covers the period 1889-1965; the book is organized
around basic curriculum changes.   The appendices
list curriculum requirements (1889-1948), list the
first faculty, dramatic productions by college groups,
1882-1965, and also presents a history and explanation of the college's coat of arms.

228.   Dearborn, Ned H.   The Oswego movement in American
education.   New York: Teachers College, Columbia
University, 1925.   189 p.   Reprinted 1972.   Bibliography: 109-18.

Attempts to evaluate and describe those educational
factors of the Oswego Movement: the needs of the
local public shools, Pestalozzian principles, object
teaching, English School materials, the maturity of
students, their training and their residence distribution after graduation, contributing to their professional importance of the school and its state-wide
and national influence, the ability of the teaching
staff, and practice teaching.   This history emphasizes the years 1861-1886 and examines each of the
above factors.   Appendices include: biographies of
teachers, reproductions of object lessons, geographi-
cal distribution of graduates.

229.   Rogers, D.   Oswego: fountainhead of teacher education; a century in the Sheldon tradition.   New York:
Appleton-Century-Crofts, 1961.   305 p.   "Notes":
p. 273-84.

For two decades the leading normal school in the
U.S.; it was also known as the "Mother of Normal
Schools" as its graduates were so prominent in the
staffing and founding of normal schools. Initiating
Pestalozzianism, Hervatianism, and progressivism,
it played a key role in the education of teachers.
This narrative is arranged by administration (1861-
1961), each reviewed in terms of curriculum, general developments, staff, and students.

230. Lahey, William C. The Potsdam tradition; a history
and a challenge. New York: Appleton-Century-
Crofts, 1966. 255 p. "Footnotes": p. 239-49.
The State University of New York, College at
Potsdam pioneered in the education of public school
music teachers in the U.S. and "common" (public)
school teachers in New York State. This history,
from the founding of St. Lawrence Academy in 1816
to 1965, is a record, by administration, of that
institution's contributions to the state, the country,
and American education.

231. Morrison, T. Chautauqua: a center for education,
religion, and the arts in America ... drawings by
Jane E. Nelson. Chicago: University of Chicago,
1974. 351 p. "Acknowledgements and Sources":
p. 337-40.
Centennial history of the Chautauqua Institution
which was originally created to improve Sunday
school teaching. Its scope was expanded to include
diverse secular interests with an emphasis upon
educational innovation and intellectual and artistic
stimulation. Leaders in the arts, sciences, government, technology, and literature have been closely
associated with its programs that range from hobbies
and religion to public discussion, music, and sports,
as well as opera and theatre. Chautauqua, as a
concept, had many local imitators and the term, in
many American towns and villages, is associated
with the travelling "cultural" companies that provided
drama, music or a speaker for the evening. Drawings and over 150 photographs complete the Chautauqua story.

SEE ALSO 127, 155, 250, 251, 541-556a, 642-644, 773, 776.

FOLKLORE

232. Thompson, Harold W. Body, boots & britches; folk-
      tales, ballads, and speech from county New York.
      New York: Dover, 1939. 530 p. Reprinted 1962.
          Tales, stories, and ballads about heroes, warri-
      ors, sailors, "uncanny critters," whalers, etc.,
      plus proverbs and explanations of place names. The
      appendix cites the source printed or otherwise of the
      information.

233. Carmer, Carl L. Listen for a lonesome drum; a York
      State chronicle. Decorations by John O'Hare Cos-
      grave, II. New York: D. McKay, 1950. 430 p.
          Very readable accounts of the history of various
      religious enterprises and sects in New York State--
      from the Covenanter and Mormons to Indian prophets,
      Spiritualists and Utopians.

SEE ALSO 287, 485, 882.

GEOGRAPHY
(general to specific)

234. French, John H. Gazetteer of the State of New York;
      embracing a comprehensive view of the geography,
      geology, and general history of the State, and a com-
      plete history and description of every county, city,
      town, village, and locality, with full tables of statis-
      tics. Port Washington, New York: I.J. Friedman,
      1969. 739 p. (Empire State historical publications
      series, no. 72). Reprint of the 1860 ed.
          Thorough, exceedingly detailed articles on state
      boundaries, state government, canals, railroads,
      lands, corporations, colleges, commerce, manufac-
      turers, agriculture, military, public schools, churches,
      religious, literary, and benevolent societies, followed
      by comprehensive profiles of each county. Excellent
      historical source.

235. Rayback, Robert J. Richard Atlas of New York State,
      Robert J. Rayback, editor-in-chief. (2nd ed.) Rev.
      and supplemented, 1965, Edward L. Towle, editor.
      Phoenix, New York: F.E. Richards, 1965. 86 p.
          Colored, detailed maps depicting not only the
      state's geologic, climatic, water and mineral

resources, but also the cultural, economic, political,
and historical factors: migrations, Indian settlements,
military campaigns, land policies, grants and patents,
politics, railroads, canals and turnpikes, as well as
literature, economics, manufacturing, state parks,
etc. There is an extensive and well-written page of
text about the topic of each map.

236. New York (State). Dept. of Transportation. Map Information Unit. Inventory of aerial photography and
other remotely sensed imagery of New York State.
Albany, 1975. 116 p.
     The purpose of the inventory is to assist the user
in identifying available and planned imagery and
aerial photography of New York State as of July, 1975.
Lists most vertical photography flown since 1968--
usually limited to complete stereo coverage of at
least one village, city, or region (river valley,
shoreline, etc.). Four parts: 1) identifies available and planned coverage on a county by county
basis; 2) description of regional projects; 3) description of satellites or high altitude imagery; 4) description of corridor and site photography. Each
project description includes date, scale, camera
focal length, film type, area of coverage, where
photos may be viewed, where purchased.

237. Stout, Neil J. Atlas of forestry in New York. Syracuse: State University College of Forestry at Syracuse University, 1958. 95 p. (State University
College of Forestry at Syracuse University, Bulletin
no. 41). Bibliography: p. 79-82.
     Criteria, twenty-seven, were selected to represent
various aspects of New York's forest economy and
were used to divide the state into nine regions and
fifty-two sub-regions. Includes description and analysis of forest economy--wood, water, recreation,
and wildlife--as well as forest statistical data by
town and counties.

238. Hedrick, Ulysses P. A history of agriculture in the
State of New York. Albany: Printed for the New
York State Agricultural Society, 1933. 462 p.
Front., illus., plates, ports, maps. Bibliography:
p. 445-50.
     Focuses upon rural life and the factors that af-
fected the farmers' quality of life--communication

and transportation, the printing press, agricultural organizations, new plants, religion, Indian agriculture. A standard history.

239. Mordoff, Richard A. The climate of New York State. Ithaca: New York State College of Agriculture, Cornell University, 1949. 72 p. (Cornell extension bulletin, no. 764). Bibliography: p. 38.
      Brief history of weather observation, an explanation of the impact of climate on agriculture, discussion of factors responsible for New York State's diverse weather followed by discussions of temperature, snowfall, droughts, thunderstorms, hail, tornadoes, winds, sunshine, humidity with historical data and tables of seasonal ranges.

240/1. Werstein, I. The blizzard of '88. New York: Crowell, 1960. 157 p.
      Emphasizing the physical and psychological impact of the snow storm that in March 1888 devastated the Eastern seaboard. Based upon magazines, newspapers, and other publications of the period. Additional information obtained from interviews. Supplemented by many photographs.

SEE ALSO 94.

HEALTH SCIENCES

Directories

242. Medical directory of New York State. New York. 19-
      Alphabetic lists of doctors of medicine and osteopathy by area (New York boroughs) and then alphabetically by city and town exclusive of New York City. Provides address, telephone number, qualifications, memberships, fellowships, and hospital affiliations. Also includes hospital staff lists.

243. Health facilities directory. 1969- (Albany). New York State Dept. of Health.
      Vol. 1: Hospitals: indicates type of ownership, the specific nature of the institution, bed capacity. Alphabetically listed within region. Vol. 2: Nurs-

ing homes: indicates type of ownership and bed
capacity. Vol. 3: Health facilities; a) Health-related
facilities; b) Diagnostic and/or Treatment centers;
c) Narcotic Addiction Rehabilitation Centers; d) Schools
for the Mentally Retarded; e) Home Health Agencies.
Indicates sponsorship, bed capacity. Alphabetically
within region.

Regulations, Rules

244. New York (State). Laws, statutes, etc. Official compilation of codes, rules, and regulations, State of
New York. 10: Health. Albany, 1962. 1 vol.
(loose leaf). Supplemented by additional or replace-
ment pages.
Contains only the current regulations and rules
together with amendments, additions, etc.

245. Medical Society of the State of New York. Relative
value scale, 1975. 2nd ed. Lake Success, New
York, 1975. 148 p.
The RVS is a method based upon statistical techniques and surveys that allows the physician to com-
pute his fees on the nature of his services, his educational background, experience, the particulars of
his practice, and the reasonable value of service in
a specific community.

History

246. Walsh, James J. History of medicine in New York;
three centuries of medical progress. New York:
National Americana Society, 1919. 5 vol.
Vol. 1: Chapters on the European background of
colonial New York medicine, medical education, first
medical society, surgery, evolution of sanitation,
nursing women as physicians. Vol. 2: Emphasis
is upon physician-writers, physician-scientists, medical education, medical colleges, and teaching hospitals. Vol. 3: Limited to Medical societies and specific hospitals. Vols 4 & 5: One to three page biographical sketches of physicians.

Dentistry

247. Directory of dental laboratories, manufacturers, deal-
      ers, New York State.   New York: New York State
      Association of Certified Dental Laboratories, Inc.,
      1970.
           Separate sections for laboratories and manufac-
      turers and dealers.   Generally geographically ar-
      ranged by area: Manhattan, Bronx, Queens, etc.
      Then alphabetically by firm.   In larger areas--West-
      chester, Upstate, etc.--it is alphabetically by city
      or town, then by company (address and telephone
      number).

248. New York (State).   Dept. of Health.   Dental public
      health in New York State; a review on the occasion
      of the American Dental Association Centennial, 1859-
      1959.   41 p.
           Covers public dental health, public health edu-
      cation, the problem of our aging population.   Also
      has a fluoridation map of New York State.

SEE ALSO 114.

Hospitals
(general to specific)

249. De La Chapelle, Clarence E. and F. Jensen.   A mis-
      sion in action; the story of the regional hospital plan
      of New York University.   New York: New York Uni-
      versity Press, 1964.   177 p.   Bibliography: p. 165-
      169.
           The "story" of a continuing education program for
      physicians, primarily those located in suburban and
      rural areas of New York, Pennsylvania, Connecticut,
      and New Jersey.   The plan functioned for seventeen
      years, 1947-1964.

250. Rochester, New York.   University.   School of Medicine
      and Dentistry.   The quarter century: a review of
      the first twenty-five years, 1925-1950.   Rochester,
      New York: University of Rochester, 1950.   144 p.
           Short descriptive chapters on each area of hospi-
      tal service or function with additional chapters de-
      voted to special educational activities, societies,
      clubs, lectureships, the medical library, honor so-
      cieties, and prizes.

251. New York (State) University.   College of Medicine at
      New York City.   Alumni Association.   History of the
      Long Island College Hospital, Long Island College of
      Medicine and the State University of New York, Col-
      lege of Medicine at New York City.   Alumni Associ-
      ation highlights, 1880-1955, and biographies of grad-
      uates, 1900-1955. [A. Jablons]. Brooklyn, 1960.
      448 p. "Index of biographies of graduates--1900-
      1955": p. 379-425.
         Brief but well-written statement of the evolution
      of an institution that has had a rather complex and
      confusing background.

Mental Health

252. Rivera, G. Willowbrook; a report on how it is and
      why it doesn't have to be that way.   New York:
      Random House, 1972.   147 p.
         A television reporter's expose of the horrendous
      conditions at the Willowbrook State School, an insti-
      tution for the mentally retarded.
         Additional documentation:

      Symposium on Ethical Issues in Human Experimenta-
      tion, New York, 1972.   The Case of Willowbrook
      State Hospital (i.e., School) research; proceedings
      ... May 4, 1972.   New York: Urban Health Af-
      fairs Program, New York University, Medical Cen-
      ter, 1973.   57 ℓ. Bibliography: p. 56-57.   While
      the emphasis is upon the ethical questions involved
      in human experimentation, it also provides some
      insight into the operation of the Willowbrook State
      School.

253. Sturm, L. The mental hospital nightmare.   New York:
      Exposition, 1973.   62 p.
         An employee in the Willard State Hospital reports
      her experience and observations.

SEE ALSO 628-640, 865, 870.

Nursing

Directory

254. New York State League for Nursing. Directory of
     schools of nursing in New York State. (Albany,
     N.Y.) 19--
       A comprehensive guide to nursing education pro-
     grams within the state. Arranged by type of pro-
     gram--college affiliation, admission dates, length
     of program, costs, etc.

Association

255. Driscoll, Veronica M. Legitimizing the profession of
     nursing: the distinct mission of the New York State
     Nurses Association. Albany: Foundation, New York
     State Nurses Assn., 1976. 80 p. Bibliography: p.
     74-79.
       The history of the organization, structure and
     creation of the New York State Nurses Association
     and its attempts to obtain statutory recognition of
     the profession, restriction of use of the title of
     nurse, licensure, and definition of nursing.

History

256. Austin, Anne L. Woolsey sisters of New York; a fam-
     ily's involvement in the Civil War and a new profes-
     sion (1860-1900). Philadelphia: American Philo-
     sophical Society, 1971. 189 p. Illus. (American
     Philosophical Society. Memoirs, v. 85). Bibliog-
     raphy: p. 171-178.
       The three Woolsey sisters, Abby, Janet, and
     Georgeanna, worked on behalf of the Union wounded
     during the Civil War and after became leaders in
     nursing education, hospital nursing service, the edu-
     cation of Negroes, and in the promotion of social
     welfare programs.

Homes

257. Thomas, William C. Nursing homes and public policy:
     drift and decision in New York State. Ithaca, New
     York: Cornell University, 1969. 287 p.
       A study of the mechanism of public policy devel-
     opment within the historical/legislative context of the
     growth of the concept of nursing homes.

Pharmacy

258. Lockie, Lawrence D. Pharmacy on the Niagara fron-
     tier; the past and the present. East Aurora, New
     York: Stewart, 1968. 264 p. Bibliography: p.
     (5-6).
         Beginning with a history of pharmacy from the
     1800's to the 1950's; then chapters on pharmacy as-
     sociations, the Buffalo School of Pharmacy, the pri-
     vate practice of pharmacy, manufacturers (by city
     and town), the oldest pharmacy in Ontario, and a
     directory of pharmacies from 1828 to 1960; listed
     by year including those discontinued or those that
     changed location.

SEE ALSO 112, 114, 360, 465, 623-649, 838.

HISTORY

259. New York State Historical Association. History of the
     State of New York (Edited by Alexander C. Flick,
     State historian). Port Washington, New York: I.J.
     Friedman, 1962 (c. 1961). 10 v. in 5. (Empire
     State historical publication no. 18). Reprint of the
     1933 edition.
         The standard history of New York State, from
     the era of exploration to the first quarter of the
     20th century, written by "the best qualified special-
     ists," covering all aspects of human endeavor--art,
     religion, literature, education, place names, etc.,
     as well as the traditional historical topics--law,
     government, politics, and economics. Each chapter
     usually has a select bibliography. Volume 10 has
     the index for all ten volumes.

260. Ellis, David M. A history of New York State. Rev.
     ed. Published in co-operation with the New York
     State Historical Association. Ithaca, New York:
     Cornell University, 1967. 732 p. "Bibliographical
     essay": p. 663-703. First published in 1957 under
     the title: A short history of New York State.
         A standard history (1609-1966) that was revised
     to be of maximum utility to teachers and students.
     Chapters and essays devoted to every aspect of so-
     cial, political, cultural, and economic endeavor
     within each time segment: 1609-1865; 1865-1966.

Bibliography

261. Dunn, James T. Masters' theses and doctoral disser-
      tations on New York history, 1870-1954. Rev. 1955.
      15 p.
        Cumulated listings that were originally published
      in the April, July, and October, 1952 issues of New
      York History. Arranged by institution conferring the
      degree, then alphabetically by the author. Only elev-
      en institutions are included, supplemented by a mis-
      cellaneous section of research completed at other
      schools.

262. Flagg, Charles A. and Judson T. Jennings. Bibliog-
      raphy of New York colonial history. Albany: Uni-
      versity of the State of New York, 1901. (289)-558
      p. (New York State Library. Bulletin, 56, Febru-
      ary, 1901).
        Covers period from discovery to 1776; includes
      references to books, articles, printed indexes and
      calendars of manuscripts, city charters and legis-
      lative journals. Classified arrangement by time
      period (discovery, Dutch period, English period,
      etc.), topic (law, medicine, printing, etc.), and
      local colonial history, subdivided by county and then
      town or city.

Colonial Period
(general to specific)

263. Fox, Dixon R. Yankees and Yorkers. New York,
      London: University Press, H. Milford, Oxford Uni-
      versity, 1940. 237 p.
        Active border disputes between New York and New
      England states existed from the 1620's to the 1790's
      and it was not until the 1870's that counter claims
      were settled--almost. These conflicts are examined
      in terms of two differing racial, religious, and po-
      litical backgrounds, each seeking a distinct social
      purpose.

264. Halsey, Francis W. The Old New York frontier; its
      wars with Indians and tories, its missionary schools,
      pioneers, and land titles, 1614-1800. Port Wash-
      ington, New York: I.J. Friedman, 1901. 432 p.
      (Empire State historical publication no. 21). Bib-
      liography: p. 403-411. Reprinted 1963.

A very detailed history of the upper Susquehanna
Valley and its role in the development of the state
from the Iroquois settlements to 1800.

265. Smith, W. The history of the Province of New York,
      by William Smith, Jr.   Edited by Michael Kammen.
      Cambridge, Mass.: Belknap Press of Harvard Uni-
      versity, 1972. 2 v.
           Originally published in 1757, emphasis is on po-
      litics, the law, assemblies, Indian relations, and
      gubernatorial struggles, at the expense of economic
      and social history, cultural commentary, and local
      and regional events. Arranged by governor's ad-
      ministration. Editor's Appendix A: The governors
      of colonial New York, 1624-1762, p. 277-282. Ed-
      itor's Appendix B: A biographical directory to
      William Smith's New York, p. 283-296.

266. Smith, Helen E. Colonial days & ways as gathered
      from family papers, by Helen Evertson Smith, with
      decorations by T. Guernsey Moore. New York: The
      Century, 1900. 376 p.
           Social life and customs of New England and New
      York colonies in pre-revolutionary times. Analytic
      table of contents compensates for the lack of an
      index.

SEE ALSO 583-587.

Revolutionary Period
(general to specific)

267. Klein, Milton M., comp. New York in the American
      Revolution; a bibliography. Albany: New York State
      American Revolution Bicentennial commission, c.
      1974. 197 p.
           Includes 1,089 entries which provide a cross-
      section of popular, scholarly, and technical pub-
      lished materials (books, articles, doctoral disserta-
      tions, government publications, etc.) about New York
      or New Yorkers in the Revolutionary era--1763 to 1789.
      Categories of publications include: general histories,
      biographies, military campaigns, Loyalists, the
      economy, ideology and propaganda, education and
      religion, women, Indians, Blacks and ethnic minor-
      ities, the Revolution locally, primary sources,

historiography, guides and bibliographic aids, and
the Revolution in New York in fiction.

268. Alper, M. Victor. America's freedom trail: a tour
      guide to historical sites of the colonial and Revolu-
      tionary War period. New York: Macmillan, 1976.
      562 p.
          Begins at Lexington and Concord and proceeds
      southward through New York and New Jersey, ending
      in Pennsylvania. Battles and events of the Revolu-
      tionary War are described. While emphasis is on
      Colonial and Revolutionary War sites, there are also
      recommended side trips exploring the area's history
      as well as suggested walking and driving tours. The
      section on New York is limited, due to the scope
      of this guide, to the eastern end of the state.

269. Scudiere, Paul J. New York's signers of the Decla-
      ration of Independence. Albany: New York State
      American Revolution Bicentennial Commission, 1975.
      30 p.
          Four biographical sketches: Philip Livingston,
      Lewis Morris, William Floyd, and Francis Lewis.

270. Swiggett, H. War out of Niagara; Walter Butler and
      the Tory Rangers. Port Washington, New York:
      I. J. Friedman, c. 1961. 309 p. Bibliography: p.
      289-295.
          Utilizing primary historical sources in both Eng-
      land and the U.S., the author, after 30 years of
      research, seeks to present an accurate and balanced
      assessment of the "villainous" Walter Butler. That
      Loyalist soldier and leader, while capturing the
      imagination, has also had almost every crime un-
      justly ascribed to him. This narrative of the fron-
      tier war in Northern New York State underscores
      the loyalists' viewpoint: they too were simply men
      fighting and defending their beliefs and a way of
      life.

271. Flick, Alexander C. Loyalism in New York during
      the American Revolution. New York: AMS, 1970.
      281 p. (Studies in history, economics, and public
      law, v. 14, no. 1). From the 1901 edition. Bib-
      liography: p. 273-281.
          Explores the religious and political basis of loy-
      alism, the organization of the Loyalist party, the

activities of the Loyalists and the Revolutionaries'
reactions toward them. Describes the confiscation
and sale of loyalist property, their emigration to
England, Canada, and Nova Scotia, and their treatment in their new homes. Appendices list and describe loyalist property, the owner, purchaser price,
and date of sale.

272.   Yoshpe, Harry B.   The disposition of loyalist estates
        in the Southern district of the State of New York.
        New York, London: Columbia University, c. 1939.
        226 p. (Studies in history, economics, and public
        law, no. 458). "Bibliographical Note": p. 210-218.
            Describes the mechanism for confiscation, how
        the Loyalists' estates were disposed of, the hardships
        and court problems of tenant-farmers, craftsmen,
        and small freeholders that were caught in the proc-
        ess, the speculation in Loyalist property, claims for
        and against those properties and the litigation in-
        volving Loyalist wealth. Detailed, systematic, with
        appendices providing names, dates, and prices of
        sale of Loyalist real estate.

273.   The Loyalist Americans: a focus on Greater New York/
        edited by Robert A. East and Jacob Judd.   Tarrytown,
        New York: Sleepy Hollow Restorations, 1975. 173 p.
        Illus. Bibliography: p. 163.
            A collection of essays concerning the British view
        of American loyalists; James DeLancey's cowboys;
        Frederich Philipse III of Westchester County; Peter
        Van Schaach; William Franklin; and a profile of New
        York loyalists. The appendix contains copies of the
        documentation provided by the Philipse family for
        their claim on the British government for the loss
        of their American property. It is both a record of
        the process and a way of life that existed along the
        Hudson River.

SEE ALSO 464, 592-595.

Civil War
(general to specific)

274.   Sorin, G.   The New York abolitionists; a case study
        of political radicalism.   Westport, Conn.: Green-
        wood, 1970. 172 p. (Contributions in American
        history, no. 11). Bibliography: p. 139-165.

Almost half of the delegates to the Second Annual
Meeting of the American Anti-Slavery Society, in
1835, were from New York State. In 1836, that
state had so much anti-slavery activity that the State
Society was formed. This study attempts to analyze
the motivational factors, sociological and psychological, of New York abolitionist leaders and determine
if their actions resulted from a personal need or
were they "normally" responding to their perceptions/
vision of America. Appendices list New York's one
hundred most prominent abolitionist leaders.

275.   Phisterer, F., comp. New York in the war of the
        rebellion, 1861 to 1865. Albany: J.B. Lyons, 1912.
        6 v.
        A massive collection of information compiled from
        official records or sources equally reliable result-
        ing in charts, lists, and statistics. Identifies mil-
        itary personnel: age, place and date of enrollment,
        ranks held, wounds, etc. Describes military units
        and officers of the regiments, battles fought, places
        and dates, numbers of wounded, dead, and missing.
        Roll of honor included. The sixth volume is the
        indices of synonyms (military units were generally
        known by local or popular names), battles, subjects,
        and names.

276.   Sullivan County (New York) Historical Society. Sulli-
        van County Civil War Commission Centennial. Brass
        buttons and leather boots; Sullivan and the Civil War.
        South Fallsburg, New York: Printed by Steingart
        Associates, 1963. 84 p.
        An account of the men of Sullivan County (143rd
        New York Volunteer Infantry Regiment) and their
        contributions during the Civil War--on the battle
        fields, the forests, and the tanneries. The Union
        Army marched and its animals pulled and were guid-
        ed by the shoes, harnesses, and saddles made from
        leather tanned in Sullivan County. Includes a sepa-
        rate section on tanneries, turnpikes, and canals;
        also a report of a Civil War soldiers' reunion.

277.   Roehrenbeck, William J. The regiment that saved the
        capital. Introd. by Allan Nevins. New York: Yose-
        loff, 1961. 244 p. Bibliography: p. 239-240.
        A general account of the Seventh Regiment, the
        "darling" of the New York newspapers; a militia unit

composed of men from the "best" families in New
York. The forty-five days (April 19 to June 3, 1961)
is emphasized when the unit rushed off to Washington
when it was being menaced by secessionist elements
and Southern military forces. Originally, 1806, a
unit of the Volunteer Militia, this regiment, now
known as the 107th Infantry, New York National
Guard, has had a long, honorable, and colorful history.

SEE ALSO 42, 43, 104, 591-601.

Spanish American War

278. New York (State). State historian. New York and the
      war with Spain. History of the Empire State regi-
      ments. Albany: Argus, 1903. 429, 192 p. Port.,
      illus.
          At the start of the Spanish American War, the
      New York State Historian sent to every New York
      regimental commander a request that a diary be
      kept about the unit's activities or its itinerary. He
      also asked for regimental reports being sent to the
      War Department. A number of officers cooperated
      and thus provided the materials of the histories of
      the New York Volunteers (1st regiment, 2nd regi-
      ment, 3rd regiment, and the 71st regiment). There
      is a separate index for each of these military units.

Genealogy

279. Robison, Jeannie Floyd J. and Henrietta C. Bartlett.
      Genealogical records; manuscripts, entries of births,
      deaths, and marriages, taken from family Bibles,
      1581-1917. Baltimore: Genealogical Pub. Co., 1972.
      331 p. Reprint of 1917 ed.
          Genealogical records found in ninety family bibles
      are represented alphabetically. Bibles are listed
      under the owner's name or the names of first de-
      scendents. Each entry identifies the language of the
      bible, its condition/location and has notes about the
      family.

280. MacWethy, Lou D. The book of names especially re-
      lating to the early Palatines and the first settlers in

the Mohawk Valley, compiled and arranged by Lou
D. MacWethy.   St. Johnsville, New York: The Enterprise and News, 1933.   209 p.

List of names extracted from various military,
church, and legal colonial documents.   Of particular
interest are: prisoner of war lists, lists of Pala-
tines in 1790 (from London manuscript) Governor
Hunter's ration list (London records) and nicknames
and their equivalents used by early German settlers
of the Mohawk Valley.

281.   Cutter, William R.   Genealogical and family history of
western New York; a record of the achievements of
her people in the making of a commonwealth and the
building of a nation, comp. under the editorial su-
pervision of William Richard Cutter ... New York:
Lewis Historical, 1912.   3 v.

Presents all the "important facts" concerning an-
cestry, careers, and family alliances of those families and individuals that were leaders in the business, professional, and social life of the area from
colonial days to the present (1912).   Also attempts
to relate their accomplishments to the growth and
development of the state.

SEE ALSO 21, 185, 276, 579.

Local History

Bibliography
(general to specific)

282.   Nestler, H.   A bibliography of New York State com-
munities, county, towns, villages.   Port Washington,
New York: I.J. Friedman, 1968.   1 v.   (Empire
State historical publications series, 51).

Emphasizing the smaller political units (larger
cities theoretically requiring their own bibliographies),
all town, county, and community histories have been
listed, "approximately 85% of the important books
and pamphlets published from 1900 through 1965, and
a large portion of those issued in the previous hundred years."   Also included are the biographical
publications (vanity "mug books") so popular in the
1800's and early 1900's.   Excluded are histories of
businesses, churches, military units, organizations,
directories, and gazetteers, as well as newspapers.

283.   South Central Research Library Council, Ithaca, New
        York Local History Committee. A guide to local
        historical materials in the libraries of south central
        New York State. Ithaca, New York: The Council,
        1976. 188 p. (SCRLC pamphlet series, no. 9).
            A union list of historical materials (atlases, bi-
        ographies, church histories, cook books, diaries,
        directories, genealogies, guide books, materials on
        folklore and Indians, maps, gazetteers, local govern-
        ment documents, periodicals, college and university
        histories, etc.) located in 122 public libraries of
        fourteen counties and the libraries of Cornell Uni-
        versity.

284.   Historical materials relating to northern New York; a
        union catalog, compiled by a committee of the North
        County Reference and Research Resources Council.
        Edited by G. Glyndon Cole with the assistance of
        Dorothy A. Plum. Plattsburgh, New York: North
        Country Reference and Research Resources Council,
        1968. 307 p.
            A bibliography of books, pamphlets, newspapers,
        journals, maps, and leaflets concerned with: North-
        ern New York or a Northern New Yorker, written
        by or closely associated as a Northern New Yorker
        or was printed in that area. Entries include history,
        geography, travel, regional histories, natural history,
        social and economic history, recreation, biography,
        genealogy, art and literature, etc., with their loca-
        tions in ninety-two libraries and six other institutions.

285.   Taub, M. and B. Sweeney. Bibliography of research
        materials on Saratoga Springs, New York. Saratoga
        Springs, New York: Saratoga Public Library, 1977.
        51 p.
            A classified bibliography (almanacs, buildings, the
        city, gambling, history, literature, organizations,
        people, racing, religion, etc.) of selective and rep-
        resentative references to books, articles, maps, and
        other items most important and useful to the student
        and researcher. Most of the citations have location
        symbols indicating libraries where the item may be
        seen.

SEE ALSO 140, 147, 148, 569, 576, 581.

286. Adirondack Mountain Club. Adirondack bibliography;
      a list of books, pamphlets, and periodical articles
      published through the year 1955. Compiled by the
      Bibliography Committee of the Adirondack Mountain
      Club. Dorothy A. Plum, chairman, Lynette S.
      Scribner, vice-chairman. Gabriels, New York,
      1958. 354 p.
      Supplement, 1966-1968. Glens Falls, New York, 1970.
      46 p.
      Supplement, 1956-1965. Blue Mountain Lake, New
      York, 1973. 198 p.
          Originally an attempt to "bring Donaldson up to
      date" (History of the Adirondacks), this regional
      bibliography covering one-fifth of the state includes
      theses and dissertations as well as printed sources.
      Newspaper articles have been excluded. An expan-
      sive classified arrangement of entries--from art
      and animals to religious history and zoology--supple-
      mented by a detailed index, provides easy access.
      The preface indicates the location of special book
      collections about the Adirondacks.

Adirondacks

287. De Sormo, Maitland C. The Heydays of the Adiron-
      dacks. Saranac Lake, New York: Adirondack Yes-
      teryears, 1974. 262 p.
          A regional history that includes many of the local
      legends, stories, and myths that result from unique
      circumstances and environment. Emphasis is upon
      the people--characters, figures--that reflected and
      contributed to the adventure and romance of the
      area--Paul Smith, Robert Schroeder, Mrs. Chase,
      etc. Based upon scrapbooks and notebooks of in-
      habitants, files of periodicals and the author's re-
      membrances, most of the topics presented are of
      personal interest to the author; thus he presents to
      us history that includes rum-running, logging river
      runs, Adirondack medicine, big hotels, and early
      steamboats, among others.

288. Donaldson, Alfred L. A History of the Adirondacks.
      Port Washington, New York: I.J. Friedman, 1963.
      2 v. (Empire State historical publication XII). Bib-
      liography: p. 299-363.
          Emphasis is placed upon only the most prominent
      aspects, generally of the early days and their

pioneers, of the Adirondacks. For example: John
Brown, Indian legends, Paul Smith, Lake Placid, Adirondack names, Mount Marry, Robert Louis Steven-
son, railroads and military roads, "Ned Buntline, "
etc. Appendices include data on Adirondack birds,
mammals, trees, heights of Adirondack mountains,
some "firsts, " etc.
Another view presented by:

Hart, L. The Sacandaga story; a valley of yesteryear.
Schenectady, New York: Riedinger & Riedinger, 1967.
69 p.
A history of the hamlets in the Adirondack Sacandaga River Valley before the waters of a modern
reservoir system covered them in the 1930's. These
brief essays, each devoted to a particular settlement
or point of interest, attempts to recreate, by word
and photography, that way of life enjoyed by the
farmers, mill hands, river drivers, lumberjacks,
housewives, and sportsmen of the area.

SEE ALSO 201.

Buffalo and Western New York
(chronological)

289. Chazanof, W. Joseph Ellicott and the Holland Land
Company; the opening of western New York. Syracuse, New York: Syracuse University Press, 1970.
240 p. (A New York State study).
Originally employed as a surveyor, Ellicott became
the Agent-general for the Holland Land Company with
the task of selling 3.3 million acres of land west of
the Genesee River. His efforts, resulting in the
settlement of 100,000 people in the area between
1800-1820, also made him wealthy and a powerful
political and social figure; involving him in public
works, taxation, elections, the Erie Canal, the War
of 1812, and all the other problems of frontier development.

290. Ketchum, W. An authentic and comprehensive history
of Buffalo, with some account of its early inhabitants, both savage and civilized, comprising historic
notices of the Six Nations or Iroquois Indians, including a sketch of the life of Sir William Johnson,

and of other prominent white men, long resident
among the Senecas. Buffalo, New York: Rockwell
Baker & Hill, 1864, 1970. 2 v. (Outlines of Niagara frontier series). Reprinted 1970.

The first volume is limited to the history of the
Indians of the Five Nations up to and including their
involvements with Europeans. Volume two continues
that history including the settlement of Western New
York, the establishment of Buffalo and its history
up to its burning by the British in 1814. Appendices
contain deeds, speeches to and by Indian chiefs, letters, and other primary sources.

291.   Bingham, Robert W. The cradle of the Queen City, a
       history of Buffalo to the incorporation of the city.
       Buffalo: Buffalo Historical Society, 1931. 504 p.
       (Buffalo Historical Society publication, v. 31).

A history of the city of Buffalo up to 1832, it is
also an account of Indian councils, French and English explorers, soldiers and ship captains, wars on
the Niagara Frontier, the investments of land companies, establishment of churches, newspapers,
schools, coffee houses, banks, and the Grand Canal.
The appendix lists date of lot sale and number in
the original Holland Land Company survey of New
Amsterdam.

292.   Spear, A. W. The Peace Bridge, 1927-1977, and re-
       flections of the past. Buffalo: The Buffalo and Fort
       Erie Public Bridge Authority, 1977. (91) p. Illus.,
       map.

A brief history of the area, early efforts at bridge
building, construction and details of finance, a description of the opening ceremonies; a history of the
ferry service is included. Has a chronology, traffic
statistics, and a summary of Peace Bridge physical
data.

SEE ALSO 205-208.

Catskills

293.   Evers, A. The Catskills, from wilderness to Wood-
       stock. Garden City, New York: Doubleday, 1972.
       821 p. "A select Bibliography": p. 781.

A regional history presented in terms of the lives
of its inhabitants--farmers, visitors, criminals, politicians, artists, miners, Indians, etc.

294.   Van Zandt, R.   The Catskill Mountain House.   New
       Brunswick, New Jersey: Rutgers University, 1966.
       416 p.   Bibliography: p. 381-397.
       A history of the "noblest wonder of the Hudson
       Valley," the Catskill Mountain House that combined
       luxury and elegance facilities, perched on the east-
       ern escarpment of the Catskill Mountains, within
       square miles of wilderness less than a day's journey
       from New York City, became a many-columned mon-
       ument of 19th-century American culture, providing
       accommodations for poets, painters, politicians, the
       wealthy, and in general the elite of society.

SEE ALSO 202, 276, 494.

                        Central New York
                      (general to specific)

295.   Melone, Harry R.   History of central New York, em-
       bracing Cayuga, Seneca, Wayne, Ontario, Tompkins,
       Cortland, Schuyler, Yates, Chemung, Steuben, and
       Tioga Counties.   Indianapolis, Indiana: Historical
       publishing company, 1932.   3 v.
       Succinct chapters, on the economic, social, in-
       dustrial, and intellectual growth of the region, from
       the earliest settlements to the 1930's.   Factual and
       detailed.   Index aids in use.   Volumes two and three
       are devoted to over five hundred biographies of con-
       temporary men (in 1932) that have significant posi-
       tions in or have made outstanding contributions to
       the area.

296.   O'Rielly, H.   Settlement in the West.   Sketches of Ro-
       chester; with incidental notices of western New York
       ... Rochester: W. Alling, 1838.   416 p.
       Characteristic of the period, these Sketches are
       actually a compendium of facts about Rochester's
       first quarter-century: its soil, climate, productions,
       geology, medical topography, the Indians (Six Na-
       tions), land grants and tracts, the development of
       the canal system, religious and social institutions,
       newspapers, associations and societies, the Bar, the

military, public works, trade and business, bath
houses, transportation, etc., and statistics of Rochester.   The appendix includes extensive information
about the Six Nations (pp. 337-404) and a biography
of Col. Rochester.

SEE ALSO 204.

Sites

297.   New York (State).   Division of Archives and History.
       Historic sites of New York State.   Albany, 1960.
       56 p.
       Descriptions, one to three pages in length, sup-
       plemented with photographs, of historic houses, bat-
       tle fields, memorials and monuments, forts, etc.

INDIANS AND ARCHAEOLOGY
(general to specific, then geographically)

298.   Parker, Arthur C.   The archeological history of New
       York.   Albany: The University of the State of New
       York, 1920.   2 v.   (New York State Museum Bul-
       letin ... nos. 235, 236, 237, 238).   Bibliography:
       p. 719-724.
       The author's objective is to relate New York ar-
       chaeology to American archaeology by a discussion
       of the importance of this discipline, an explanation
       of the origin of material culture and human progress,
       the distribution of man in North America, aboriginal
       life in New York, and a detailed explanation and de-
       scription of New York sites.

299.   Ritchie, William A.   The archaeology of New York
       State.   Revised edition.   Garden City, New York:
       Natural History Press, 1969.   357 p.   "References":
       p. 325-343.
       Covers the periods from circa 8000 B.C. (Paleo-
       Indian hunters) to circa 1000 B.C.-A.D. 1600 (wood-
       land stage) with emphasis upon examination of whole
       cultures within archaeological limits.   Each culture
       description includes such categories as: physical
       characteristics of related peoples, economy, housing,
       dress, and ornaments, artifact technology, trans-
       portation, trade, warfare, recreational activities,

organizations (social and political), mortuary cus-
toms, religio-magical activities. A detailed study
including descriptions and finds of sites in the state.

300. Ritchie, William A. An introduction to Hudson Valley
      prehistory. Albany: University of the State of New
      York, State Education Dept., 1958. 112 p. (New
      York State Museum and Science Service Bulletin no.
      367). Bibliography: p. 110-112.
          Individual discussion of eight archaeological/pre-
      historic sites; each one follows essentially the same
      format: description of location, excavation, arti-
      facts, artifact inventory, and conclusion.

301. Weinman, Paul L. A bibliography of the Iroquoian
      literature, partially annotated. Albany: University
      of the State of New York, 1969. 254 p. (New York
      State Museum and Science Service. Bulletin no. 411).
          Citations include books, articles, pamphlets, and
      the publications of societies, associations, and other
      academic and scholarly organizations. Only the
      "readily available" entries have summarizing anno-
      tations.

302. Pratt, Peter P. Archaeology of the Oneida Iroquois.
      George's Mill, New Hampshire: Man in the North-
      east, 1976. 303 p. (Occasional publications in
      northeastern anthropology; no. 1). Bibliography: p.
      289-303.
          While this study is an expanded dissertation con-
      cerned with determining the validity of the possibil-
      ity that Nichols Pond was the site of the historic
      Champlain-Iroquois battle of 1615, a controversial
      issue among scholars and natives of Central New
      York, it is also a detailed introduction to archaeo-
      logical research as well as providing a great deal
      of information about the Iroquois (from early pre-
      historic time to the early historic period) and their
      adaptation resulting from European contacts.

303. Beauchamp, William M. A history of New York Iro-
      quois, now commonly called the Six Nations. Port
      Washington, Long Island: I.J. Friedman, 1961.
      337 p. Originally published as University of the
      State of New York. Bulletin 329. Feb. 1905; and
      New York State museum. Bulletin 78. Archeology
      9. Bibliography: p. 308-310.

Presents details of all aspects of Iroquois life
and their modifications from the time of discovery
and exploration up to the 20th century. Quotes primary sources and observers.

304. Graymont, B. The Iroquois in the American Revolu-
      tion. Syracuse, New York: Syracuse University,
      1972. 359 p. (A New York State study).
      "Bibliographical Essay": p. 327-343.
      Based in central New York, the Six Nation Con-
      federacy or the League of the Iroquois, described as
      the most powerful Indian group in North America,
      because of geography and military strength, controlled
      important waterways west and north. During the
      American Revolution both the British and the Amer-
      icans recognized the value of the League as an ally
      and the danger of it as an enemy. Neither could
      endure the neutrality of the Six Nations. This is
      an account, with stress on the military and political
      factors, of the cultural elements that destroyed the
      Confederacy.

305. Wallace, Anthony F. C. and Sheila C. Steen. The
      death and rebirth of the Seneca. New York: Knopf,
      1969. 384 p. Illus. Bibliography: p. 369-384;
      index: p. iii-xi.
      A history of the Seneca Indians (late colonial and
      early reservation period) and of the religious and
      moral revitalization of that Iroquois society achieved
      by the prophet Handsome Lake and his followers
      around 1800.

306. Wissler, C. The Indians of Greater New York and
      the Lower Hudson. New York: The Trustees, 1909.
      242 p. (Anthropological papers of the American mu-
      seum of natural history, vol. III).
      Describes and interprets the significance of archaeo-
      logical sites, rock shelters, the ethnography of the
      Mohegan and Niantic Indians, with discussion of ar-
      ticles and implements of bone, stone, shell, clay,
      metal, and antler.

SEE ALSO 290, 296, 418, 578, 662.

Biography
(chronological)

307. Walworth, Ellen H. The life and times of Kateri Tek-
      akwitha, the Lily of the Mohawks. 1656-1680. Buf-
      falo: P. Paul & Brother, 1891. 314 p.
      The life and influence of an Indian girl converted
      to Christianity.

308. Weiser, Francis X. Kateri Tekakwitha, with a pref-
      atory note of John Cardinal Wright. Montreal:
      Kateri Center, 1972, 1971. 167 p. Bibliography:
      p. 167.
      Detailed biography of the famous Mohawk girl,
      born at what is now Auriesville, New York, that
      was declared "Venerable" by Pope Pius XII on Janu-
      ary 3, 1943. This is the first of three stages lead-
      ing to official sainthood.

309. Kelsay, Isabel T. "Joseph Brant (1742-1807): The
      legend and the man. A foreword." New York His-
      tory, 40 (1959): 368-379.
      More of a profile of the character and spirit of
      Joseph Brant than a biographical sketch of a man
      who associated with the influential and important
      men of his time: George Washington, John Graves
      Simcoe, Sir William Johnson, Ethan Allan, Gilbert
      Stuart, Robert Morris, James Boswell, George
      III, etc. The contradictions in the various accounts
      of his life are underscored.

310. Manley, Henry S. "Red Jacket's last campaign, and
      an extended bibliographical and biographical note."
      New York History, 31 (1950): 149-168.
      Emphasis is on the issues of the 1826 Treaty and
      the sale of Indian lands. The bibliographical and
      biographical sections provide the references to more
      comprehensive and other specialized studies of Red
      Jacket.

311. Rickard, C. Fighting Tuscarora; the autobiography of
      Chief Clinton Rickard, edited by Barbara Graymont.
      Syracuse, New York: Syracuse University, 1973.
      182 p. "Notes": p. 169-178.
      Based upon interviews and taped conversations,
      the text was compiled and edited by Ms. Graymont,
      Chief Rickard's close friend and noted Indian

historian. Chief Rickard, a founder of the Indian
Defense League of America, an advocate of Indian
nationalism and intertribal cooperation, was a noted
warrior in the struggle for Indian rights and justice.
The photographs are from his personal collection.

LAW
(general to specific)

312. New York (State). Laws, statutes, etc. The consol-
     idated laws of New York annotated; with annotations
     from State and Federal courts. Brooklyn: E. Thomp-
     son, 1942. v. 1.
         On cover: Mckinney's Consolidated Laws of New
     York annotated. Arranged alphabetically by numbered
     "titles" or sections of the law, penal code education,
     criminal procedure law, etc. Kept current by pocket
     parts and special pamphlet supplements. Multivol-
     umed index provides easy access to different aspects
     of New York law relating to one subject.

313. Badner, Jeffrey A. The New York handbook on small
     claims courts: an essential guide to fighting your
     case. New York: Hawthorn Books, 1975. 158 p.
     Forms.
         In plain English, written by a practicing lawyer,
     the functions and processes of the small claims court
     are explained and what one should do when involved
     in its operations: how to sue, how to prepare a
     defense, the trial, the judgement, and making an ap-
     peal. The appendix lists city courts (throughout the
     state), New York City Civil Courts, and the district
     courts of Suffolk and Nassau counties. Includes
     sample copies of forms needed.

314. How to live, and die, with New York probate, edited
     by Ralph D. Semerad. Houston, Texas: Gulf, c.
     1975.
         In plain language, New York citizens are provided
     with ways to avoid taxes, trouble, and wasted time
     and money concerning probate laws. Some of the
     topics explained are: who needs a will, what a will
     contains, tax savings, will substitutes, marital de-
     ductions, probate costs, how estates are taxed, etc.
     Prepared by twenty-five members of the Trusts and
     Estates Law Section of the New York Bar Association.

History

315. Chester, A. Legal and judicial history of New York.
      New York: National Americana Society, 1911. 3
      vol.
          Vol. 1: Chronological exposition of the three
      hundred years of history concerning legal institutions
      in the Colony and State of New York. Vol. 2: Con-
      cerned with constitutional conventions and the events
      that made constitutional revision necessary. Vol. 3:
      Legal history of the state by county; much descrip-
      tive detail with emphasis upon the biographical as-
      pects of the individuals connected with the courts.

316. Scott, Henry W. The courts of the State of New York;
      their history, development and jurisdiction, embrac-
      ing a complete history of all the courts and tribunals
      of justice, both colonial and state, established from
      the first settlement of Manhattan Island and including
      the status and jurisdiction of all the courts of the
      state as not constituted. New York: Wilson Publish-
      ing, 1909. 506 p.
          Part I: Colonial period, 1623-1777. Part II:
      Constitutional period (1777-1909). Part III: Chron-
      ological listing of each court to its present status
      and jurisdiction (1909) or its final abolition.
          This can be supplemented by:

      Chester, A. and E. Melvin Williams. Courts and
      lawyers of New York; a history, 1609-1924. New
      York, Chicago: American Historical Society, 1925.
      3 vol. Chronological, the basis of this narrative
      is the biographical method. Focus is upon people
      rather than events.

Legal Education

317. Hamlin, Paul M. Legal education in colonial New York.
      New York: New York University. Law Review Quar-
      terly, 1939. 262 p. Bibliography: p. 217-332.
          With the thesis that before any evaluation of the
      institutions of American Jurisprudence can be made,
      the cultural and educational background of the men
      that created and interpreted colonial law must be
      examined--the education of the colonial lawyer, the
      law student's education, accessibility of law library

facilities, legal curriculums, other educational opportunities, etc. The Appendices have a wealth of
information about the educational backgrounds of
colonial lawyers, law libraries (catalogs of books),
laws and legislation affecting law students, bar agree-
ments, etc.

Courts

318. Smith, Franklin A. Judicial review of legislation in
      New York, 1906-1938. New York: Columbia Uni-
      versity, 1952. 251 p. (Studies in history, econom-
      ics, and public law, edited by the Faculty of Polit-
      ical Science of Columbia University, no. 574). Bib-
      liography: p. 247-250.
          The economic, cultural, and political importance
      of New York State, its population, size, and the
      number of cases in its courts involving judicial re-
      view was the basis for examining the process of judi-
      cial review in New York State. Primary source of
      information are court reports; the author hopes that
      this study will answer some of these questions: which
      constitutional clauses are most often interpreted by
      the courts; do the courts protect civil liberties from
      legislative attacks; what are court attitudes toward
      economic, cultural, and social issues?

319. Breuer, Ernest H. The New York State Court of
      Claims; its history, jurisdiction, and reports. Al-
      bany: University of the State of New York, 1959.
      55 p. (New York State Library. Bibliography bul-
      letin no. 83). Bibliography: p. 49-54.
          In the adjudication of disputes between the individ-
      ual and the state, New York has been a pioneer with
      the creation of its Court of Claims. This study
      provides a record of its antecedents and the Legis-
      lative and Constitutional history of that court, its
      published reports, and cites those sources where its
      opinions are published. A bibliography of commen-
      taries, reported cases cited in the text, law review
      articles and treatises are included.

SEE ALSO 101, 109, 116, 244, 368.

LITERATURE
(general to specific, then by
form: stories, plays, and poetry)

320. Turco, L.   The literature of New York; a selective
      bibliography of colonial and native New York State
      authors.   Binghamton, New York: New York State
      English Council, c. 1970.   98 p.
         Literary and scholarly writings are cited, includ-
      ing those of historians, journalists, political writers,
      children's authors, and other genres that were sig-
      nificant to American letters or the state's cultural
      life.   Only the most important of each author's works
      are listed.

321. Carmer, Carl L.   The tavern lamps are burning; lit-
      erary journeys through six regions and four centuries
      of New York State.   New York: D. McKay, 1964.
      567 p.
         It was the compiler's intent to highlight the "unique,
      peculiar and especial qualities" of the people of up-
      state New York with this anthology of short stories,
      letters, extracts, essays, etc. by such diverse au-
      thors as Henry James, Brooks Atkinson, Charles
      Dickens, Theodore Dreiser, Oliver Goldsmith, and
      Rudyard Kipling.

322. Albany Institute of history and art, Albany, Library.
      Albany authors.   A list of books written by Albanians
      contained in the collection of the Albany institute and
      historical and art society.   1902.   With biographical
      data.   Librarian: Cuyler Reynolds.   Albany, 1902.
      107 p.
         Inclusion as an Albanian based upon the published
      work (book, paper, journal article) being the result
      of "personal research and expression" and the writer
      either being a native or residing in Albany longer
      than required during a term of office (Albany being
      the state capital) or a period of official employment.
      Arranged alphabetically by author in three parts:
      books (372 are listed), magazines, articles, and pam-
      phlets.   Each entry has brief biographical data--birth/
      death dates and full bibliographic information.

323. Ishmole, J. and S. Ronsheim.   New York portrait; a
      literary look at the Empire State.   Illustrated by
      Dorothy B. Morse.   New York: Holt, Rinehart and

Winston, 1965.   592 p.   Illus.   Bibliography: p.
588-590.

Plays, stories, poems, articles, essays, letters,
speeches, excerpts from diaries, newspapers, etc.,
written either by contemporaries of the period described or an author has simply used an historical
fact as a point of departure.   Arranged into six
categories concerned with Indians, the Revolutionary
period, the colonial period, the 19th century, immigration, and modern times.

324.   Frederic, H.   Stories of York State.   Edited by Thomas
F. O'Donnell, with an introd. by Edmund Wilson.
Syracuse, New York: Syracuse University, 1966. 340 p.

These stories, located in the Mohawk Valley during
the period of the Civil War, were the author's fa-
vorites.   Depicting the ordinary individual's mixed
feelings about the war, these carefully crafted and
realistic short stories, written before the turn of
the century, without sentiment, romance, or melo-
drama, were modern before their time.

325.   Drummond, Alexander M. and Robert E. Gard.   The
lake guns of Seneca and Cayuga, and eight other
plays of upstate New York.   With an introd. by
Harold W. Thompson.   Port Washington, New York:
I.J. Friedman division, Kennikat Press, 1972, c.
1942.   (Empire State historical publications series,
no. 8).

A collection of nine regional plays selected from
the Project for New York State Plays.   Written by
New Yorkers about New York, the subject matter
spans the state--from the Hudson to Lake Erie,
covering a time period from 1750 to 1941.   Comedies,
dramas, farces, etc. about romantic love, rent, and
milk wars, Indians, and horse thieves.

326.   Berbrich, Joan D.   Sounds and sweet airs; the poetry
of Long Island.   Port Washington, New York: I.J.
Friedman, 1970.   179 p.   (Empire State historical
publications series no. 89).   Bibliography: p. 174-176.

Collection of poetry about Long Island, written by
poets who had lived on Long Island sometime during
the last 150 years.   Chronologically arranged by
poet's birth date; for each a brief biographical sketch
followed by a selection of their poems.

SEE ALSO 2, 267, 604-622.

POLITICS AND GOVERNMENT

327.   League of Women Voters of New York State. New
       York State, a citizen's handbook/ League of Women
       Voters of New York State; (Jeanne Richman, editor).
       New York: The League, 1974. 112 p. Bibliog-
       raphy: p. 111-112.
           Outlines the structure of state government, delin-
       eates its powers and responsibilities, and describes
       the administrative and fiscal relationships. Provides
       an overview of the executive, legislative, and judicial
       branches and describes the bureaus and agencies
       within those divisions. Also identifies the relation-
       ships between the three branches of government and
       those between the State and its political subdivisions.
       Updated about every five years.

328.   Bonomi, Patricia U. A factious people; politics and
       society in colonial New York. New York: Columbia
       University, 1971. 342 p. Bibliography: p. (317)-
       330.
           Attempts to assess political events and activities
       within the economic, cultural, geographic, and social
       contexts during the period after Leisler's Rebellion
       (1689) and up to but excluding the Revolution.

Constitution
(general to specific, then chronological)

329.   Breuer, Ernest H. Guide to manuscript and printed
       materials by and about New York State Constitutional
       Conventions available in the New York State Library.
       Albany: New York State Library, 1957. 29 p.
           Publications relating to constitutional conventions
       (1777-1938), manuscripts (1777-1938), the 1938 con-
       stitution and its revisions as of 1956. Also citations
       and bibliographies concerning constitutional and state
       history, state government, and other related topics--
       education, family, home rule, legislation, local gov-
       ernment, military, race, wiretapping, etc.

330.   Polf, William A. 1777: the political revolution and
       New York's first constitution. Albany: New York
       State Bicentennial Commission, 1977. 63 p. "Fur-
       ther Study": p. 62-63.
           Includes the complete text of New York's Consti-
       tution of 1777; a discussion of the conditions in which

it was created with separate chapters on the legislature, the executive, the creation of the courts,
legal rights, and ballots.

331. Breuer, Ernest H. Constitutional developments in New
      York 1777-1958; a bibliography of conventions and
      constitutions with selected references for constitu-
      tional research. Albany: University of the State of
      New York, 1958. 103 p. (New York State Library
      Bibliography bulletin no. 82).
          Chronological arrangement of all official publica-
      tions relating to constitutional commissions and con-
      ventions (proceedings, manuals, journals, reports,
      proposed amendments, etc.). To this basic bibliog-
      raphy selected materials concerned with constitutional
      revision and problems are added, covering such top-
      ics as civil defense, civil rights, education, home
      rule, military, press, wiretapping, etc. Each sub-
      section has its own select bibliography.

332. Shalala, Donna E. The city and the constitution: the
      1967 New York Convention's response to the urban
      crisis. New York: National Municipal League, 1972.
      132 p. (State constitutional convention studies no.
      7).
          The explanation that state governments are unable
      to respond to urban problems due to antiquated con-
      stitutions is accepted and examined within this con-
      text--how did the New York Constitutional Convention
      seek to overcome this problem? The resulting anal-
      ysis delineates that the interests attempting to main-
      tain the status quo or change it were quite different
      from those manifested in the legislature and that
      legal and fiscal constitutional constraints, in terms
      of urban crisis, can have both positive and negative
      values.

333. League of Women Voters of New York State. Seeds of
      failure; a political review of New York State's 1967
      Constitutional Convention. New York, 1973. 66 p.
          An analysis of those factors that defeated the pro-
      posed Constitution in the form of a case history of
      the Convention.

Legislature
(current to retrospective,
general to specific)

334. New York State legislative annual. New York: New
      York legislative service, 1948. Annual.
         Record of primary sources, arranged by topic/
      subject, concerning the activities of the New York
      legislation, including reports and memoranda filed
      by agencies, entities, or individuals relevant to
      bills and proposals plus the intent of the Governor's
      veto memoranda, etc.

335. New York (State). Dept. of State. Manual for the use
      of the Legislature of the State of New York. Albany,
      1840.
         New York State constitution, description of state
      administrative departments, miscellaneous authorities,
      commissions, etc. The legislative section, lists of
      county, town, and village officials, by function; sta-
      tistical data--school enrollments, population voting
      records--by district, county, and ward. Photographs
      of government officials.

336. The New York red book, containing latest information
      relating to the state government. Albany: J. P.
      Lyons, 18--
         Annual publication providing biographical data on
      the administrators of the various political subdivi-
      sions of New York State government. Brief descrip-
      tion of the functions of the agencies, departments,
      commissions, and authorities, etc. Lists members
      of political parties, has election returns, by county
      and New York City. Photographs of administrative
      heads as well as assemblymen and senators are in-
      cluded. Also biographies of New York congressmen.

337. New York (State). Legislature. Assembly. The As-
      sembly; genesis, evolution and history (by) William
      J. Embler, director of research for the Legislature,
      and others. Albany, 1960. 52 p. Illus., ports,
      map, diagr.
         Brief history of the Assembly with lists of the
      Speakers (1777-1959), majority leaders (1901-1959),
      minority leaders (1901-1959), chairmen of commit-
      tees of ways and means (1917-1959). Also has an
      organizational chart of the Assembly. Many

photographs and illustrations of buildings and interiors associated with the Assembly.

338. New York (Colony) Council. Journal of the Legislative
      council of the colony of New York. Began the 9th
      day of April, 1691; and ended the (3rd of April,
      1773). Published by order of the Senate of the State
      of New York. Albany: Weed, Parsons, 1861. 2 v.
         A chronological record of the proceedings and votes
      of the council, including relevant documents.

339. New York Public Interest Research Group. Legislative
      profile project. New York, 1974. 6 v.
         Legislator's profile includes: background, election
      campaign, legislative record, interest group ratings,
      voting record, quotes on various issues.

340. Hevesi, Alan G. Legislative politics in New York State:
      a comparative analysis. New York: Praeger, 1975.
      245 p. (Praeger special studies in U.S. economic,
      social, and political issues). Bibliography: p. 224-
      236.
         Covering the period 1954-1974, this study of the
      New York State Legislature attempts to ascertain the
      structure and effectiveness of decision-making power
      to determine if that institution can and does meet
      the needs and challenges of the voters. Included in
      this analysis are the elected lawmakers, the gover-
      nor, legislative leaders, and the impact of others,
      i.e., the press, political party organization, the ju-
      diciary, and lobby groups.

341. Lehne, R. Reapportionment of the New York Legisla-
      ture: impact and issues. New York: National Mu-
      nicipal League, 1972. 58 p.
         Analysis of the impact of reapportionment as re-
      flected in state legislation, the relationship between
      political behavior and reapportionment, and the links
      between constituency changes and legislative action.
      Attempts to identify the socio-economic characteris-
      tics of legislation and looks at state aid in terms of
      policy decisions.

342. Chamberlain, Lawrence H. Loyalty and legislative ac-
      tion; a survey of activity, by the New York State
      Legislature, 1919-1949. Ithaca, New York: Cornell
      University, 1951. 254 p. (Cornell studies in civil
      liberty).

New York State, for a variety of reasons, has
the dubious distinction of having had more legislative "subversive" investigations within the period
1919-1949 than any other state and all, to an extent,
concerned themselves with education.   Based upon
committee hearings and reports, supplemented by
interviews, newspaper and private files, this study
reviews the Lusk investigations, the Rapp-Coudert
investigations, the Feinberg Law, and the trials, dis-
missals, and investigations involving the New York
City Board of Education.

343.   New York (State).   Legislature.   Senate.   Cumulative
index to joint legislative committees and selected
temporary State commissions and alphabetical list
of chairmen and vice-chairmen thereof, 1900-1950.
Albany, 1966.   229 p.
Entries are limited to the main subject concern
of the various committees and commissions.   Under
each entry is: name of agency, committee, etc.,
date established, statement of purpose, name of chairman, date and identifying number of the report(s)
made.   The supplement 1951-1965 updates this very
useful document.

344.   Prescott, Frank W. and Joseph F. Zimmerman.   The
Council of Revision and the veto of legislation in New
York State: 1777-1822.   Albany: Graduate School of
Public Affairs, State University of New York at Albany, 1972.   61 p.   (State University of New York at
Albany.   Graduate School of Public Affairs.   Occa-
sional paper no. 1).   Notes: p. 45-61.
The objectives of this study are to review the history and record of the Council and its veto record;
includes tabulations of the voting behavior of its members.

345.   New York (State).   Office for Local Government.
County charters in New York State, a comparative
guide to leading charter provisions.   Albany, 1963.
69 p.
Comparison of the principal provisions of the
charters of seven counties.   A provision is presented, for example, the Board of Supervisors, and then
how each of the counties defines and limits its powers
and functions is presented.

Governors
(general to specific, then
alphabetically by governor)

346.   New York (State).   Office of General Services.   Gov-
        ernors of the State of New York.   Albany, 1967.
        32 p.
           Brief biographies and colored portraits of New
        York's first forty-nine governors (Clinton to Rocke-
        feller) with descriptive text and photographs of the
        Executive Mansion, the State Capitol, and the South
        Mall.

347.   New York (State).   Governor.   State of New York.
        Messages from the governors, comprising executive
        communications to the Legislature and other papers
        relating to legislation from the organization of the
        first colonial Assembly in 1683 to and including the
        year 1906, with notes.   Ed. by Charles Z. Lincoln;
        pub. by authority of the state...   Albany: J.B. Lyon,
        1909.   11 v.
           With some exceptions, provides full text of the
        executive communications with notes and explanations
        of action by the people or the Legislature.   Chron-
        ologically arranged.

348.   Alexander, De Alva S.   Four famous New Yorkers; the
        political careers of Cleveland, Platt, Hill, and Roo-
        sevelt, forming volume four of the Political history
        of the State of New York, 1882-1905.   Port Wash-
        ington, New York: I.J. Friedman, 1969.   488 p.
        (Empire State historical publications series, no. 69).
           Focus is upon the types of public men (Cleveland,
        Roosevelt-reform law makers; Hill and Platt, crea-
        tors of political machines) that shaped, controlled,
        and directed the political parties of New York State
        for nearly a quarter-century--1883-1905.

349.   Wesser, Robert F.   Charles Evans Hughes; politics
        and reform in New York, 1905-1910.   Ithaca, New
        York: Cornell University, 1967.   366 p.   Bibliog-
        raphy: p. 349-359.
           A study of New York politics, the reform move-
        ment and its effects upon the state's political parties
        provides the context for an analysis and assessment
        of Hughes' political career and his contribution to
        party reform and to progressive government.

350. Nevins, A. Herbert H. Lehman and his era. New
      York: Scribner, 1963. 456 p. "Footnotes": p.
      421-438.
          A biography of one of the three men (the others:
      Alfred E. Smith, Franklin D. Roosevelt) that, be-
      tween World Wars, raised New York to national em-
      inence; a chronicle that spans sixty years: of public
      service, national concerns, labor, business, state
      affairs, and philanthropy.

351. Governing New York State: the Rockefeller years.
      Edited by Robert H. Connery and Gerald Benjamin.
      New York: Academy of Political Science, 1974.
      262 p. (Proceedings of the Academy of Political
      Science, v. 31, no. 3).
          Twenty experts in brief papers evaluate and de-
      lineate the major processes and institutions of New
      York State government and how they have changed
      during the fifteen years of Governor Rockefeller's
      leadership. The focus is upon intergovernmental
      relations, political change, education, finance, hous-
      ing, health care, transportation, prison reform, and
      environmental protection.

352. Rodgers, William H. Rockefeller's follies; an unau-
      thorized view of Nelson A. Rockefeller. New York:
      Stein and Day, 1966. 224 p. Index: p. 219-224.
          An assessment of Nelson Rockefeller that pene-
      trates the circle of secrecy that protects the Rocke-
      feller families by an analysis of his public conduct
      and his use of power in public office and in his pri-
      vate life that leads to the conclusion "that he is a
      rather ordinary man, capable of folly, cupidity, de-
      ception, and self-delusion, as well as acts of gener-
      osity and humanity."

353. Bellush, B. Franklin D. Roosevelt as Governor of
      New York. New York: Columbia University, 1955.
      338 p. (Columbia studies in the social sciences, no.
      585).
          While F.D.R.'s political behavior and administra-
      tion is considered by some to be overshadowed by
      predecessors and successors this analysis examines
      his political achievements and behavior in terms of
      his presidential plans and expectations.

354. Chessman, G. Wallace. Governor Theodore Roosevelt:
      the Albany apprenticeship, 1898-1900. Cambridge:
      Harvard University, 1965. 335 p. "Bibliographical
      Note": p. (313)-320.
          The author contends that it was during the Albany
      years that T. R. developed the basic concepts of
      his "Square Deal," where he tested his talents, sharp-
      ened administrative skills, and learned to work with
      party leaders and political factions. Arranged by
      topic--the nomination and campaign, his relations
      with political machines, franchise-tax bill, trusts,
      the Erie Canal, labor, housing, education, conser-
      vation, administrative reforms, etc.
          A less political viewpoint is presented:

      Hagedorn, H. Sagamore Hill; an historical guide.
      Oyster Bay, New York: Theodore Roosevelt Asso-
      ciation, 1977. 67 p. Bibliography: p. 63. The
      home of Theodore Roosevelt from 1884 to 1919. This
      guide is both a history and biography of T. Roose-
      velt and his family as they live in and from this home
      in Oyster Bay. The second half of the guide is de-
      voted to descriptions and photographs of the furnish-
      ings and design of each room and architectural fea-
      tures, including comments on the prevailing life
      styles and historic associations. Lists other sites,
      with brief annotations, associated with T. R. Saga-
      more Hill was made a national shrine in 1955 and
      an Historic Site in 1963.

355. Smith, Alfred E. Alfred E. Smith; an anthology,
      (edited by) Richard M. Lynch. New York: Vantage,
      1967, 1966. 133 p.
          Essays and excerpts about: theories of govern-
      ment, Catholicism, "Isms" and the KKK, personal
      liberty, social justice and education, government and
      dictatorship, and a selection of his aphorisms.

356. Irwin, Ray W. Daniel D. Tompkins: Governor of New
      York and Vice President of the United States. New
      York: New York Historical Society, 1968. 334 p.
      Bibliography: p. 313-328.
          Scholarly assessment of this statesman as supreme
      court judge, governor, military commander, univer-
      sity chancellor, and vice president.

Offices, Departments, etc.
(alphabetical by department)

357. New York (State). Dept. of Health. Your New York
      State Department of Health. Albany, 1961. 40 p.
          Organizational history of the Department supple-
      mented by a description of the activities and func-
      tions of its various divisions.

358. New York (State). Dept. of Public Works. A short
      history of the New York State Department of Public
      Works. Albany, 1961. 22 p.
          Created in 1923, this public agency is responsible
      for the administration, construction, operation, main-
      tenance, and architecture of New York State's water-
      ways, canals, highways, expressways, and public
      buildings.

359. Fediuk, S. Bibliography of publications by and about
      New York State Division of Human Rights: 1945-
      1970. New York: Division of Human Rights, 1971.
      41 p.
          Lists about 500 titles, of which 400 were published
      by the agency. All stress the operation, activities,
      and successes of the agency.

360. Sexton, Anna M. A chronicle of the Division of Lab-
      oratories and Research, New York State Department
      of Health; the first fifty years: 1914-1964. Lunen-
      burg, Vermont: Stinehour, 1967. 252 p. Illus.
          The second state public health laboratory to be
      established; this is an account of its triumphs over
      disease and its discoveries in the area of preventive
      medicine.

361. Todd, Frederick P. and Kenneth C. Miller. Pro patria
      et gloria; the illustrated story of the one hundred
      and fifty years of the Seventh Regiment of New York
      (107th Infantry Regiment, N.Y.N.G.). Hartsdale,
      New York: Published for the Seventh Regiment by
      Rampart House, 1956. 1 v.
          Separate chapters devoted to honors and symbols,
      customs and traditions, field training, etc.
          Additional and associative historical information
      provided by:

Carroll, John F. A brief history of New York's famous Seventh Regiment and the events surrounding
its march to the defense of the National Capital.
New York, 1960. 1 v. Bibliography: 3 ℓ. This
narrative includes the explanations of this military
unit's association with Mathew B. Brady, photogra-
pher, General Lafayette and the origins of the
phrases "National Guards" and the "West Point of
the National Guard." Most of this publication is an
annotated chronicle (September 5, 1860-May 30, 1861)
of the events leading up to the Seventh Regiment's
participation in the Civil War.

SEE ALSO 126, 127, 750, 751.

RECREATION, CONSERVATION, AND NATURAL RESOURCES

Exhibitions, Fairs, etc.
(alphabetical by name of event)

362. Buffalo. Pan-American Exposition, 1901. Official
catalogs and guide book to the Pan-American exposition ... Buffalo, New York, U.S.A., May 1st to
Nov. 1st, 1901. Buffalo, New York: C. Ahrhart,
1901. 251 p.
      The first fair that did not commemorate a histor-
ical event but had as its objective the promotion of
the commercial and social interests among states
and Western Hemisphere countries. The guide describes the various exhibits and also functions as a
guide book to the city of Buffalo (pictures of important landmarks, civic buildings and institutions, a
directory of streets) and the general area of Western
New York (Niagara Falls, Chautauqua, etc.). Lists
the officers, directors, standing committees, members, etc. of the Exposition, dates of various conventions, sport days, etc. Maps of the exhibit halls
have numeric keys to lists of exhibitors.

363. Barry, Richard H. Snap shots on the midway of the
Pan-Am expo, including characteristic scenes and
pastimes of every country there represented ... with
vivid pen descriptions. Buffalo, New York: R.A.
Reid, 1901. 157 p.
      The performers--American Indians, Africans,
Japanese, midgets, couchee-couchee dancers, cowboys,

etc.--the buildings and exhibits--the Cardiff Giant,
Trip to the Moon, the Johnstown Flood--and the
promoters and stars--Cora Beckwith, Frank C.
Bostoch (Animal King), W. Maurice Tobin, "King of
the Midway," William Jennings Bryan, H. F. Mc-
garvie--are all here and more. The photographs
and text succeed in recreating perhaps the most
interesting aspects of the Pan-Am Expo.

364.   Clark, H.   The tall ships: a sailing celebration/ text
        by Hyla Clark; introduction by Frank O. Braynard
        and Tony Gibbs.   New York: Two Continents, 1976.
        125 p.
            An account of Operation Sail of July 4, 1976, a
        festival involving sixteen tall ships, some fifty me-
        dium-size tall ships, one hundred smaller sailing
        craft, classic yachts, and other historic vessels
        representing dozens of nations plus 53 warships of
        26 nations, representing the International Naval Re-
        view.   The event--July 4th, New York Harbor, a
        Bicentennial celebration--recorded by colored photo-
        graphs of the ships, the festivities, the fireworks,
        the Hudson River parade, etc.

365.   Tyng, Francis E.   Making a world's fair; organization,
        promotion, financing and problems, with particular
        reference to the New York World's Fair of 1939-
        1940.   New York: Vantage, 1958.   118 p.
            Intended as a guide for future organizers of exhi-
        bitions, based on sixteen volumes of the Board of
        Directors' minutes and interviews with fair officers,
        this publication presents the problems of engineering,
        financing, organization, and operations of a modern
        fair.   Appendix: lists of directors, charter mem-
        bers, and committeemen.
            This can be supplemented by:

        Cummings, Carlos E.   East is East and West is West;
        some observations on the world's fairs of 1939 by
        one whose main interest is in museums.   East Auro-
        ra, New York: Printed by the Roycrofters, 1940.
        382 p.   Illus., plates.   A very different perspective
        is presented here.   Funded by the Rockefeller Foun-
        dation, this is an analysis of the similarities and
        differences of presenting exhibits by fairs and mu-
        seums, for the purposes of identifying problems that
        overlap and where museums can utilize or adapt fair

techniques to solve their own problems. Two fairs
were studied: the Golden Gate International Exposition and the New York World's Fair, the World of
Tomorrow. Unfortunately, the concerns of museums
and fairs--visitor participation, traffic flow, light,
attendants, etc.--determine the format of this book,
consequently, references to particular exhibits or
aspects of the New York Fair are made only when
relevant to these professional/museum concerns.

366. Time, inc. New York World's Fair, 1964/1965; official souvenir book, by the editors of Time-Life books.
Editor: Norton Wood. New York, 1964. 117 p.
Illus., maps.
    Cartoons, paintings, photographs (most in color),
and text are used to record the variety of things and
events that was the Fair--science and technology, art
masterpieces, history, New York City as host and
attraction. Also includes two essays--one by Robert
Moses, Mr. Fair, and the other by Loren Eisely
on the emergence of life. Lists also 150 pavilions
at the Fair--their designers and architects.
    Other selected reading includes:

Time, inc. Official guide: New York World's Fair,
1965; all new for 1965 by the editors of Time-Life
books. New York, 1965. 280 p. Description of
fair exhibits and tourist attractions of New York City
with lists of exhibitors, concessionaires, fair directors and officials, and pavilion designers and architects.

Sorel, E. Sorel's World's Fair, 1964. New York:
McGraw-Hill, 1964. 1 v. Combining cartoons,
caricatures, satire, this is a delightful spoof of the
most obvious self-serving aspects of some of the
pavilions and exhibits. The drawings are great fun
and are almost as ascerbic as the text.

New York (City). World's Fair, 1964-1965. The Fair
in 1965. New York, 1965. 48 p. Lists U.S. and
foreign exhibitors and concessionaires with brief descriptions of their attractions, explanation of the
Fair's administrative and operating divisions, the
marina, details of special engineering problems, profile of attendees, charts about costs and post fair
plans, lists of directors, administrators, and an organization chart.

National Research Council. Special Advisory Committee on Full-Scale Testing of New York World's Fair
Structures. Full-scale testing of New York World's
Fair Structures. Washington: National Academy of
Sciences, 1969. 3 v. As costs prohibit the construction of full-scale buildings solely for testing
purposes--improved design criteria and techniques,
building economy and efficiency, and development of
realistic safety factors--a representative selection
of conventional structures built for the Fair provided
a unique opportunity. Bourbon Street (v. 1), the
Rathskeller (v. 2), and the Chimes Tower (v. 3) were
subjected to such tests.

Land, Use, Needs, Control

367.   Planning and zoning officials in New York State direc-
       tory. Albany, Bureau of Communication, New York
       State Office of Planning Coordination. 1969- Annual.
           Lists technical directors and chairmen of planning
       and zoning boards for villages, towns, cities, coun-
       ties, and regions.

368.   Natural Resources Defense Council. Land use controls
       in New York State: a handbook on the legal rights
       of citizens. New York: Dial/J. Wade, 1975. 368 p.
           Oriented to what New York State citizens can do
       about land development, its impacts upon the quality
       of life and nature, based upon existing laws. A
       guide through and to the land laws and regulations at
       the local, state, and federal levels.

Olympics

369.   Ortloff, George C. and S. Ortloff. Lake Placid: the
       Olympic years: 1932-1980: a portrait of America's
       premier winter resort. Lake Placid, Hollywood:
       Macromedia, 1976. 204 p. Illus., col. plates.
           History of this center of winter sports and a his-
       tory of the development of those sports. Also pro-
       vides some insight into the complexity of staging the
       Olympics; the coordination and cooperation involved.
       Some commentary about the 1980 Winter Olympics.

370.   Third Olympic winter games committee. Official re-
        port, III Olympic winter games, Lake Placid, 1932,
        issued by III Olympic winter games committee ...
        compiled by George M. Lattimer. Lake Placid, New
        York, c. 1932. 291 p.
           Attempts two objectives: the complete story of
        the Winter Olympics at Lake Placid (plans and logis-
        tics of staging such an event) and a history of winter
        sports at that resort. Actually a catalog of all the
        activities involved in the organization and presenta-
        tion of an international sporting event.

Sports

Automobile Racing

371.   Schuster, George N. and T. Mahoney. The longest
        auto race. New York: J. Day, 1966. 160 p.
           A chronicle of a Thomas Flyer that won a 22,000-
        mile race from New York City across the United
        States, Alaska, Siberia, and Europe to Paris in 1908.
        Written by the mechanic for the American entry, he
        relates the details of the race around the world be-
        fore snowplows, filling stations, and in many places,
        no roads.

372.   Long Island Automobile Club. Official programme of
        the 100-mile endurance test to be held on Long Is-
        land April 20, 1901, under the auspices of the Long
        Island Automobile Club. Brooklyn, New York, 1901.
        31 p.
           Brief history of the club, list of race officials,
        list of entries, including horse power, number of
        passengers and owners, directions for the race with
        photographs of the cars. Illustrated advertisements
        of clothing and tools remind us that automobile owner-
        ship and riding were a very specialized function.

Baseball
(general to specific, then
alphabetical by team)

373.   Cooperstown, New York. National Baseball Hall of
        Fame and Museum. National Baseball Hall of Fame
        and Museum. Cooperstown, New York, 1972. 71
        p.

History of the origins of the game of baseball,
establishment of the Baseball Hall of Fame, brief
biographies with statistical data of those immortals
elected to the Hall with reproductions of the plaque.
Also lifetime records of Hall of Fame members,
rules for elections.

374/5. Jennison, C. Wait 'til next year; the Yankees, Dodg-
ers, and Giants, 1947-1957. New York: Norton,
1974. 169 p.
A chronological recap of those eleven years that
New York baseball dominated the national scene--a
narrative of characters, personalities, down-to-the-
wire pennant races, outstanding players and worship-
ing fans all sharing proud traditions. Includes a
photo essay on the ball parks and the appendix has
the statistics for selected teams and individuals.

376.   Kiernan, T. The miracle at Coogan's Bluff. New
York: Crowell, 1975. 284 p.
An account of the Giants winning the pennant, October, 1951, when they were $13\frac{1}{2}$ games behind with
only forty-four games left to play. Thus the title!
Interviews with sports writers and players. Appendix has player/team statistics.

377.   Koppett, L. The New York Mets. Rev. ed. New
York: Collier, 1974. 384 p.
The author, sports writer for the New York
Times, presents a complete history of the Mets
from 1960 through to the 1973 World Series. Includes personality sketches, statistics, numerous
photographs.

378.   Fishman, L. New York's Mets: miracle at Shea.
Englewood Cliffs, New Jersey: Prentice-Hall, 1974.
126 p.
History of the Mets with many full-page action
photographs. Also profiles of Gerald Wayne Grote,
John David Milner, Jonathan Trumpbour Matlack,
Daniel Joseph Staub, George Thomas Seaver, Cleon
Joseph Jones, Frank Edwin McGraw, Jr., Derrel
McKinley Harrelson, Jerry Martin Koosman, Felix
Bernado Martinez Millan, Willie Howard Mays, Jr.

379.   Allen, M. Now wait a minute, Casey! Garden City,
New York: Doubleday, 1965. 254 p.

Biography of Casey Stengel and a history of the
New York Mets, baseball politics and personalities.

380. Golenbock, P. Dynasty: the New York Yankees, 1949-
      1964. Englewood Cliffs, New Jersey: Prentice-Hall,
      1975. 394 p.
      Based upon interviews of ex-players, executives
      and former executives, this is an attempt, incorpo-
      rating the events of the period and the personalities
      of the players, to describe the circumstances that
      produced the 1949-1964 baseball dominance of the
      New York Yankees.

381. Mosedale, J. The greatest of all: the 1927 New York
      Yankees. New York: Dial, 1974. 220 p. Illus.
      Attempts to answer the query: why were and are
      the 1927 Yankees considered the greatest baseball
      team of all time? What did that team do, whom did
      they beat and how? The author explores possible
      answers to these questions with some concessions to
      the social history of the period of the roaring twen-
      ties.

382. Robinson, R. The greatest Yankees of them all. New
      York: Putnam, 1969. 223 p.
      The biographies, fifteen, of great Yankees ball
      players from 1920 to 1968--Mantle, Ford, Ruffing,
      Ruth, Maris, Reynolds, Pennock, Rizzuto, Gomez,
      Berra, Dickey, Rolfe, Lazzeri, Di Maggio, Gehrig.

Basketball

383. Fishman, L. The New York Knicks, pride of Gotham
      ... photography by Bruce Curtis, Kevin Fitzgerald,
      Ron Koch. Englewood Cliffs, New Jersey: Prentice-
      Hall, 1974. 127 p. Illus.
      Brief history with extensive full-page action photo-
      graphs. Also biographical profiles of: Bill Bradley,
      Dave Debusschere, Walt (Clyde) Frazier, John
      Gianelli, Phil Jackson, Jerry Lucas, Earl Monroe,
      Willis Reed, and coach William (Red) Holzman.

384. Jackson, P. and C. Rosen. Maverick: more than a
      game. New York: Playboy, 1975. 249 p.
      Autobiographical account of a player for the New
      York Knicks that provides an insider's view about
      team mates, other basketball teams, the NBA and

social/economic aspects of the game less well-known
to the sports spectator.

Bicycling

385. Tobey, E. and R. Wolkenberg. Northeast bicycle tours.
New Canaan, Conn. Tobey Pub. Co., 1973. 280 p.
Most of the in-state trips are circular so can eas-
ily be reversed. Each trip has a map, stated mile-
age, terrain description, very specific directions,
camping sites and fees noted, "fun spots" located,
and the addresses of bicycle shops on the route.
Specific section for tours in New York City and Long
Island as well as the state in general.

Canoeing

386. Manley, A. and Paul F. Jamieson. Rushton and his
times in American canoeing. Syracuse: Syracuse
University, 1968. 203 p. Illus., plans, ports.
A biography of a northern New York boat builder
whose name is synonymous with canoeing. He also
built other small watercraft but his fame rests with
regional, national, and international canoeing history.
Appendices provide construction details, plans, etc.
Excellent photographs of his famous designs and
canoe types.

387. Jamieson, Paul F. Adirondack canoe waters, north
flow ... with a chapter on camping by Robert N.
Bliss. Glens Falls, New York: Adirondack Mountain Club, 1975. 299 p.
Describes over 700 miles of canoe water in the
St. Lawrence River Basin and the Lake Champlain
Basin. Arranged by river and branches, provides
explicit directions to launching sites, different trips
on each river are described--length, class of river,
conditions, historical background, comments about
natural history of the area; recommends side trips
to points of interest. Map references are to USGS.
7. 5 minute series.

Camping

388. New York (State). Dept. of Commerce. Camping in
New York State, 1977. Albany, 1977. 32 p.
Arranged into ten geographic areas--Catskills,
Niagara Frontier, etc. A chart provides mailing

address of parks and camping sites, telephone numbers, daily fees, number of sites, and indicates availability of facilities--electricity, fire places, show-
ers, fishing, boat rentals, children's areas, rec.
building, camp store, ice blocks, ice cubes, laundry.
Periodically revised.

Fishing

389. Wilcoxson, Kent H. Angler's guide to freshwater fish-
      ing in New York State. Lexington, Mass.: Stone-
      wall, 1973. 144 p. Maps.
         Two sections: 1) lakes and ponds; 2) rivers and
      streams. Within each section, the arrangement is
      alphabetical, each entry including name, location,
      types of fish, boating facilities, and a general in-
      formation section supplemented by maps indicating
      access roads, etc. Separate section lists additional
      sources of maps and publications about fishing in
      New York State.

390. New York (State). Department of Environmental Con-
      servation. Freshwater fishing in New York. Albany,
      197-? Folder. Illus., map.
         Chart of lakes and reservoirs and rivers indicat-
      ing which of the twenty-four types of game fish listed
      are available in those waters. Also illustration and
      descriptions of twenty-seven freshwater game fish
      found in New York State. Includes list of fifty of
      the top trout streams in the state and a list of record
      fish caught (ten categories)--weight, year taken,
      place, and the angler.

Football
(alphabetical by players, then by team)

391. Namath, Joe W. and B. Oates. A matter of style.
      Boston: Little, Brown, 1973. 196 p. "Glossary":
      p. 188-189.
         Hundreds of action photographs and text devoted
      to the techniques, philosophy, and strategies of Joe
      Namath's style as a quarterback. Step-by-step anal-
      ysis of passing techniques--grip, arm action, foot-
      work, etc. Instructions also on faking, passing vs.
      running, calling plays, leadership, responsibility,
      etc. Includes some personal observations by and
      about the famous quarterback off the field.

392.   Baker, J.   The Buffalo Bills: O. J. Simpson, rushing
       champion.   Englewood Cliffs, New Jersey: Prentice-
       Hall, 1974.   128 p.   Illus.
          A brief history of the Buffalo Bills, supplemented
       with many full-page and double-page action photo-
       graphs.   Also an overview of O. J. Simpson's foot-
       ball career, his records plus profiles of Lou Saban,
       Jim Cheyunski, Earl Edwards, Joe Ferguson, J. D.
       Hill, Robert James, Reggie McKenzie, Walt Patulski,
       John Skorupan, and Jim Braxton.
          For a more extensive biography see:

       Fox, L.   The O. J. Simpson story: born to run, in-
       troduction by Weeb Ewbank.   New York: Dodd, Mead,
       1974.   173 p.   Biographical, but with emphasis upon
       the football career of "the Juice."   Many photographs
       and the Record section (pp. 166-173) should settle
       most questions.

393.   Alfano, P.   The New York Giants; a new tradition.
       Photography by Dan Rubin.   Englewood Cliffs, New
       Jersey: Prentice-Hall, 1975.   144 p.   Illus.
          Emphasis is upon the current team (1973) with
       many full-page action photographs.   Special section
       on Coach Alex Webster with one-page biographies of
       Ron Johnson, Norman Snead, Bob Tucker, Doug Van
       Horn, Pete Gogolak, Jack Gregory, John Mendenhall,
       Jim Files, Carl Lockhart, and Willie Williams.

                            Hiking
                     (general to specific)

394.   New York walk book.   4th ed., completely rev. under
       the sponsorship of the New York-New Jersey Trail
       Conference and the American Geographical Society.
       Pen sketches by Robert L. Dickinson and Richard
       Edes Harrison.   With an introd. to the geology of
       the region by Christopher J. Schuberth.   Garden
       City, New York: Doubleday, 1971.   Illus., maps.
       Bibliography: p. 307-311.
          Arranged by area (Palisades, Bear Mountain,
       Storm King, The Catskills, The Taconics, Hudson
       Highlands, Perimeter parks of New York City, east-
       ern Long Island, etc.), then by trail.   Entries vary:
       where appropriate some history presented, geologic
       details, directions to the trails (by car, bus, or
       subway), length of trail, color of blazes, particular
       views to seek, etc.

395.   Volgstadt, George M.   Gateways to solitude: a back-
       packing trail guide to western New York and N. W.
       Pennsylvania; cartoons by Bryan Schultz, photos by
       George M. Volgstadt.   Bemus Point, New York,
       1977.   34 p.   Illus., maps.
            Intended only to give length of trails, their gen-
       eral direction, and access points whereby trails can
       be reached from intersecting roads.   For most of
       the trails described maps are included.   Also sec-
       tions on: equipment checklists, how to read a com-
       pass, trail hints, first aid, etc.   The resource unit
       lists sources of maps.

396.   Healy, T.   A climber's guide to the Adirondacks; rock
       and slide climbs in the high peak region.   2nd ed.
       rev.   (Glens Falls, New York: Adirondack Mountain
       Club, 1971).   108 p.   Illus., maps.   "Recommended
       reading"; p. 12-13.
            Arranged by categories of rock climbs and slide
       climbs and then by geographic area.   Each climb
       includes: grade, directions, and ratings (UIAA) of
       ascents; also names of those making the first ascent.

397.   Patterson, Barbara M.   Walks and waterways: an
       introduction to adventure in the East Canada Creek
       and the west branch of the Sacandaga River sections
       of the southern Adirondacks.   Glens Falls, New York:
       Adirondack Mountain Club, 1974.   171 p.   Illus.,
       maps, (5 fold. in pocket).
            Covers the area comprising northern Fulton Coun-
       ty and southern Hamilton County.   Most of these
       walks are one day in length.   Description includes
       reference to maps, directions for finding the "path"
       or bushwhack, advice about the area, notes on nat-
       ural features (wild flowers, waterfalls, lakes,
       streams, etc.).

Horse Racing

398.   Manning, L.   The noble animals; a look into the past
       of events of the turf at Saratoga, New York.   Sara-
       toga Springs, New York: Saratoga Printing, 1973.
       139 p.   Bibliography: p. 124.
            A history of Saratoga horse racing and the people
       involved.   Many excerpts from primary sources--
       newspapers, programs, etc.   The appendum is a special
       chapter on the great intercollegiate regatta of 1874.

Hockey
(alphabetically by team)

399. Fischler, S. The Buffalo Sabres: swashbucklers of
      the ice ... photography, Melchior DiGiacomo, Joe
      Bongi, Jr. Englewood Cliffs, New York: Prentice-
      Hall, 1974. 127 p.
          History of the team with many full-page action
      photographs. Includes profiles of Rick Martin, Gerry
      Meehan, Gil Perreault, and Jim Schoenfeld.

400. Fischler, S. The triumphant Islanders: hockey's new
      dynasty/ photography, Kalish/Mecca/Bereswill. New
      York: Dodd/Mead, 1976. 126 p. Illus.
          History and assessment of the team and its pro-
      gress followed by biographical profiles of Roy Boe
      (owner), William Arthur "Bill" Torrey (manager),
      Jean Potvin, Eddie Westfall, Gary Howatt, Bryan
      Trottier, Denis Potvin, J. P. Parese, Jude Drouin,
      Chico Resch, Billy Smith, Billy Harris. Many photo-
      graphs.

401. Fischler, S. New York's Rangers: the icemen cometh
      ... photography, Melchior DiGiacomo; introd. by
      Mary Albert. Englewood Cliffs, New Jersey: Pren-
      tice-Hall, 1974. 127 p.
          History of the team 1926-1974 with many full-page
      action photographs. Also profiles of Eddie Giacomin,
      Rod Gilbert, Brad Park, Derek Sanderson, Walt
      Tkaczuk, Steve Vickers.

402. Boucher, F. When the Rangers were young by Frank
      Boucher with Trent Frayne. New York: Dodd,
      Mead, 1973. 244 p.
          A history of the New York Rangers from 1925 to
      1955 by one of the original players.

Hunting

403. New York (State). Dept. of Environmental Conservation.
      Small game hunting, 1975-1976. Albany, 1975.
      Folder.
          Colored maps for game seasons, general hunting
      regulations, list of unprotected wildlife, gun laws,
      lists of regional offices and law enforcement officers,
      popular hunting areas arranged by region/county,
      sun rise-sun set tables.

Rowing and Skulling

404. Young, Charles Van P. Courtney and Cornell rowing.
      Ithaca, New York: Cornell Publications, 1923. 107
      p.
          Biography of Charles E. Courtney, considered to
      be the greatest living oarsman of his day, and the
      history of his contribution to the sport of rowing and
      college athletics as coach of Cornell's crews. Ap-
      pendix cites Cornell's rowing record from 1872 to
      1920.

Skiing

405. New York (State). Dept. of Commerce. Ski New York,
      1976, 1977. Albany, 1977. Folder, map.
          Arranged into three areas, charts list name of
      ski resort/park, telephone number, height of slopes,
      number of trails and slopes, number of chairs, lifts,
      and tows, and the availability of snowmaking, cross-
      country, rentals, babysitting, overnight camping, the
      operating schedule, and the basic weekend fees. Also
      has telephone numbers for ski reports and explanation
      of symbols used on ski runs. Includes national ski-
      er's courtesy conduct code. Frequently revised edi-
      tions.

Yachting

406. New York (State). Office of Parks and Recreation.
      The inland sea: cruise 'n chart--Lake Erie, Lake
      Ontario, the St. Lawrence River. Albany, 1974.
      46 charts.
          Includes New York State boating rules and regu-
      lations, locking procedures, the seaway profile, and
      locks, charts of the lakes, harbors, the Welland
      Canal, the Niagara River, and the St. Lawrence Riv-
      er.

407. Parkinson, J. and Robert W. Carrick. The history of
      the New York Yacht Club: from its founding through
      1973. New York: The Club, 1975. 2 v. Illus.,
      photos.
          The New York Yacht Club was founded in 1844 and
      its history is also the history of yachting in America.
      Chronological treatment with many illustrations, de-
      tails of races, the social aspects of yachting, etc.

Appendices provide tremendous amounts of information, lists of flagships, vital statistics of America's Cup yachts, officers, and standing committees (1844-1973), record of America's Cup matches, regulations concerning yacht models, etc.

SEE ALSO 762-768.

Water

Directory

408. United States. Great Lakes Basin Commission. 1976 Great Lakes directory of universities, research institutes and agencies concerned with water and land resources in the Great Lake Basin.... Ann Arbor, Michigan: The Commission, 1976. 66 p.

Updates and is more extensive than the 1969 edition. Has three sections: an alphabetic arrangement of U.S. and Canadian agencies (name, address, telephone number, activities code); a directory of libraries, research institutions, and universities (address, telephone numbers), and the final section again lists the agencies with a description of programs, purpose, members, staff, etc.

Resources
(general to specific)

409. United States Geological Survey. Water resources data for New York/United States, Department of the Interior, Geological Survey; prepared in cooperation with the state of New York and with other agencies. Albany: U.S. Geological Survey, 196-? 1 v.

Now in two parts. Part 1 (begun in 1961), Surface water records, includes data about stream flow, reservoir storage, partial record status, lake elevations, etc. Part 2, Water quality records (a separate report since 1964) provides data about the characteristics of surface, ground, and precipitation water (chemical and physical).

410. United States. Geological Survey. Quality of public water supplies of New York, November 1970-April 1972. Open file report. United States Dept. of the Interior, Geological Survey, prepared in cooperation

with the New York State Dept. of Health. Washington, The Survey, 1974. 198 p. Tables, illus.,
maps. Selected reference: p. 4.

The first of a planned series to analyze samples
of water taken from some 1500 water supplies within
the state. The data is arranged by county, citing
the major constituents, the spectographically analyzed
minor constituents, and the related constituents in
New York public waters.

411. Water Symposium, State University of New York at
      Buffalo, 1966. The fresh water of New York State:
      its conservation and use; proceedings. Lauren B.
      Hitchcock, editor. Dubuque, Iowa: W.C. Brown,
      1967. 255 p. Illus., maps, ports.

The advancement of water resources management
was the objective of this interchange between profes-
sionals from divergent disciplines. Some sixty-five
speakers, representing many viewpoints (engineering,
water resources management, economics, urban planning, government, etc.) covered such topics as: pol-
lution, energy, conservation, the Great Lakes, planning, regional problems, and water quality.

SEE ALSO 942-944.

RELIGION

History
(general to specific)

412. New York (State). State historian. Ecclesiastical rec-
      ords, State of New York. Pub. by the State under
      the supervision of Hugh Hastings, state historian....
      Albany: J.B. Lyons, 1901-1916. 7 v.

Translations and copies of colonial records and
documents, extracts of research in the ecclesiastical
archives of the Hague and Amsterdam, and excerpts
of religious publications supporting essays presented
by each religious denomination's representative. Vol.
1 & 2 cover the period 1621 to 1700. Vol. 3-6 cover
the period 1701-1801. Vol. 7 is subject and personal
name index. The documents are arranged chronologically.

413. Disosway, Gabriel P.   The earliest churches of New
      York and its vicinity.   New York: James G. Greg-
      ory, 1865. 416 p.
      "Vicinity" is broadly defined to include histories
      of denominations as far north as Albany and in New
      Jersey: Protestant, Catholic, Jewish, and Quaker.
      Biographical data on many ministers, priests, clergy-
      men, and others closely associated with the estab-
      lishment (pro or con) of early religious bodies and
      their institutions.

414. Cross, Whitney R.   The burned-over district; the so-
      cial and intellectual history of enthusiastic religion
      in Western New York, 1800-1850. New York: Har-
      per & Row, c. 1950. 383 p. Maps.
      A microcosmic study of economic, ideological,
      political, and social factors influencing the religious
      forces that provided the thrust of the social forces
      and movements of the period.

Lutheranism

415. Kreider, Harry Julius.   Lutheranism in colonial New
      York. New York: Arno, 1972. 158 p. (Original-
      ly author's thesis, Columbia University, 1942). Bib-
      liographical essays: p. 149-158.
      Beginning with European antecedents and the re-
      lationships with Dutch and English colonial govern-
      ments this discussion of New York Lutheranism in-
      cludes such topics as various aspects of internal
      discord, the language controversy, slaves and Indi-
      ans, and comparisons of Muehlenberg and Berken-
      meyer leadership.

Mormons

416. Hill, D.   Joseph Smith, the first Mormon. 1st ed.
      Garden City, New York: Doubleday, 1977. 527 p.
      Bibliography: p. 495-513.
      Without attempting to resolve the controversial
      issues, this major study, based upon original
      sources, presents the human and dramatic facets of
      Joseph Smith's life--as prophet, city planner, seer,
      banker, instrument of divine revelation, and politi-
      cian. This portrayal of a complex man, his will,

and his weaknesses, also narrates the courage and
sacrifices of his followers. Born in Vermont, it
was in Palmyra, New York that he had his first
visions and it was there he translated the Book of
Mormon.

Roman Catholic Church

417.   Douglas, P. Saint of Philadelphia: the life of Bishop
       John Neumann (1811-1860). Cambridge, Mass.:
       Ravengate, 1977. 180 p. Illus., port.
          Biography of the first male American saint. Born
       in Bohemia, educated in Europe, ordained in New
       York City, he functioned as a parish priest in the
       Buffalo area (900 square miles) before he became a
       Redemptionist. Declared Venerable (1921), Blessed
       (1963), his sainthood was established June 19, 1977.

418.   Egan, Thomas F., Father, S.J. ed. The National
       Shrine of the North American Martyrs: Auriesville,
       New York ... and Father Robert L. Fleig, S.J.
       Revised ed. 1978. Baltimore, Maryland: Shrine of
       Our Lady of Martyrs of Auriesville, New York, 1978,
       1964. 65 p.
          The text, supplemented by many colored photo-
       graphs and drawings, presents the history of Amer-
       ica's first and only canonized Martyrs--St. Rene
       Goupil (1642), St. Isaac Jogues (1646), and St. John
       Lalande (1646)--and the establishment of the National
       Shrine of the North American Martyrs at Auriesville,
       New York.

Spiritualism

419.   Brown, Slater. The heyday of spiritualism. New
       York: Hawthorn Books, 1970. 264 p. Bibliography:
       p. (249)-256.
          Chapters, biographical and evaluative, are devoted
       to such New York seers as Andrew Jackson Davis
       (Poughkeepsie), the Fox sisters (Rochester), and the
       Davenport brothers (Buffalo).

SEE ALSO 769-811.

SCIENCES

Astronomy

420. Boss, B. History of the Dudley Observatory, 1852-1956.
      Albany: Dudley Observatory, 1968. 123 p.
         History of the third oldest observatory in the United
      States, detailing the acquisitions of buildings, instru-
      ments, and the creation of the "General Catalogue" of
      stars and the research generated by it. Also note the
      contribution of the Observatory to the Astronomical
      Journal and lists of research papers contributed to
      other journals by staff. Appendices also list trustees,
      directors, and staff through 1956.

Geology

Handbooks, Outlines
(general to specific)

421. New York (State). State Museum and Science Service.
      Geology of New York; a short account. Adapted from
      the text of "Geologic map of New York State" by J. G.
      Broughton (and others). Albany: University of the
      State of New York, State Education Dept., New York
      State Museum and Science Service, 45 p. Illus., maps.
      (Its Educational leaflet, no. 20).
         Intended originally for the teacher of secondary
      school earth science courses but also useful to the in-
      terested layman, this is a simplified and adaptive pre-
      sentation of New York's geologic history. Covers the
      Pleistocene epoch, Precambrian, Paleozoic, Mesozoic,
      and Cenozoic eras with a section on economic mineral
      deposits--non-metals, metals, and mineral fuels. A
      color-coded generalized geologic map of the land forms
      indicates the relationships of topography and bedrock
      characteristics.

422. Miller, William J. ... The geological history of New York
      State. Albany: University of the State of New York,
      1924. 148 p. (New York State museum bulletin ... no.
      255). Bibliography: p. 120-129.
         Presents in a simple yet readable format an outline
      of the physical development of New York State. A
      knowledge of geology or physicography is not assumed
      on the reader's part. Emphasis is upon the geologic
      history of geographic forms.

423. New England Intercollegiate Geological Conference, 61st
      Albany, New York, 1969. Guidebook for field trips in
      New York, Massachusetts and Vermont. Editor John
      M. Bird. Albany: State University of New York at Al-
      bany, 1969. (Various paging).
         The editor acknowledges that these field trips "go
      considerably west of geographical New England." A
      justified position as at least fourteen of the twenty pa-
      pers are devoted to New York geology--Schoharie Val-
      ley, Albany area, Washington County, Mohawk River
      Valley, Southern Adirondacks, Utica, Taconic Moun-
      tains, Herkimer County, etc. Each paper has its own
      bibliography and road log.

424. Broughton, John G. Geology and mineral resources of the
      middle and lower Hudson River Valley by John G.
      Broughton, James F. David (and) John H. Johnsen. Al-
      bany: Hudson River Valley Commission, 1966. 92 p.
      Illus., maps. "Notes and references": Appendix 3.
         A general description of the geology, mineral re-
      sources, and their commercial uses with summaries
      of the history and current production of each mineral.
      Also discussion of factors (scenic value, land use,
      depletion of resources) that influence the mineral in-
      dustries. Has lists of quarries, location, commodity
      produced, activity/size status.

Specific Areas

425. Fuller, Myron L. The geology of Long Island, New York.
      Washington, Govt. Print. off., 1914. 231 p. (U.S.
      Geological Survey. Professional paper 82).
         A study of the underground waters developed new
      geologic data requiring the complete revision of the
      views and opinions regarding the geologic history and
      structure of Long Island. The results, compared with
      New England and New York coast investigations, indi-
      cated that the formations of the Pleistocene epoch and
      its sequence of events were nowhere else so well and
      clearly delineated as on Long Island. With the excep-
      tion of the Iowan all stages are represented. N.B.:
      There is a separate section on the development of the
      geologic literature on Long Island from 1750 to 1908.

Specific Areas--Finger Lakes

426.   Engeln, Oscar D. V.   The Finger Lakes region: its
       origin and nature.   Ithaca, New York: Cornell Uni-
       versity, (1961).   156 p.   "Glossary" (p. 139-147).
          The geologic history of the Finger Lakes resulted
       in not only a scenically distinctive system of lakes
       but a topographically unique area, one without prec-
       edent in the world.   This process is explained in a
       very readable manner, supplemented with helpful
       charts, photographs, and drawings.

427.   Fairchild, Herman L.   Geologic story of the Genesee
       Valley and Western New York.   Rochester, New York:
       The author, 1928.   215 p.   Illus., fold. map, draw-
       ings.
          Written for the general reader, the text is well-
       supported by illustrative materials.   References to
       other bibliographic sources are included within the
       text.

Specific Areas--Niagara Falls

428.   Forrester, Glenn C.   Niagara Falls and the glacier
       ... with illustrations by William Zannie and John
       Bjarnov.   Hicksville, New York: Exposition, 1976.
       140 p.   Bibliography: p. 139-140.
          Describes the origins of Niagara Falls, its evo-
       lution for the past 12,000 years, the factors that
       have been influential in that process and the possi-
       bilities of the future.   The walking tour of the Falls
       and the Lockport Field trip are particularly inter-
       esting.   The diagrams of geologic events are also
       very useful.

Caves

429.   Perry, Clair W.   Underground empire; wonders and
       tales of New York caves, by Clay Perry (pseud.).
       New York: Stephen Daye, 1948.   221 p.   Illus.,
       ports., map.   (The American cave series, 2).
          Utilizing the resources of historians, geologists,
       speleologists, spelunkers, and folklorists, the author
       presents a many-faceted narrative of the caves and
       mines of New York State supplemented by his own
       extensive knowledge and experience.

SCIENCES, NATURAL

430. Boyle, Robert H. <u>The Hudson River; a natural and un-</u>
      <u>natural history.</u> New York: Norton, 1969. 304 p.
      Bibliography: p. 282-296.
      An account of the life in and on the banks, both
      flora and fauna, of the Hudson, from its headwaters
      (Adirondack Mountains) to the sea, and its origins
      seventy-five million years ago to the present with
      man treated as simply another environmental factor--
      positive and negative.

<u>Botany</u>

431. Krieger, Louis C. C. <u>A popular guide to the higher</u>
      <u>fungi (mushrooms) of New York State.</u> Albany: Uni-
      versity of the State of New York, 1935. 538 p.
      (New York State Museum Handbook 11).
      Comprehensive approach to the topic--conditions
      required for growth, where they flourish, how, the
      study and life history of mushrooms, their economic
      and environmental importance, poisonous types, ed-
      ible mushrooms of New York State, and a key to the
      classes, orders, families, and genera of fungi. Also
      a glossary of related technical terms.

432. Gleason, Henry A. <u>Plants of the vicinity of New York.</u>
      <u>Rev. ed.</u> New York: Published for the New York
      Botanical Garden by Hafner Publishing, 1962.
      "Vicinity" is defined as being within two hundred
      miles of New York City. Designed to assist those
      interested in learning the names of wild plants. A
      section on the structure of plants, a glossary, and
      a section on how to use this book, plus illustrations
      enable the reader to begin. The arrangement is by
      groups--woody plants, vines, ferns, aquatic plants,
      etc.--then within group by characteristics.

<u>Zoology</u>

Invertebrate--Insects

433. Metcalf, Clell L. and W. E. Sanderson. <u>Black flies</u>
      <u>and other biting flies of the Adirondacks</u> ... <u>Control</u>
      <u>of biting flies in the Adirondacks.</u> Albany: University

of the State of New York, 1932.   78 p.   (New York
State museum bulletin ... no. 289).   Bibliography:
p. 39, 40, 72.

That great park, created by New York State in
the Adirondacks, had its recreation/business potential
reduced by forty to fifty percent by a plague of biting
flies that successfully challenged man's use of the
area.   This is a preliminary report of the efforts to
develop effective measures of control.   Detailed data
about the conditions, life cycles, and importance of
various kinds of flies, i.e., deer flies, mosquitoes,
black flies, etc.

434.   Leonard, Mortimer D.   A list of the insects of New
York with a list of the spiders and certain allied
groups.   Ithaca, New York: Cornell University,
1928.   1121 p.

Data gathered from published records and public
as well as private collections of specimens, listing
some 15,449 insects.   Arranged by class, order,
family, and subfamily.   Each entry includes the
name of the collector and/or the person responsible
for the determination.   Also indicates month(s) that
adults can be collected and the areas of the state
where they can be found.

435.   Needham, James G.   Aquatic insects in New York State;
a study conducted at the entomologic field station,
Ithaca, New York under the direction of Ephraim
Porter Felt ... Alex D. MacGillivray ... O. A.
Johansen ... K. C. Davis.   Albany: University of
the State of New York, 1903.   517 p.   Illus., plates.
(New York State museum.   Bulletin 68.   Entomology
no. 18).

A collection of seven monographs based upon a
field study; emphasis is upon the young or immature
forms of aquatic insects with particular reference as
to their importance as fish food.   Detailed scientific
descriptions supplemented with line drawings.

Invertebrates--Mollusca

436.   Leton, Elizabeth J.   Check list of the Mollusca of New
York.   Albany, New York State education department,
1905.   112 p.   (New York State museum ... Bulletin
85, Zoology 11).

Arranged by class, order, suborder, family, and
genus, the species is listed followed by bibliographic

references to books or other publications providing
relevant detailed and descriptive information. Scope:
cephalopoda, gastropoda, pulmonata, polyplacophora,
pelecypoda.

437. Robertson, Imogene C. and Clifford L. Blakeslee. The
      Mollusca of the Niagara Frontier region and the ad-
      jacent territory. Buffalo: Buffalo Museum of Science,
      1948. 191 p. Illus., plates, fold., map. (Buffalo
      Society of Natural Sciences, Bulletin, v. 19). Bibliog-
      raphy: p. 121-124.
          A list of mollusca taken from wayside ditches,
      streams, lakes, ponds, and woods from within a fifty-
      mile radius of Buffalo. Major part of text is devoted
      to a "Systematic account of the Species" (terrestrial
      gastropod, aquatic pulmonates, fresh water opercu-
      lates, fresh water mussels, and the white clams);
      each description includes references to collection
      sites. There is a separate section describing those
      collection sites. A brief history of the Conchological
      section of the Buffalo Society of Natural Sciences with
      lists of past and present members concludes this
      monograph.

                    Vertebrates--Birds
          (general to specific geographic areas)

438. Bull, John L. Birds of New York State. 1st ed. New
      York: Doubleday, 1974. 655 p. Maps, col. plates.
      The Federation of New York State Bird Clubs, Inc.
      published a Supplement to Birds of New York State
      by John Bull. Special Publication (1976, 51 p.) that
      updates the major breeding changes up to July, 1975.
      Bibliography: p. 627-636.
          Main body of text devoted to the 410 species of
      birds located in the state: name (scientific and com-
      mon), range, changes in status (occurrence, frequency,
      abundance), breeding, banding, and remarks. The
      text is supplemented by reproductions of paintings of
      representative birds, more than eighty photographs
      and 164 breeding and banding maps. Breeding data
      for this work valid up to 12/31/1972.
          Less extensive but useful is:

      Reilly, Edgar M. and K. C. Parkes. Preliminary an-
      notated checklist of New York State birds. Albany:
      New York State Museum and Science Service, State

Education Dept., 1959. 42 p. Illus., maps. Su-
persedes E. H. Eaton's The Birds of New York
State (1914). Limited to New York State, 429 species
are recorded. Each entry includes all or part of the
following: English name, Latin name, areas where
sighted, breeding sites, a symbol indicating rarity/
abundance.

439. Beardslee, Clark S. and Harold D. Mitchell. Birds of
the Niagara frontier region: an annotated checklist.
In cooperation with the Buffalo Ornithological Society.
Buffalo: Buffalo Society of Natural Sciences, 1965.
478 p. Illus., fold, col. map. (Buffalo Society of
Natural Sciences, Bulletin, v. 22). Bibliography:
p. 453-467.
The order of species and use of vernacular and
scientific names follow the "Checklist of North American Birds," fifth of the American Ornithologists
Union. Area includes the territory west of the Genesee River Valley and that part of the Niagara Pen-
insula in the Ontario Province. A section is devoted
to ornithological territorial localities of special interest in the area with numeric keys to a fold-out
map. Entries for each species include dates more
frequently seen, nesting times, status (summer resident, winter resident, etc.), text about habits, quotes
from observers, references to printed sources, numbers seen with dates.
A publication that complements the above in scope:

Pettingill, Olin S. Enjoying birds in upstate New York;
an aid to recognizing, watching, finding and attracting
birds in New York State North of Orange and Putnam
counties, ... and Sally F. Hoyt. Ithaca, New York:
Laboratory of Ornithology at Cornell University, 1963.
89 p. Illus. "Sources of information on birds": p.
84-85. Some eighty birds are described, and nesting,
migration, and food habits noted. The section on
where to locate birds divides upstate New York into
areas (eastern New York, central New York, etc.)
with careful directions to sites where particular species may be observed at different seasons. The
"Check-list and calendar graph" lists 250 species, the
habitat where they can be seen during designated
months. Final section devoted to attracting birds:
feeders, food, houses, baths, etc.

Vertebrates--Mammals

440. Connors, Paul F. The mammals of Long Island. Al-
      bany: University of the State of New York, 1971.
      78 p. Illus., maps. (New York. State Museum &
      Science Service, Bull. 416).
         Based upon a field survey (1960-1963) concerned
      primarily with native and naturalized Long Island
      mammals and those in the adjacent waters. Discuss-
      es thirty-five land mammals and twenty-four marine
      species.

Vertebrates--Snakes

441. Eckel, Edwin C. and Frederick C. Paulmier. Cata-
      logue of New York reptiles and batrachians. Albany:
      University of the State of New York, 1902. 414 p.
      Illus. (New York State museum. Bulletin 51). Bib-
      liography: p. 357-359, 389.
         The purpose of this publication is to assist the
      non-specialist in the identification of these species.

SEE ALSO 651, 665-671.

SOCIAL SCIENCES

Psychology, Psychiatry

442. Directory of psychiatric clinics in New York State.
      1952- Albany, Dept. of Mental Hygiene.
         Alphabetic by county and then alphabetically by
      name of the clinic. Identifies the clinic by type--
      all purpose, child guidance, children, etc.

443. Elinson, J. Public image of mental health services
      (by) Elena Padilla (and) Marvin E. Perkins. New
      York: Mental Health Materials Center, 1967. 288 p.
         A household survey that recorded the public's
      knowledge and opinions about mental health care, at-
      titudes toward the mentally ill, appraisals of mental
      health facilities, and professional, personal experi-
      ences with the mentally ill, hospitalization and rec-
      ognition of personal problems. The second part of
      the study is a detailed profile of selected adults in
      greater New York--demographic, socioeconomic, and
      educational factors, health-related habits, religious

and political affiliations, community participation,
personal social preferences and values. The appendices include the procedures and methods of the
study, sampling plan, the questionnaires used, cost
of field work, etc.

444. Wangh, M. Fruition of an idea; fifty years of psychoanalysis in New York. Samuel Atkin, Edith L. Atkin,
and David Kairys, coeditors. In honor of the fiftieth
anniversary of the New York Psychoanalytic Society,
1911-1961, and the thirtieth anniversary of the New
York Psychoanalytic Institute, 1931-1961. New York:
International Universities, 1962. 124 p. Illus.
Chapters by different authors review and evaluate
the process, impact, and contribution of the science/
art of psychoanalysis in America, particularly by way
of the "Society" and the "Institute" and the various
publications and periodicals they generated. Appendices list presidents, charter members, and officers
of both institutions; also the contributor and title of
papers presented at "Society" meetings from 1950 to
1961.
A related publication:

Schulman, J. Remaking an organization; innovation in
a specialized psychiatric hospital. Albany: State
University of New York, 1969. 255 p. Bibliography:
p. 255. A study of the reorganization of the Psychiatric Institute just before and during the period when
it was directing its efforts toward the teaching of new
therapies and the testings of experimental approaches
to psychiatry.

SEE ALSO 252, 253, 469, 873, 874.

Parapsychology

445. Gourley, J. Great Lakes triangle. Greenwich, Conn.:
Fawcett, 1977. 192 p. "Notes": p. 179-187.
A collection of narrative concerning peculiar/mys-
terious events involving the aircraft, men, and ships
associated with the Great Lakes. Organized around
phenomena--disappearances, memory loss, mechanical
problems, etc. The author relies heavily upon speculation to create relationships to the Unknown.

Sociology

Prisons
(retrospective, then autobiographical)

446. New York (State). Special Commission on Attica. At-
      tica; the official report of the New York State Special
      Commission on Attica. New York: Bantam Books,
      1972. 533 p. Bibliography: p. 507-515.
         Documents in great detail every aspect of prison
      life of a major prison; one that is representative of
      every prison. The findings and recommendations of
      this commission are based upon "more precise infor-
      mation than has ever been assembled about any single
      institution." Examines the factors that resulted in
      the riot, delineates the events, the negotiations, and
      the retaking of the prison and the aftermath. Exten-
      sive photographs supplement the already graphic de-
      tails of the narrative.

447. Wicker, T. A Time to die/ Tom Wicker. New York:
      Quadrangle/New York Times, 1975. 342 p.
         An account of the prison riot at Attica, New York,
      by the reporter that the prisoners requested to pre-
      sent their views and demands. Appendices include:
      chronology, the five demands, the fifteen practical
      proposals, a comprehensive list of observers, the
      twenty-eight points that Commissioner Oswald said
      he would accept.

448. New York (State). Dept. of Correction. Reception
      Center, Elmira. The New York State Department
      of Correction Reception Center, Elmira, New York.
      Albany, 1958. 65 p. Illus.
         The legal basis of the Center, its functions, ad-
      ministration, classification of inmates, problems,
      early release procedures. Includes statistical data
      about test results, intake by type of offense, classi-
      fication reports.

449. Brockway, Zebulon R. Fifty years of prison service,
      an autobiography, by Zebulon Reed Brockway, super-
      intendent of the Elmira reformatory from the time
      of its opening in 1876 to the year 1900. New York:
      Charities publications committee, 1912. 437 p.
         This autobiography also includes information about
      the prisons at Albany and Rochester, progress of

penal reforms and a "contemporary" perspective re-
garding prisoners and their treatment.

450. Osborne, Thomas M. Within prison walls; being a
      narrative of personal experience during a week of
      voluntary confinement in the state prison at Auburn,
      New York. (Thomas Brown, Auburn n. 33, 333x).
      New York and London, D. Appleton, c. 1914. 327 p.
          A serious attempt by the chairman of the State
      Commission on Prison Reform to learn the needs of
      the inmates and the conditions of the prisons and to
      assess the effects of the penal system, in part or
      whole, upon the prisoners.

451. O'Brien, Edna V. So I went to prison. New York:
      Frederick A. Stokes, 1938. 282 p.
          Personal account of the author's prison term at
      the New York State Reformatory for Women at Bed-
      ford Hills.

SEE ALSO 718, 758-761.

Race Relations and Minorities

452. New York (State). University. Information Center on
      Education. Bureau of Statistical Services. Racial/
      ethnic distribution of public school students and staff
      in New York State. Albany, 1968- Annual.
          Percentage and numerical distribution of Black,
      Spanish-surnamed, American Indian, and Oriental
      students, by city and school district; race and ethnic
      origins of staff, etc.

SEE ALSO 461, 543, 672, 676, 829-861.

Race Relations and Minorities--Italians

453. Yans-McLaughlin, V. Family and community: Italian
      immigrants in Buffalo, 1880-1930. Ithaca: Cornell
      University, 1977. 286 p. Bibliography: p. 267-
      279.
          Study of the transition and adjustment of agricul-
      tural Italian families to an urban community; their
      occupations, institutions, attitudes, and family rela-
      tionships.

SEE ALSO 838.

Race Relations and Minorities--Jews
(general to specific)

454.   Levitan, Tina N. The firsts of American Jewish his-
       tory. 2nd. ed. Brooklyn: Charuth, 1957. 285 p.
       Bibliography: p. 267-271.
          First institutions, people, places, and things con-
       cerning Jewish contributions of American history and
       growth. Due to the concentration and long history
       of Jews in New York many of the firsts occurred in
       the Empire State and in New York City.

455.   Adler, S. and Thomas E. Connolly. From Ararat to
       suburbia; the history of the Jewish community of
       Buffalo. Philadelphia: Jewish Publication Society of
       America, 1960. 498 p. (The Jacob R. Schiff li-
       brary of Jewish contributions to American democracy,
       no. 12). Glossary: p. 463-466. Bibliography: p.
       467-479.
          Covers the period from 1813 to after the Second
       World War, attempts to present and assess within
       the three contexts of American, Jewish, and world
       developments local Jewish history in New York State's
       second largest city.

456.   Rosenberg, Stuart E. The Jewish community in Roch-
       ester, 1843-1925. New York: Columbia University,
       1954. 325 p. (American Jewish Communal Histo-
       ries, No. 1). Bibliography: p. 301-309.
          A narrative of the development of a sense of unity
       and community between the German Jews and those
       from East Europe that evolved into an American
       indigenous American Jewish community--one that has
       made its contributions to its fellow American citizens
       during the cultural, economic, political, and social
       development of this country in general and the city
       of Rochester in particular.

SEE ALSO 22, 29, 509, 514, 628, 629, 802, 803, 839-850.

Race Relations and Minorities--Blacks
(chronological by scope of each title)

457.   McManus, Edgar J. A history of Negro slavery in
       New York. Foreword by Richard B. Morris. Syr-
       acuse: Syracuse University, 1966. 219 p. "Bibli-
       ographical Notes": p. 201-212.

An account, well documented, of urban slavery;
Negroes trained in diverse occupations and skills,
working, often, side by side with free whites and
making substantial contributions to the growth of the
state. Also considers the accomplishments of the
Negro slaves, their sense of self-identity, and the
immediate problems and hardships created by emancipation.

458.   Bradford, Sarah E.   Harriet Tubman, the Moses of her
        people.   Introd. by Butler A. Jones.   New York:
        Corinth Books, 1968.   149 p.   Reprint of the expand-
        ed second edition of 1886.
            Biography of a "conductor" of the Underground
        Railroad, one who led more than 300 Negroes out of
        the South to their freedom in the North.   So success-
        ful, so resourceful that the complement of a reward
        of more than $40,000 was offered for her capture.
        She also acted as a Union spy, scout for Union troops
        in Southern swamplands, and as a practical nurse in
        Union hospitals.   After the Civil War she returned
        home to Auburn, New York to establish a home for
        aged and indigent Negroes.   Appendix contains letters
        from Gerrit Smith, Wendell Phillips, and Frederick
        Douglass.

459.   Seifman, E.   A history of the New York State Coloni-
        zation Society.   New York: Sponsored by the Phelps-
        Stokes Fund, 1966.   201 p.   Bibliography: 189-201.
            The Society published the New York Colonization
        Journal for thirteen years, had the responsibility for
        colonizing freed Negroes in Africa, established an
        independent colony that eventually became the Repub-
        lic of Liberia.   The Society also became a force in
        the shift of emphasis from African colonization to
        African education.   This study, utilizing historical
        methods, also examines: 1) colonization plans during
        the Lincoln Administration; 2) the 1894-1896 Mexican
        colonization movement; 3) the Marcus Garvey period;
        4) the Black Muslim movement; and 5) the Commu-
        nist Party and Negro self-determination.

460.   New York (State).   State Commission Against Discrim-
        ination.   Research Division.   Negroes in five New
        York cities; a study of problems, achievements, and
        trends by Eunice and George Grier.   New York,
        1958.   110 p.   Bibliography: p. 103-110.

Based upon analysis of data compiled by Federal,
state, and local government agencies and private
ones. Supplemented by the opinions of "knowledgeable" local people (white and Black). A profile of
the status of white-Negro relations was attempted
for Albany, Binghamton, Rochester, Syracuse, and
Troy.

SEE ALSO 851-856.

Race Relations and Minorities--Welsh

461. Thomas, I. Our Welsh heritage. New York: St.
      David's Society of the State of New York, 1972. 56
      p. "Recommended books": p. 53.
         Compendium of information relating to the history
      of the Welsh, their contribution to the world and in
      particular the growth and development of the United
      States. Includes chapters on: St. David's Society,
      lists of presidents and life members, pre-Columbian
      Welsh explorers, historical background of the Prince
      of Wales, Welsh surnames, Welsh language, distin-
      guished Americans of Welsh origins (Thomas Jeffer-
      son, General Morgan Lewis), Welsh history, the
      Welsh alphabet and guide to pronunciation, etc.

Race Relations and Minorities--Women
(general to specific)

462. Vance, M. The lamp lighters; women in the Hall of
      Fame. Foreword by Sarah Gibson Blanding. Illus-
      trated by J. Luis Pellicer. New York: Dutton,
      1960. 254 p. Illus.
         Of these eight biographies, five of these women
      have personal New York associations: Emma Willard
      (Troy Female Seminary), Charlotte Saunder Cushmen
      (actress), Maria Mitchell (astronomy/Vassar), Susan
      B. Anthony (women's suffrage), Fran Elizabeth
      Willard (women's suffrage, temperance).

463. Gurko, M. The ladies of Seneca Falls; the birth of
      the women's rights movement. New York: Mac-
      millan, 1974. 328 p. Bibliography: p. 316-320.
         The contributions and impact of New Yorkers and
      New York events--the Seneca Falls Convention, the
      Rochester Convention, the "New York group" are all
      delineated in this history of the women's rights move-
      ment in the 19th century.

464. DePauw, Linda G. Four traditions: women of New
      York during the American Revolution. Albany: New
      York State American Revolution Bicentennial Com-
      mission, 1974. 39 p. Bibliography: p. 38-39.
          Explores the limits that four cultures--Iroquois,
      Dutch, African, and English--had imposed upon co-
      lonial women, the role women had in the Revolution,
      and the impact that war had on their lives and status.

465. Wilson, Dorothy C. Lone woman: the story of Eliz-
      abeth Blackwell, the first woman doctor. Boston:
      Little, Brown, 1970. 469 p. Bibliography: p. 447-
      453.
          In 1847, the students of the Geneva Medical Col-
      lege in upstate New York (forerunner of the Cornell
      Medical School) voted to admit Miss Blackwell to
      medical studies. This radical action and its conse-
      quences, for medicine, women, and Miss Blackwell,
      are the subjects of this rather detailed biography.

Social Concerns
(general to specific)

466. Schneider, David M. The history of public welfare in
      New York State. Chicago: University of Chicago,
      1938-1941. 2 v.
          A review of all fields of social work controlled
      or financed by either federal, state, or local agencies
      and those influences generated by private social work.
      Vol. 1: 1609-1866; Vol. 2: 1867-1940.

467. New York (State). Office for the Aging. A plan of
      action for older Americans; the final report of the
      New York State Committee for the 1971 White House
      Conference on Aging. Editor: James J. O'Malley.
      Albany, 1973. 249 p. Illus., charts, maps.
          A compilation of both state and national recom-
      mendations. In 1970 persons sixty-five and over in
      New York accounted for 9.8 per cent of all such
      persons in the U.S. Conference focused on need
      areas (income, health and mental health, housing,
      employment, etc.).

468. Fenton, J. and Robert E. Ayers. Residential needs of
      severely physically handicapped non-retarded children
      and young adults in New York State; a report to the

Honorable Nelson A. Rockefeller, Governor of the
State of New York. New York: Institute of Rehabil-
itative Medicine, New York University, Medical Center, 1972. 184 p.
   Identifying 2,565 severely disabled non-retarded
individuals, this fourth and final report profiled them
in terms of age, sex, marital/family status, education, services needed/received. Includes a special
study of 5,000 proprietary nursing homes. Also
investigated needs/costs and problems concerning
long-term facilities, including some in Europe. Concludes with summaries of findings and recommendations.

469.   Wilber, Robert C. Rome State School, 1894-1969.
       Rome, New York, 1969. 46 p. Illus., map, ports.
          The first New York institution created especially
       to meet the needs of the mentally retarded. This
       seventy-five-year history reviews this institution's
       residential program and its contributions to New
       York State's increasing commitment to the care of
       its less fortunate citizens.

                          STATISTICS

Yearbooks
(general to specific)

470.   New York (State). Division of the Budget. Office of
       Statistical Coordination. New York State statistical
       yearbook. 1967- Albany. Maps.
          Compilation of the statistical data series of thirty-
       three different State agencies arranged by such topics
       as: population and vital statistics, employment, per-
       sonal income, banking, commerce, transportation,
       agriculture, state and local finances, construction,
       public health, natural resources, and elections. Ret-
       rospective data included. Most data presented in
       terms of New York City, the five boroughs, and the
       counties.
          An excellent supplement is:

       New York (State). Dept. of Commerce. Business fact
       book. Albany, 1957. Part 1 is based upon the U.S.
       censuses of Business, Manufacture, and Agriculture.
       Part 2 is based upon the U.S. censuses of Population

and Housing.   Both parts present basic statistical
data about communities, counties, economic areas,
and metropolitan area.   Biennial.   There are annual
supplements.   A separate volume for New York state
and one for each of the following localities: Binghamton, Buffalo, the Capital area, Elmira, Mid-
Hudson area, Mohawk Valley, New York City, Nassau-
Suffolk district, Northern area, Rochester, Syracuse,
Westchester-Rockland-Putnam district.   There are
tables for population, labor force, income, income
of persons, education, county of origin, housing,
fuels, and appliances.

471.   New York (State).   Dept. of Commerce.   Basic sta-
       tistics for counties and metropolitan areas of New
       York State.   Albany, 1973.   1 v.
            One data sheet for each county or SMSA.   Con-
       tains: General Information (county seat, land area,
       population for 1950, 1960, 1970, percentage change;
       names largest communities, etc.), Characteristics
       of Employed Workers (total number, percent female,
       distribution by industry, personal income, per
       capita, percent of state, etc.), Manufacturing Sta-
       tistics, Trade and Selective Service Statistics, Ag-
       ricultural Statistics, and also lists the principal
       industrial and commercial employers.   Population
       chart for 1870, 1890, 1910, 1950, 1970.

472.   New York.   Agricultural Experiment Station, Ithaca.
       Dept. of Rural Sociology.   The People of Albany
       County (and other counties in) New York; trends in
       human resources and their characteristics, 1900-
       1960.   (Prepared by Ali A. Paydarfar and Olaf F.
       Larson).   Ithaca, New York: Dept. of Rural Soci-
       ology, Cornell University.   Agricultural Experiment
       Station.   New York, State College of Agriculture,
       1963.   57 v. in 6 illus., maps.
            Arranged alphabetically by county, the data is
       based upon U.S. Census of Population and U.S. Cen-
       sus of Agriculture sources with the intent of pro-
       viding selected information about population trends
       and characteristics which in turn are considered
       social and economic indicators, valid means and
       measures of the human resources of a county, thus
       creating the basis for planning in the future of the
       county and its communities.   Each county profile
       includes analysis by age, place of residence, color,

nativity and parentage, sex, occupation, net changes
in population; percentages and ratios are presented
for the combinations of the above factors. Each report has a selected bibliography on population. The
counties of New York City have been excluded from
this study.

Census
(chronological)

473. Jacobsen, Edna L. New York State and Federal census records; an inventory. Rev. 1956. Albany:
University of the State of New York, 1957. 8 p.
(New York. State Library, Albany. Bibliography
bulletin 81).
    Listed by county, census records and data are
arranged retrospectively from the 1925 schedules.
Location and/or county clerk's office is indicated.

474. New York (State). Secretary of State. Census of the
State of New York for 1875. Albany: Weed, Parsons
and Company, printers, 1877. 465 p.
    A very carefully compiled document detailing as-
pects of Population (race, nationality, foreign born,
by county, votes), Birthplace (county, state, foreign
country, by city, town and ward), Age (sex, birthplace), Mortality (class of disease, sex, age, race,
nationality), Blind, Deaf, and Dumb, etc. (nativity,
sex, age, county, race), Sex, Marriages, Areas,
Dwellings, Families (county, towns, city wards, value), Churches (members, property value, salary of
clergy), Agriculture (county, towns, value, size,
sheep, butter, cheese, yield per acre), Occupations
(age, sex, nativity), Public debt (city, town, village),
Census of Indian Reservations (sex, nativity, unfor-
tunate classes, dwellings, church statistics, occupations, etc.). Maps for population, nativity, agriculture graphically highlight distribution of census factors.

475. McMullin, P. New York in 1800; an index to the Federal census schedules of the State of New York with
other aids to research. Pref. by Winston DeVille.
Provo, Utah: Gendex, 1971. 272 p.
    References are to family names, first name, reel
number, page number, and county. Particularly

useful for micro-history studies and the needs of
the genealogist and family historian.

476.   U.S. Bureau of the Census.   Heads of families at the
       first census of the United States taken in the year
       1790: New York.   Baltimore, Genealogical Pub.,
       1966. 308 p.
            By county and minor civil division, lists heads
       of families, number free white males over sixteen;
       free white males under sixteen, free white females,
       all other free people, slaves.   Has summaries of
       categories by county and town.

477.   New York (State).   Office of Planning Coordination.
       Demographic projections for 0-24 age group, by one-
       year age intervals to 1995 A.D.   Albany, 1969.   92
       p.
            County projections providing one-year age-sex
       distributions from ages 0-24 for SMSA's, counties,
       and regions.   The 1960 Census of Population, vol.
       1, pt. 34, N.Y., provides similar data for the state
       and the 1-20 age group for counties.   The 21-24 age
       group by county is not available in that publication.
            Supplemented by:

       New York (State).   Office of Planning Coordination.
       Demographic projections for New York State counties
       to 2020 A.D.   Albany, 1968.   183 p.   Illus., maps.
       Population projections, male and female, with inter-
       vals of five years age grouping by SMSA's, counties,
       and region.   This effort was an attempt to establish
       a "most probable future" based upon figures that
       would be annually reviewed, modified, and validated
       as required.

SEE ALSO 539, 540, 857.

                        TRANSPORTATION

Aviation

478.   Bostock, P.   The great Atlantic air race: the adven-
       ture and its lessons.   New York: Morrow, 1970.
       224 p.
            Written by one of the organizers of the race that
       commemorated the 50th anniversary of the first

non-stop flight across the Atlantic. The race, involving 390 competitors during eight days in May,
1969, was from the top of the Empire State Building
to the London Post Office Tower. Appendices list
winners of various categories, data on the participat-
ing aircraft.

479. O'Neill, Ralph A. and Joseph F. Hood. A dream of
      eagles. Boston: Houghton, Mifflin, 1973. 324 p.
         The author's personal account of how he created
      the world's longest airline, the New York, Rio, and
      Buenos Aires Line, when aviation was in its infancy.
      Surviving Latin American politics, hurricanes, and
      tropical rains, this company was taken over by Pan
      American Airways by Wall Street intrigues and un-
      ethical government officials.

Canals
(chronological)

480. Shelton, Ronald L. The New York State Barge Canal.
      Ithaca, New York: Dept. of Conservation, New York
      State College of Agriculture, Cornell University,
      1965. 60 p. (Current topics in conservation, series
      II, no. 3). Bibliography: p. 63-66.
         This study explores the question of who shall con-
      trol and use the state or the federal government--
      the water resources represented by the Barge Canal
      System. Includes an historical sketch of the Canal
      System, and a description of its present uses and
      operations in relation to recreation, flood control,
      agriculture, industry, commercial barge navigation,
      and hydroelectric power. Extensive quantitative data.

481. Hill, Henry W. An historical review of waterways and
      canal construction in New York State. Buffalo: Buf-
      falo Historical Society, 1908. 549 p. Front. (Port.),
      fold. , map.
         Written by the legislator, Senator Hill, who was
      very active in the establishment of canals and water-
      ways, and is thus able to present a very unique
      viewpoint as well as political insight into events. In-
      cludes two of his famous "canal speeches. "

482. New York (State). Legislature. Joint Committee on
      Historic Sites and Historic Canal Preservation. Re-
      port. Albany. 1957/58--

Brief description and commentary on historic sites, including the Erie Canal. Includes recommendation about historic marker program, the possibility of a Canal Museum, etc.

483. Buffalo and Erie County Historical Society. Canal en-
      largement in New York State: Papers on the barge
      canal campaign and related topics. Buffalo: Buffalo
      Historical Society, 1909. 446 p.
           Collection of monographs about the politics, im-
      pact, and businesses associated with the New York
      canal system and the importance of inland navigation
      to the state's commercial/population growth.

484. Condon, George E. Stars in the water; the story of
      the Erie Canal. Garden City, New York: Doubleday,
      1974. 338 p. Bibliography: p. 323-325.
           A delightful and detailed history of the Erie Canal
      --its construction, the politics involved, its impact
      upon the nation and the people of New York State
      with anecdotes of the famous and near famous asso-
      ciated with the cities and villages along the Canal,
      such as Sam Patch, Jonathan Bass, the Ossified
      Man, Samuel Clemens, Chauncey Olcott, etc.

485. Wyld, Lionel D. Low bridge! Folklore and the Erie
      Canal. Syracuse, New York: Syracuse University,
      1964. 212 p. "Notes": p. 182-206.
           History of the Erie Canal, its construction, life,
      and entertainments on it, famous men and women
      associated with it, the specialized vocabulary it
      contributed to American English, and impact and
      place in lore, literature, and music.

486. Garrity, Richard G. Canal boatman: my life on up-
      state waterways. Syracuse, New York: Syracuse
      University, 1977. 222 p. (A York State Book).
           Beginning with a boyhood spent on the Erie Canal
      (1905-1916) working on his father's canal boats, to
      a life as a canaller on the Barge Canal System until
      his retirement in 1970, the author provides descrip-
      tions of canal boat drivers, steermen, famous canal
      boat mules, anecdotes and recollections of farmers,
      grocers, and others along the water ways, defines
      terms, and discusses a wide range of work activity
      associated with the canals. He also comments on
      family life on a canal boat.

Railroads
(chronological, then alphabetical
by railroad company)

487.   Shaughnessy, J.   Delaware & Hudson; the history of an
       important railroad whose antecedent was a canal net-
       work to transport coal.   Berkeley, Calif.:   Howell-
       North, 1967.   476 p.   Bibliography: p. 471.
          An impressive history (1825-1967), lavishly illus-
       trated with photographs, maps, reproductions of
       schedules, documents, etc.   Final section is a roster
       of the motive power of the D & H, 1913-1967, with
       details on cylinders, driving pressure, weights, trac-
       tive efforts.

488.   Taber, Thomas T.   The Delaware, Lackawanna & West-
       ern Railroad, the Road of Anthracite, in the nine-
       teenth century, 1829-1899: the history of the formation
       and development of the D. L. & W. "family" of rail-
       roads, and their locomotives which, in the following
       century, became one of our most admired and be-
       loved railroads.   Muncy, Pa.:   Taber, 1977.   407 p.
       Plates, illus., maps.
          A history of the "family" of railroads that became
       one strong unit--the story of each is told, moving
       geographically from East to West.   Also chronicles
       activities and kinds of traffic usually not seen or
       known by the travelling public.   A special section is
       devoted to the locomotives of the various branches
       and divisions with detailed data.   Many illustrations,
       maps, photographs, and reproductions of tickets,
       schedules, etc. complete this very detailed account.

489.   Weller, John L.   The New Haven Railroad: its rise
       and fall.   New York: Hastings House, 1969.   248 p.
       Bibliography: p. 239-241.
          History of the New York, New Haven and Hartford
       Railroad Co.--primarily the financial, political, ad-
       ministrative aspects--its predecessors and its looting
       and decline between 1914 to 1968.

490.   Beebe, Lucius M.   20th Century, the greatest train in
       the world.   Berkeley, Calif.:   Howell-North, 1962.
       180 p.
          Lavishly illustrated with photographs and repro-
       ductions, this history is actually a detailed tribute to
       The Century, that standard of speed, comfort, and

excellence and prestige. This train was the best,
its passengers the famous and infamous from all the
worlds of literature, art, finance, entertainment,
sports, society, etc. While it was a Vanderbilt
train, a New York train, in fact, it became a national institution, the epitome of rail travel.

491.   Harlow, Alvin F.   The road of the century; the story
       of the New York Central.   New York: Creative Age
       Press, 1947.   447 p.   (The railroads of America 2).
       Bibliography: p. 430-439.
       A detailed history of the trials, failures, problems,
       and successes of the first twenty years of those early
       railroads (ten) that in 1853, by consolidation, became
       the New York Central Railroad.   Individual chapters
       devoted to each "road," and such subjects as: tracks,
       freight, and passenger rates, fuel, credit, cars, and
       bridges.   The appendices include a summary of the
       consolidation agreement with brief sketches of the
       leaders involved.

492.   Staufer, Alvin F. and Edward L. May.   Thoroughbreds:
       New York Central's 4-6-4 Hudson, the most famous
       class of steam locomotive in the world.   Medina,
       Ohio: Staufer, c. 1974.   336 p.   Illus., plates.
       A history of locomotives (and cars) with emphasis
       upon the Hudson.   Profusely illustrated with photo-
       graphs, reproductions of posters, paintings, and
       plans.   Individual chapters devoted to wrecks, model
       and toy trains, the engineers and firemen and other
       aspects of railroading.

493.   Edson, William D. and Edward L. May.   Steam and
       electric locomotives of the New York Central Lines:
       numbering and classification.   Irvington-on-Hudson,
       New York: 1966.   136 p.
       Arranged by class (wheel arrangement), almost
       15,000 electric and steam locomotives that operated
       on New York Central and its subsidiary lines are
       listed.   Each engine is cited once with builder's data
       and a complete record of renumbering.   Specifica-
       tions, dimensions, and weights for each are also
       included.

494.   Wakefield, Manville B.   To the mountains by rail; peo-
       ple, events and tragedies ... the New York, Ontario
       and Western Railway and the famous Sullivan County

resorts. Foreword by Irwin Richman. Grahams-
ville, New York: Wakefair, 1970. 415 p. Illus.,
maps, ports. Bibliography: p. 405-410.
    Lavishly illustrated with photographs, drawings,
paintings, maps, reproductions of advertisements,
time tables, etc., this history of the role that railroads played in the development of the Sullivan County hotel resort industry includes details and anecdotes
about fires, entertainment, railroad disasters, personalities, the life style of the Catskills, bridges
etc.

495.   King, Shelden S. The New York State Railways. El-
       mira, New York: Distributed by Whitehall Mail
       Service, 1975. 128 p. Bibliography: p. 128.
           The New York State Railways, in terms of miles,
       was the largest electric railway company in New York
       State. Located in central and western New York, it
       was the result of a number of mergers of firms from
       Rochester, Syracuse, Schenectady, and other smaller
       communities. This is a detailed, factual history
       (1887-1929), emphasizing statistics, numerous photo-
       graphs of trolley cars, reproductions of time tables,
       tickets, etc.

496.   Arcara, R. Westchester's forgotten railway, 1912-
       1937; the story of a short-lived short line which was
       at once America's finest railway and its poorest: the
       New York, Westchester & Boston Railway. Rev. and
       expanded ed., including When the Westchester was
       new. New York: Quadrant, 1972. 136 p.
           A detailed and profusely illustrated history (photo-
       graphs, reproductions of time schedules, facsimiles
       of plans, etc.) of this electric railway. Includes
       When the Westchester Was New, another history which
       consisted of nine articles about the New York, West-
       chester & Boston Railway that originally appeared in
       the Electric Railway Journal and the Railway Age Ga-
       zette.

497.   Hilton, George W. The Great Lakes car ferries.
       Berkeley, Calif.: Howell-North, 1962. 282 p.
           The "car" of the title refers to railroad cars, this,
       in fact, being a centennial history of those companies
       and railroads that ferry railroad cars, at fourteen
       miles per hour, across the lakes. Emphasis is on
       the car ferries' accidents and the men who demonstrated

resourcefulness and heroism during such disasters.
Arranged by the history/activities of the individual
companies. The fleet lists indicate: owner, builders
of the boats, type/size of engines and/or boilers,
car capacity and disposition.

Roads

498. New York State Thruway Authority. Facts ... the New
 York Thruway. Albany, 1961. 20 p.
 Concise figures and explanations about Thruway
 construction, operation, revenues, laws, services,
 etc.
 Additional information is provided by:

 Thomas, Lowell J. The New York Thruway story.
 1st ed. Buffalo: H. Steward, 1955. Illus., maps.
 Prefaced by brief history of New York State, this
 account includes details of Thruway construction and
 operations, the organization and structure of the Authority and concludes with "A Tourist Guide to the
 Thruway"--descriptions of points of interest, natural
 wonders, and historic sites near the Thruway from
 one end of the state to the other.

Ships
(specific to general)

499. Ringwald, Donald C. The Mary Powell; a history of
 the beautiful side-wheel steamer called "Queen of the
 Hudson." Berkeley, Calif.: Howell-North, 1972.
 212 p. Illus. Bibliography: p. 208-209.
 A history of steamboats on and along the Hudson
 with the Mary Powell as the epitome of that mode of
 travel. Many photographs, illustrations, drawings,
 and paintings recreate the era. The appendices include data about the Mary Powell's construction, various measurements, enrollments, fast runs, models,
 poems, and the details of her dismantling.

500. Ringwald, Donald C. Hudson River Day Line; the story
 of a great American steamboat company. Berkeley,
 Calif.: Howell-North, 1965. 228 p. Bibliography:
 p. 223.
 Detailed history of the Day Line from 1863 to the
 close of its operations in 1948, supplemented with an

account of its successors. Many photographs, reproductions, maps, interior views. Appendix provides: statistical data about Day Line steamboats
and others, biographical sketches of Day Line ship
officers.

501. Boyer, D. Ships and men of the Great Lakes. New
      York: Dodd, Mead, 1977. 208 p. Bibliography:
      p. 195-197.
      Based upon both research and personal acquaint-
      ance, these accounts of the shipwrecks, fires, and
      disasters of Great Lakes shipping span a time period
      from 1841 to the tragedy of the sinking of the Edmund
      Fitzgerald in 1975.
      The above can be supplemented by:

      Boyer, D. True tales of the Great Lakes. Illustrated
      with photos and maps. New York: Dodd, Mead,
      1971. 340 p. Illus. Bibliography: p. 325-327.
      Detailed narrative of shipping disasters--one even at
      dockside. Photographs of ships lost on the lakes.

SEE ALSO 933-941.

PART II: NEW YORK CITY

GENERAL WORKS

502. City almanac, v. 1- 1966- New York Center for New
York City Affairs. New School for Social Research.
Bimonthly.
Each issue is devoted to a particular aspect or
problem of New York City--anti-poverty programs,
decentralization, book publishing, city finance, etc.
Factual, statistics, graphs.

Directories

503. New York (City). Official directory of the city of New
York. New York, 1918.
Statistical and historical data about New York City.
Extensive directory of New York City government
and New York State. Identifies directors, members
of committees, commissions, with addresses, telephone numbers, etc. Even contains some U.S. government directory information.

504. Directory of directors in the city of New York. 1898-
Annual. New York, Directory of Directors Co.
Alphabetic lists of important business executives
of companies capitalized at 100,000 or more. Includes residential addresses as well as the name of
the firm with which each director, partner, or trus-
tee is most closely associated. Second part includes
companies who maintain their principal offices in
New York City or whose boards of directors included
New York City directors. Also cites names and
titles of senior officers and the names of all directors. Address of corporation included.

505. The New York woman's directory, by the Womanpower
Project. New York: Workman, 1973. 262 p.

Compiled by feminists for feminists who, when
they seek a service, make a purchase, or need help,
want to employ a woman and support the cause.
This group effort provides access to practitioners,
services, and items from such categories as: employment, managing money, self-defense, medical
needs, the home, courses to take, the law, publishing, finance, theatre, funding and grants, and fem-
inism in New York.

Bibliographies

506.   Eiberson, H. and S. Ditzion. Sources for the study
       of the New York area. With a chapter on the study
       of population distribution and composition. New York:
       City College, 1960. 128 p. (Institute of New York
       Area Studies, the City College of New York. Mono-
       graph no. 5).
          An annotated list of the more important indexes,
       guides, bibliographies, the chief reference sources,
       outstanding books and documents; also indicates those
       organizations and libraries that may be of value to
       the researcher. Classified arrangement by broad
       subject area: law, government, business, population,
       etc.

507.   Reynolds, James B.   Civic bibliography for Greater
       New York. New York: Charities publication Com-
       mittee, 1911. 296 p.
          Arrangement in broad categories and then sub-
       divided, books and articles are listed on a variety
       of subjects; just about every aspect of human activ-
       ity that occurs in a city: population, history, gov-
       ernment, art, finance, transportation, public health,
       crime, education, religion, recreation, etc. Some
       entries have one line annotations.

Charities

508.   New York Foundation.   Forty-year report, 1909-1949.
       New York, 1950. 70 p.
          Limiting the major part of its philanthropy to
       metropolitan New York City, avoiding the areas and
       problems well-served by other agencies and govern-
       ment, this foundation seeks and has sought new areas

of public advancement, supporting new endeavors, taking risks with untried possibilities for social betterment. Its emphasis upon the innovative; an interesting attitude for one of the oldest philanthropic foundations.

509.   Federation of Jewish Philanthropies of New York. The Golden heritage; a history of the Federation of Jewish Philanthropies of New York from 1917 to 1967. New York, 1969. 395 p.
        A significant social force, a centralized organization mobilizing the community's resources and coordinating the activities of member agencies in order to meet the welfare and health needs of the city. This history of the Federation is based upon the four most important events of its past. Also included is a section with one- or two-page descriptions of its member agencies and service organizations.

Description and Travel
(general to specific)

510.   Simon, K. New York places & pleasures; an uncommon guidebook. 4th ed. rev. New York: Harper & Row, 1971. 417 p.
        Delightful guidebook emphasizing the lesser-known attractions of the City. The author orients the visitor with some historical facts, profiles the psyches of taxi drivers, saleswomen, and waiters, and provides other clues to survival. The rest of the text is devoted to parks, walking tours, museums, eating and dining, children in the city, bargains, shops, entertainments, with a chronology of "Perennials"-- a monthly record of events, celebrations, etc. The appendix is an alphabetic listing of items (aduki beans to thumb screws and zithers) and where they can be obtained.

511.   Horowitz, Harold H. Hart's guide to New York City. Illus. by Ruby Davidson. Maps by Hilda Simon. New York: Hart Pub., 1964. 1331 p. Illus., col. maps.
        Alphabetically by topic, from "After Theatre" places to "Zoos." Brief descriptive reports on over 2,200 stores, services, and activities. Much of the

information--prices, schedules, etc.--is now out of
date, but much does remain valid. Extensive map
section of various subway systems and specific neighborhoods, i.e., Chinatown, Greenwich Village, etc.
More valuable now as a historical document profiling
the City.

512. New York (City). City Commission for the United Na-
      tions and for the Consular Corps. New York, your
      host: a New York handbook ... 2nd rev. ed. New
      York: The Commission, 1974. 68 p. Bibliography:
      p. 62-63.
          While written for a very special audience, the
      advice and comments are useful to any new resident
      or visitor--covering first days in the city (hotels,
      restaurants, etc.), finding a place to live, your fam-
      ily (schools, churches, etc.), shopping, recreation,
      meeting New Yorkers, transportation.

513. Shepard, Richard F. Going out in New York: a guide
      for the curious. New York: Quadrangle/New York
      Times, 1974. 366 p. Illus., map. Bibliography:
      p. 343-348.
          Emphasis is on theatre and ethnic sights and pro-
      grams with many old favorites (Empire State Building,
      U.N., etc.) included as this is a guide for the New
      Yorker, who takes his city casually, rather than for
      visitors. Like most guide books, sections are de-
      voted to the standard topics of interest: music, mu-
      seums, art, libraries, film, churches, lectures,
      shopping. Descriptions of events, places, and sites
      include directions for getting there. No nonsense
      commentary. The section on "Guide to Guidebooks"
      is useful and refreshingly candid.

514. Postal, B. and L. Koppman. Jewish landmarks in New
      York; an informal history and guide. Illus. by Lynette
      Logan. New York: Hill and Wang, 1964. 277 p.
      Illus. Index of Synagogues: p. 275-277.
          Prefaced by a general history of Jews in New York
      City from 1654 to 1963, the rise of the Jewish com-
      munity and its religious, cultural, and philanthropic
      institutions. The guide itself includes walking tours,
      descriptions of synagogues, places to visit, entertain-
      ment, dining out, shopping, local institutions, and
      national and international organizations--all reflecting the
      character and accomplishments of the Jews in New York.

SEE ALSO 143, 196, 199, 667, 766, 767.

Description and Travel
(general to specific)

Specialized Guides

514a. Night people's guide to New York; a Darien House pro-
    ject. Introd. by Jean Shepherd. New York: Bantam
    Books, 1965. 160 p.
       City-wide directory for very unique or special
    services not limited to one area of the city; then the
    Neighborhood Directory divides Manhattan into eleven
    sections with subdivisions on apparel, automobile ser-
    vices, bakeries, bookstores, home furnishings, res-
    taurants, etc. Brief description of each business.
    The introduction reminds us that New York City is
    ever-changing and ever the same; consequently, this
    guide is very much outdated. Its value is primarily
    in its use in identifying a business or service (re-
    ferred to in a novel, history, or conversation) that
    no longer exists.

514b. Ch'ên, T'ien-ên, ed. Welcome to Chinatown. Official
    Chinatown guide book, New York 1964-1965; official
    guide book for World's Fair visitors, year of dragon.
    Henin Chin, editor. James Boyle, associate editor.
    New York: Heinin, 1964. 64 p. Illus., maps,
    ports.
       History of Chinatown, explanation of Chinese cus-
    toms, foods, festivals, some brief information about
    the World's Fair, interesting places to visit in New
    York.

514c. Fang, John T. C. Chinatown handy guide, New York
    City. New York, 1958. 96 p. Illus.
       Brief sections on the history, customs, culture,
    food, music, holidays, folklore, etc. of the Chinese
    of Chinatown.

514d. Petronius, pseud. New York unexpurgated; an amoral
    guide for the jaded, tired, evil, non-conforming,
    corrupt, condemned, and the curious, humans and
    otherwise, to underground Manhattan. New York:
    Matrix House, c. 1966. 246 p.
       A clever, amusing, tough-minded look at New
    York and the attitudes, techniques, mores, and places

involved in the success of the world's oldest game/
sport. As warned in the preface, many of the names
and addresses may be just "history" now but they
have been replaced. Aside from the brittle wit,
many useful clues to interesting but non-sexual New
York.

514e. Chiang, Yee. The silent traveller in New York. Written and illustrated. With a pref. by Van Wych
Brooks. New York: John Day, 1953. 281 p.
Illus., map.
A Chinese painter and author of many travel books
about England visits New York City and by drawing,
water color, and written word provides us with another perspective--one of charm, cosmopolitan urban-
ity, and fresh insight--concerning the usual and tourist attractions--Harlem, Central Park, Greenwich
Village, Chinatown, the George Washington Bridge,
etc.

514f. Federal Writers' project. New York (City). New York
panorama; a comprehensive view of the metropolis,
presented in a series of articles prepared by the
Federal Writers' Project of the Works Progress Administration in New York City. New York: Random
House, c. 1938. 526 p. Illus.
Twenty-six essays about the social, economic,
political, intellectual aspects of the City as well as
its art, mass media, history, and the World's Fair
of 1939. Useful for historical perspective now.

New York for Children

515. Shaw, Ray. New York for children; an unusual guide
for parents, teachers, and tourists. Rev. ed. New
York: E. P. Dutton, 1974. 167 p.
Arranged into four categories (brief annotation describing the school, shop, store, factory, office,
etc.; admission information, reservations (?), and
appropriate age levels): On the Job--airlines, fashions, hotels, textiles, etc.; Being Made--bagels,
ballet slippers, stained glass, etc.; Once a Year--
annual events listed by month; To Be Seen--bottle
collections, doll library, Fire Dept. museum, etc.

516. Levinson, S. and M. Levinson. Where to go and what
to do with the kids in New York. Los Angeles:
Price/Stern/Sloan, 1972. 126 p.

Arranged in categories: Outdoor adventures; Back
to nature; Restaurants with small fry appeal; Tours
and exhibits; Concerts, films, TV, and theater;
Classes and clubs; Museums with attractions for kids;
Special places outside the City; Where to take young
out-of-towners; Miscellany. Brief descriptions of
attractions and activities, addresses, telephone numbers and directions.

517.   Berman, C. A great city for kids; parents' guide to a
child's New York. Illus. by Shelly Sacks. Indianapolis: Bobbs-Merrill, 1969. 360 p.
Arranged by interest categories (outdoor/indoor
activities, the arts, services, tourist attractions,
tours) for children three to thirteen. All entries
have age recommendations, travel directions, financial data.

Architectural and Historical Tours

518.   The heritage of New York; historic-landmark plaques
of the New York Community Trust. Pref. by Whitney North Seymour. New York: Fordham University, 1970. 402 p.
Explanation of the efforts of the Landmark Pres-
ervation Commission and the New York Community
Trust. The Heritage Plaque locations, 178, are
illustrated also with a close-up of the plaque and its
inscription on the opposite page. Arranged alphabetically within borough. Each section is preceded by
a borough map. Detailed, numerically-keyed street
maps pinpoint locations. A separate collection of
the maps, by borough, provides a walking-guide to
historic sites and buildings.

519.   American Institute of Architects. New York Chapter.
AIA guide to New York City. Norval White, Elliot
Willensky, editors. New York: Macmillan, 1968.
464 p.
Limited to largely permanent places and things,
natural and man-made, several thousand structures,
monuments, places, and events have been described,
located on detailed maps and organized into walking
tours. Criteria for inclusion: it be an example of
historical, social, or technical significance, and it
be interesting and/or pleasurable to a wide variety
of people. Arranged geographically by borough, then

subdivided; brief descriptions, symbols, and codes
provide a wealth of information. Use of special
lists such as (Street spectacles) and indexes (Architectural Style Guide) are a must.

520.   Federal Writers' Project, New York (City). New York
       City guide; a comprehensive guide to the five boroughs
       of the metropolis--Manhattan, Brooklyn, the Bronx,
       Queens, and Richmond. With a new introd. by John
       V. Lindsay. New York: Octagon, c. 1939. 708 p.
       Reprinted 1970. Bibliography: p. 649-659.
       A detailed description of the points of interest
       (some) and the communities in all five boroughs of
       New York City. Each borough is divided into Sec-
       tions, and those are subdivided into Localities (Hell's
       Kitchen, Times Square District, etc.). The Section
       introduction includes a historical sketch and contem-
       porary description (1939). Landmarks are noted,
       important buildings and sites are commented upon,
       and in general the unique aspects of the Localities
       are highlighted and explained. Maps and careful
       street directions aided the tourists. The bibliography
       is a classified list of books about various aspects
       of New York life.

SEE ALSO 663.

                   ECONOMICS AND COMMERCE
                        (chronological)

521.   New York Herald Tribune. New York City in crisis
       (a study in depth of urban sickness). Prepared by
       the New York Herald Tribune staff under the direc-
       tion of Barry Gottehrer. New York: D. McKay,
       1965. 212 p.
       Initially a series of newspaper articles devoted to
       what was wrong, how it got that way, and what could
       be done about it, rewritten, updated, and reorganized
       into twenty-three individual topical chapters: from
       business, pollution, and crime to health, youth and
       politics. Written just before John Lindsay became
       mayor. Appendix includes the New York Herald Trib-
       une's indictment of New York City which was pub-
       lished 1/25/65.

522.   New York (State). Chamber of Commerce of the State
       of New York. Colonial records of the New York

Chamber of Commerce, 1768-1784. With historical
and biographical sketches, by John Austin Stevens,
Jr. New York: John F. Trow, 1867. 404, 172 p.
The organization of the "Society of Merchants"
into the Chamber of Commerce, a register of proceedings followed by brief biographical sketches of
those mentioned in the minutes of the meetings.
Notes to the register identify individuals, explain
business procedures, provide information about cur-
rency, impact of legislation, etc. Lists members
of the Chamber of Commerce and the location of
their businesses. Final section is devoted to biographies of the presidents of the Chamber.
Reprinted by B. Franklin press: Burt Franklin
research and source works series, 729. American
classics in history and social science, 188.

523. Pound, A. The golden earth; the story of Manhattan's
landed wealth. New York: Macmillan, 1935. 316 p.
Bibliography: p. 305-308.
A detailed economic and financial history from
1609 to the mid-1930's.

524. Beach, Moses Y. The wealthy citizens of New York.
New York: Arno, 1973. 83 p. Reprint of the edition
(1845) published under the title: Wealth and biography of the wealthy citizens of New York City, by the
Sun office, New York, and of the 1855 edition published by the Sun office under the title: The Wealth
and biography of the wealthy citizens of the city of
New York.
An alphabetical listing of New York City residents
"worth $100,000 and upwards," with brief genealogi-
cal and biographical notes. The fifth (1845) edition
was thirty-two pages long with no less than twenty
entries per page. The twelfth edition (1855) was
eighty-three pages in length with no less than ten
entries per page.

525. Bahl, Roy W. Taxes, expenditures, and the economic
base; case study of New York City (by) Roy W. Bahl,
Alan K. Campbell (and) David Greytak. New York:
Praeger, 1974. 351 p. (Praeger special studies in
U.S. economic, social, and political issues).
Focus is upon economic, demographic, and social
change aspects related to the city fiscal position.
City employment is examined, personal income (level

and distribution) is analyzed, the population compo-
sition profiled, and land use changes are noted--as
property tax is the single most important source of
revenue. Many tables, statistics--wealth of data
even if somewhat technical at times.

526.   De Voe, Thomas F. The market book; a history of
       the public markets of the city of New York. New
       York: A. M. Kelly, 1970. 621 p. (Library of
       early American business and industry, 40). General
       index: p. 607-621.
           This volume, one of two, is devoted to some
       forty market places and public markets within the
       limits of the City of New York (1629-1857), their
       history, owner(s), descriptions of buildings, products
       sold, fires, finance, etc. In broader terms, this
       is also an economic history of the city. First edi-
       tion was printed in 1862.

SEE ALSO 213, 574, 663, 752, 753, 840.

Finance and Banking
(general to specific, then alphabetically
by name of exchange)

527.   Levinson, L. Wall Street; a pictorial history. New
       York: Ziff-Davis Pub., 1961. 376 p.
           From the founding of New Amsterdam to the
       1950's, this chronicle, extensively illustrated, in-
       cludes the facts, details, statistics, traditions,
       myths, and life styles that characterize the finan-
       cial center of America and its responses to the
       triumphs and disasters that are part of U. S. history.

528.   Sobel, R. Amex: a history of the American Stock Ex-
       change, 1921-1971. New York: Weybright and Tal-
       ley, 1972. 382 p. "Bibliographical essay": p. 353-
       360.
           The people, the psychology, and the circumstances
       that resulted in the secure establishment of "Amex"
       as the second financial market in the City.

529.   Boston College, Boston, Mass. College of Business
       Administration. New York Coffee and Sugar Ex-
       change, Inc.: its role in the marketing of sugar; an
       analysis performed by the College of Business

Administration, Boston College, Chestnut, Mass.
New York: Hobbs, Dorman, 1965. 96 p. Bibliography: p. 85-99.
A study commissioned by the Exchange's Board
of Managers. Chapters four and five are specifically
concerned with procedures and routines of the Exchange with some recommendations for tightening up
operations.

530.   Hamon, H. New York Stock Exchange manual, containing its principles, rules, and its different modes
of speculation: also, a review of the stocks dealt
in on 'change, government and state securities, railway, mining, petroleum, etc., etc. Westport,
Conn.: Greenwood, 1970. 405 p. Reprint of 1865
edition.
Constitution and by-laws of the Stock Exchange,
Gold Exchange, Open Board of Stock Brokers, the
Evening Exchange, Public Petroleum Exchange, Petroleum Stock Board, with lists of stock jobbers,
stock brokers, explanation of the operation of the
exchanges, and financial concepts defined. Part II
has lists of various companies and types of stock
available, and a list of banks with officers and assets
cited.

531.   Eames, Francis L. The New York Stock Exchange.
New York: Greenwood, 1968. 139 p. Reprint of
1894 ed.
Originally written "solely" for members of the
Exchange that had an interest in the development
and history of the organization. A chronological
presentation (1792-1894) that includes: cost of membership, use of the telegraph, failures of the Exchange, officers of the Exchange. Members of the
Exchange in 1894 are listed by year of admission.
Similar data is provided about the Open Board of
Stock Brokers, the New York Gold Exchange, and
the Evening Exchanges.

532.   Sobel, R. N.Y.S.E.: a history of the New York Stock
Exchange, 1935-1975. New York: Weybright and
Talley, 1975. 398 p. Bibliography: p. 379-382.
This history is divided into three stages: 1) sur-
vival and change (1935-1941); 2) the period of power,
confidence, and expansion (1941-1966); 3) stress,
problems, slow change, (1967-1975). An attempt at

perspective and comprehension of an institution that
has faithfully reflected America's attitudes, problems,
and values.

533. New York. Stock Exchange. Dept. of Public Relations
      and Market Development. Fact book. 1956- Annu-
      al. New York.
          Summary of various statistical publications of the
      Exchange plus data generated by other organizations
      on such topics as market activity, stock prices, the
      investing public, the Exchange community, Capital
      markets, etc. Has a section on the organization of
      the NYSE and a historical section on volume, prices,
      dividends, market value, credit, short sales, etc.

534. Garside, Alston H. Wool and the wool trade ... with
      twenty-three reproductions from photographs and
      three graphic charts. New York: Frederick A.
      Stokes, 1939. 331 p.
          Author had two objectives: to provide a descrip-
      tion of the production, manufacturing, and marketing
      of apparel wools in the U.S. and to explain the or-
      ganization and operation of the New York Wool Top
      Exchange; how it benefits and is used by those in the
      trade.

SEE ALSO 840.

Occupations

535. Personnel research federation. Occupational trends in
      New York City; changes in the distribution of gainful
      workers, 1900-1930, prepared for the Adjustment
      service of New York City by the Personnel research
      federation, W. V. Bingham, director, in cooperation
      with O. M. Hall, Bryce Haynes and Bruce Alexander.
      New York: National Occupational Conference, 1933.
      15 p.
          New York City data is compared with national
      figures; some 110 occupations charted for each dec-
      ade, 1900-1930, for manufacturing, transportation,
      trade, professional services, public services, do-
      mestic and personal services, and clerical. Some
      data goes back to the 1870's.

536. Ginzberg, E. New York is very much alive: a man-
      power view (by) Eli Ginzberg and the Conservation of

Human Resources staff, Columbia University. New
York: McGraw-Hill, 1973. 318 p. Illus., tables.
"Notes": p. 297-309.

New York as the sample, this study explores the
problems of and operation of metropolitan economics
and labor markets with the belief that what is learned
about New York City manpower situations will be
relevant to other metropolitan areas. The essays
are arranged into four parts: 1) Perspective--New
York City as a unique metropolis, assessment of
manpower, etc.; 2) Problems--minorities, their occupational and employment opportunities and con-
straints; 3) Planning--explorations in decision making,
informational services, educational planning, relationships between manpower institutions, etc.; 4) Policy--
recommendations for more effective development and
utilization of manpower.

Real Estate

537. Makielski, Stanislaw J. The politics of zoning; the New
York experience. New York: Columbia University,
1966. 241 p. Bibliography: p. 229-233.

Traces the major events in the history of New
York City zoning, identifies and analyzes the operant
factors (social, economic, ideological, and governmental), and attempts to relate them to the process
of decision making in this area of public policy.
Sources of information are direct personal interviews,
newspapers, and the records and reports of nongov-
ernmental interest groups and government agencies.
Covers the period 1010 to 1960.

538. A history of real estate, building and architecture in
New York City during the last quarter century. New
York: Arno Press, 1967. 704 p. Illus., maps.
Reprint of 1898 edition.

Statistical data (price of lots, auction sales, etc.)
and almost a directory of real estate firms, lawyers,
builders, architects, and materials companies. Includes assessment of leading architects and the review of architecture contains a chronological list of
building constructed from 1868 to 1897. Many line
drawings and photographs of famous and outstanding
structures.

158   New York City

SEE ALSO 367, 368.

Statistics

539. Shannon, Michael O. New York urban statistics. Mon-
      ticello, Ill.: Council of Planning Librarians, 1975.
      9 p. (Council of Planning Librarians. Exchange
      bibliography, no. 873).
      Historical background is provided by:

      Rosenwaike, Ira. Population history of New York City.
      Syracuse, New York: Syracuse University, 1972.
      224 p. Tables, maps. Bibliography: p. 207-216.
      Reports, from its founding to 1970, on the popula-
      tion changes and the physical expansion of the City.
      Social and economic factors are simply noted; em-
      phasis is upon the extensive historical census data
      available-- 1) tables; and 2) appendices provide
      almost every combination of census factors.

540. New York (State). Office of Biostatistics. Selected
      health statistics for hospitals: New York State (ex-
      clusive of New York City), 1973/ New York State
      Dept. of Health, Robert D. Whalen, Acting Com-
      missioner. Albany: New York State Dept. of Health,
      between 1974 and 1976. 147 p. Tables.
      An analysis of birth-related statistics by hospitals
      within six health regions.

SEE ALSO 470-477.

EDUCATION

Public Schools
(general to specific,
current to retrospective)

541. Sheldon, Eleanor H. and Raymond A. Glazier. Pupils
      and schools in New York City; a fact book. New
      York: Russell Sage Foundation, 1965. 151 p.
      The New York City school system is reviewed
      within the national context of social change. Indi-
      vidual chapters devoted to demographic changes and
      enrollments, the organizations of the educational sys-
      tem, its major programs, open enrollments, staffing,

and an analysis of student performance (permissive zoning/compensatory programming).

542.   Rogers, D.   110 Livingston Street; politics and bureau-cracy in the New York City schools.   New York: Random House, 1968.   584 p.   Bibliography: p. 527-544.
        A study of the politics and administration of the New York City school system within the context of the desegregation/decentralization struggle (1963-1968).

543.   Berube, Maurice R. and M. Gittell.   Confrontation at Ocean Hill-Brownsville; the New York school strikes of 1968.   New York: Praeger, 1969.   340 p.   "Chronology of Events":   p. 335-340.
        Arrangement is by documents completely reproduced, followed by "viewpoints"; magazine articles, speeches, advertisements, etc. commenting on the issues that generated the documents.   Basic questions are decentralization and community control, with other sections on due process, racism, and anti-Semitism.

544.   Swanson, Bert E.   The struggle for equality; school integration controversy in New York City.   With a foreword by Bert James Loewenberg.   New York: Hobbs, Dorman, 1966.   146 p.
        Delineates the reaction/response of the white community to proposed desegregation policies, the social and political conflicts generated by the "threats" to ethnic, economic, social, and political factions, and the antagonisms revealed between diverse groups. Reviews the decade, 1954-1963, of integration controversy, examines the position and power of the school board, the teachers, the superintendency, the various community groups, the proposed alternatives, and suggests techniques for further study.

545.   Fuchs, E.   Teachers talk; a view from within inner city schools.   New York: Project True, Hunter College, City University of New York, 1967.   222 p.
        Attempts to provide, for teachers and administrators, insights into the needs of new teachers in inner city schools.   The approach is anthropological, emphasizing "cultural awareness," unusual, but as a consequence is very informative about New York City

public schools and the various relationships therein--
teachers, administrators, parents, students, peers,
the community, and the interactions in and between
these groups.

546. Steigman, Benjamin M. Accent on talent; New York's
      High School of Music and Art. Detroit: Wayne State
      University, 1964. 370 p.
          History (25 years) of the HSMA, how students are
      selected, what they study, profiles of the students
      themselves, their interests, and outside activities;
      what becomes of them after graduation; the limits
      of the school--financial, bureaucratic, and otherwise,
      with an assessment of the school, its students, and
      HSMA's hopes for the future.

547. Bourne, William O. History of the Public School So-
      ciety of the City of New York. New York: Arno
      Press, c. 1869. 768 p. Port. (American education:
      Its men, ideas, and institutions. Series II). Re-
      printed 1971.
          A chronological (1817-1853), detailed history that
      includes, in full, speeches, reports, papers, me-
      morials, and addresses. Chapters 16, 17, 18, 19
      are exceptions as they are limited to the administra-
      tion of the Society, normal and high schools, infant
      schools and primary schools, and schools for colored
      children. Final chapter is devoted to the history of
      public schools, established by the Society--public
      schools nos. 1-18.

Private Schools

548. Waterbury, Jean P. A History of Collegiate School,
      1638-1963. 1st ed. New York: C.N. Potter, 1965.
      160 p.
          Established in 1638 by the Reformed Protestant
      Dutch Church, it was and became, under various
      flags and circumstances, an official school, a char-
      ity school, a city school, and in 1887 began to func-
      tion as a private secondary school. This history is
      based upon translated records of the Reformed Prot-
      estant Dutch Church, a previous history and histories
      of Dutch education in colonial New York. Includes
      lists of Masters, dates, and location of the school
      when they served.

549. Pratt, C. I learn from children; an adventure in pro-
      gressive education. New York: Simon and Schuster,
      1948. 204 p.
         A history and the philosophy of the City and Coun-
      try School by its founder.

550. Horace Mann School, New York. The country day
      school; history, curriculum, philosophy of Horace
      Mann School. Edited by R. A. McCardell. Dobbs
      Ferry, New York: Oceana Publications, 1962. 111 p.
         Prefaced by a history/explanation of the country
      day school concept, this is a seventy-five-year chron-
      icle of the Horace Mann School with special sections
      devoted to its curriculum and philosophy.

Universities and Colleges
(alphabetical by institution)

551. New York (City). City College. Problems and pros-
      pects of an urban public university; a report by
      Robert E. Marshak, president of the City College of
      the City University of New York, biennium. 1970-
      1972. New York, 1973. 173 p.
         The City College developed out of the Free Academy
      --first free municipal institution of higher education
      in the U.S. This is a review of the issues, devel-
      opments, practices, and aspirations of a new admin-
      istration (1970-72) during a period of great change
      and difficulties--SEEK, open admissions, sense of
      community, institutional relationships, new programs,
      etc.

552. Rudy, Solomon W. The College of the City of New
      York, a history, 1847-1947. New York: City Col-
      lege, 1949. 492 p. Reprint edition 1977 by Arno
      Press, Inc. Bibliography: p. 465-477.
         A centennial history of the first free public insti-
      tution of higher education maintained by a municipal-
      ity, delineating the personalities and philosophical
      conflicts and differences that shaped the growth of
      this institution.

553. Heller, Louis G. The death of the American univer-
      sity, with special reference to the collapse of the
      City College of New York. New Rochelle, New York:
      Arlington House, 1973. 213 p.

Description and interpretation of the attack on the
educational system, utilizing the events that occurred
in 1969 at City College to illustrate that process and
its consequences. The appendices present source
documents--memoranda, flyers, posters, etc.--
representative of the period of violence and disrup-
tion.

554.   Meier, Elizabeth G. A history of the New York School
       of Social Work. New York: Columbia University,
       c. 1954. 154 p.
       This institution's development is traced from its
       predecessor's activities in 1898 (Charity Organization
       Society, New York School of Philanthropy) to the
       granting of the first degree of Doctor of Social Wel-
       fare conferred by Columbia University in 1952. Ap-
       pendices list faculty, trustees, and deans.

555.   Hug, Elsie A. Seventy-five years in education; the
       role of the School of Education, New York University,
       1890-1965. New York: New York University, 1965.
       276 p.
       A review of the founding and development of the
       first school, established in a major university for
       the preparation of educational administrators, spe-
       cialists, and teachers.

556.   Jones, Theodore F. New York University, 1832-1932.
       New York City, London: New York University, H.
       Milford, Oxford University, 1933. 459 p. Bibliog-
       raphy: p. 431-437. Index: p. 441-459.
       Limited to the educational process, the students'
       social and athletic activities are excluded. A chron-
       ological format by administration. There are sep-
       arate histories for the University College, the Med-
       ical College, College of Engineering, School of Edu-
       cation, School of Commerce and Retailing, and the
       Washington Square College. Appendices include
       material on the Laboratory Clock, history of Uni-
       versity Heights, letters and addresses, and accounts
       of non-academic tenants of the building on Washing-
       ton Square--artists, writers, and Samuel F. B.
       Morse.

556a. Davis, James L. Foreign students look at International
       House, New York. New York: International House,
       1965. 95 p. Tables.

International House, founded in 1924, is the first
and largest residence and program center for both
foreign and American graduate students. The objectives of International House include: fostering the
concept of brotherhood, providing educational assistance, and developing an understanding of the United
States. This study and evaluation is based upon a
questionnaire (included in the appendix) sent to foreign
residents of a ten-year period. Also included is a
brief history of the institution, its officers and organization, and an evaluation of the success of its
objectives.

SEE ALSO 219-231.

FINE ARTS

Artists
(general to specific)

557. McDarrah, Fred W. The artist's world in pictures.
      Introd. by Thomas B. Bess, commentary by Gloria
      Schoffel McDarrah. New York: Dutton, 1961. 191 p.
      Illus. (A Dutton paperback original, D84).
          The artist and his world in New York: all aspects,
      working, the critics, the galleries, parties, family
      life, companions, etc.

558. Filsinger, C. Locus: a cross-referenced directory
      of New York galleries and art sources with their
      current stables of artists and art, the place to find
      everybody's work. New York: Filsinger, 1975.
      192 p.
          Part 1: Artists listed alphabetically if their "gal-
      lery" was selected. Part 2: Galleries were selected
      because of their reputation, activity, or importance.
      Gallery entry also lists which artist they represent.

559. Post, N. and R. Harcourt. On permanent view; a
      cross-referenced guide to the New York galleries ex-
      hibiting contemporary artists. New York: P. Glen,
      1971. 95 p. Illus.
          Lists over 1,000 artists with reference to the
      galleries (103) where their works can be seen. Lists
      only galleries open to the public, having reasonable
      viewing hours, etc. Maps indicate gallery locations.

Lists of special galleries (tapestry, portrait, rental,
etc.) and lists of special services--appraisers, art
transportation, framing, restorers, etc.

560.   Solomon, Alan R.   Painting in New York: 1944 to
       1969.   Exhibition dates: November 24, 1969 to Jan-
       uary 11, 1970, Pasadena Art Museum.   Pasadena,
       1969.   76 p.   Illus.   Bibliography: p. 72-75.
       Seventeen artists represented including A. Gorky,
       Jackson Pollock, C. Still, and Andy Warhol.

561.   Los Angeles Co. Calif. Museum of Art, Los Angeles.
       New York School, the first generation; paintings of
       the 1940's and 1950's.   Foreword by Maurice Tuch-
       man.   Los Angeles, 1965.   253 p.   Bibliography: p.
       209-252.
       Includes individual statements by the artists (fif-
       teen) and a group statement followed by comments of
       critics.   Each of the fifteen artists is represented
       by an average of eight paintings.   The bibliography
       includes references written by the artist, material
       about him, and a listing of catalogues and reviews of
       his work.

562.   Association of American Painters and Sculptors, New
       York.   The Armory Show; international exhibition of
       modern art, 1913.   New York: Arno, 1972.   3 vol-
       umes.   (Arno Series of Contemporary Art).
       Vol. 1:   Reproduced catalogues of the show at New
       York, Chicago, and Boston.   Vol. 2:   Contains the
       pamphlets written for the show by Faure, Paul
       Gaugin, Walter Pack, and Frederick James Gregg.
       Vol. 3:   Reprints some twenty-one articles written
       for, against, and about the show from 1913 to 1958.
       Includes Walter Kuhn's pamphlet, The Story of the
       Armory Show.

SEE ALSO 604.

New York School

563.   Ashton, D.   The life and times of the New York School.
       Bath, New York: Adams and Dart, 1972.   246 p.
       Illus.   "References":   p. 235-240.
       Examines the idea and the myth of the New York
       School by placing it in historical and cultural context,

emphasizing, not particular artists, but their collective history. Many intimate details and insights about painters are included in the philosophical/intellectual structure of this study.

564.   Rosenberg, B. and N. Fliegel. The vanguard artist, portrait and self-portrait. Chicago: Quadrangle Books, 1965. 366 p.
   An attempt to study the psychological and social situation of the artist--in this instance, twenty-nine artists of the New York School or at least "established," financially prospering, known to those familiar with contemporary art, and residing in Manhattan.

565.   Friedman, Bernard H. School of New York: some younger artists. New York: Grove Press, 1959. 83 p. Illus., col. plates. (An Evergreen Gallery Book, no. 12).
   Some eleven artists, each represented by three reproductions (one in color), with several pages of text--critical and biographical.

Sculpture

566.   Fried, F. New York civic sculpture: a pictorial guide, photos by Edmund V. Gillon, Jr. New York: Dover, 1976. 180 p. Illus. Bibliography: p. 175-176.
   Black and white photographs; the annotations include the physical details (height, material, pedestal, etc), name of sculptor/architect, interpretation of the sculpture, circumstances of the presentation to the city. If it is a statue, the biographical data concerning the subject is included.

567.   Jacoby, Stephen M. Architectural sculpture in New York City with an introd. by Clay Lancaster. New York: Dover, 1975. 150 p. Chiefly illus.
   Photographs, 159, of architectural decoration, figures, friezes, doors, windows, iron railings, etc. from the last 100 years. The introduction provides the interpretation and analysis--styles, trends, etc. Each plate's caption includes: present and former names of the building, address, name of the architect or architectural firm, date of building, name of sculptor.

568.   Lederer, J. All around the town: a walking guide to
        outdoor sculpture in New York City. Photos by
        Arley Bondarin. New York: Scribner, 1975. 243 p.
        Photographs of outdoor statuary viewable without
        charge, arranged by geographic areas--Battery Park,
        West Side, Central Park--with a numerical key to
        section maps of the city. Text includes the biograph-
        ical/historical background of the individual/idea event
        represented by the sculpture and the sculptor's bio-
        graphical data.

                    HISTORIC SITES, HOUSES
                       (general to specific)

569.   Goldstone, Harmon H. and M. Dalrymple. History
        preserved; a guide to New York City landmarks and
        historic districts. New York: Simon and Schuster,
        1974. 576 p. Bibliography: p. 530-532.
        Based upon, but going beyond, the Landmark and
        Historic District designation reports of the Landmark
        Preservation Commission of the City of New York,
        the guide is divided geographically and then subdi-
        vided by types of structures. Historic districts,
        when they occur, are described at the end of chap-
        ters. Chronological charts, 1650-1930, for the land-
        marks not only provide dates but also indicate trends
        in types and styles.

570.   Burnham, A., ed. New York landmarks; a study & in-
        dex of architecturally notable structures in greater
        New York. Middletown, Conn.: Published under the
        auspices of the Municipal Arts Society of New York
        by the Wesleyan University Press, 1963. 430 p.
        Illus. Bibliography: p. 391-412.
        Provides the name of the building or its owner,
        address, name of architect, important date of the
        structures, style, and outstanding features of the
        building (ironwork, stained glass, mosaics, etc.).
        1930 is the terminal year for inclusion. Discussions
        and definitions of architectural styles precede the
        numerous plates. The "Index of Architecturally No-
        table Structures ..." is arranged according to: 1)
        structures of national importance, local or regional
        value; 2) those designated for preservation; and 3)
        those of "note."

571. Lockwood, C. Manhattan moves uptown: an illustrated
      history. Boston: Houghton Mifflin, 1976. 343 p.
      Illus.
         March of the City northward up the island--the
      neighborhoods, the elegant streets, row houses, ten-
      ements, hotels, stores, architectural firsts, slaughter
      houses, shanty towns, and parks--from 1783 to the
      twentieth century. Illustrations include photographs,
      engravings, and drawings. This chronicle does not
      ignore the City's problems--historic and contempo-
      rary--lack of water, disease, slum housing, etc.
      and points out the problems that have resulted because
      the residents, while proud of their city, have loved
      it as few other cities are loved by their citizens.

572. Silver, N. Lost New York. Boston: Houghton Mifflin,
      1967. 242 p.
         Not limited to buildings, this book of photographs
      also notes and records the other "lost" aspects of
      the City by categories: Public Places; Private Gath-
      ering Places; Civic Architecture; Great Houses; the
      New York Row House, Churches; Movement (Train
      shed, Hudson Ferries, etc.), Commerce; Public
      Amusements. Final section: "Landmarks in Danger"
      (Ellis Island, Metropolitan Opera, etc.).

573. New York (City). Dept. of Public Works. The re-
      nascence of City Hall; commemorative presentation,
      rededication of City Hall, the City of New York, July
      12, 1956. Published with the cooperation of the co-
      sponsor Downtown Manhattan Association, inc. ...
      New York, 1956. 94 p.
         Many interior views of the building plus close-ups
      of architectural details. Thirteen essays devoted to
      various aspects of City Hall--its history, construction,
      restoration, its place in New York City history, its
      role in national events, relationship to the Civic Cen-
      ter, the development of downtown Manhattan, the City
      Hall park and its function as a museum. Also has
      list of mayors from 1665 to 1954.

574. Rosebrock, Ellen F. Counting-house days in South
      Street: New York's early brick seaport buildings.
      New York: South Street Seaport Museum, 1975. 48
      p. Illus., maps, plans, drawings. Bibliography:
      p. 43-44.

History of 19th-century New York harbor commercial setting, details and explanation of materials
and construction of the new "Fire Proof Store" along
the harbor (brick, granite, and iron) with brief look
at the disparity between the life styles of counting
house clerks and their masters--the "calico aristocracy" and other great merchants of the city.

575.   Sloane, E. and E. Anthony. Mr. Daniels and the
       Grange. New York: Funk & Wagnalls, 1968. 119
       p. Illus.
       "The Grange," the house Alexander Hamilton built
in upper Manhattan for his family a few years before
his death. Declared a national monument in 1962,
this fine and historic house had been allowed to de-
teriorate. Interior views, plans, line drawings, and
photographs contribute to recreating what was once
an elegant structure. Extensive research by the
author has resulted in many vignettes about the house
and its history. The Mr. Daniels of the title is the
caretaker of the property--a most knowledgeable
gentleman about "the General" and his home.

SEE ALSO 141-146, 519, 520, 664, 896.

                            HISTORY
                    (general to specific;
                       chronological)

576.   Still, B. New York City, a students' guide to localized
       history. New York: Teachers College Press, Colum-
       bia University. 1965. 52 p. (Localized history
       series).
       Four sections: 1) The Dutch Background; 2) The
Provincial City; 3) The Advancing City: 1783-1860;
4) The Metropolitan Era. Each one has a brief historical introduction followed by a bibliography which
is arranged topically and is annotated. Part of each
section is a series of "field trips" or relevant walking tours of the city. The final segment describes
historic sites, landmarks, buildings, battlefields, or
neighborhoods that have associations with the time
period.

577.   Tooker, William W. The origin of the name Man-
       hattan, with historical and ethnological notes ... with

map. New York: F. P. Harper, 1901. 75 p. (The
Algonquin series).

Part of an effort to uncover the significance of
Algonquin names for the purposes of understanding
local history, myths and gaining some insight into
the Indian mind. This particular volume is an extensive review tracing the history of the name "Manhattan." Lacks bibliography but the many footnotes
are more than adequate.

578. Bolton, Reginald P. Indian life of long ago in the city
of New York with illustrations. New York: J. Graham, 1934. 167 p. Front., illus. (incl. maps).
Bibliography: p. 165-167.

A description of Indian life prior to European
settlement. Particularly interesting is the chapter
on Indian settlements in the New York City area with
individual sites described and located on a map of
the appropriate borough. If the diggings have been
recorded and material about the site published, the
annotations include bibliographical references.

579. Bailey, Rosalie F. Guide to genealogical and biographical sources for New York City (Manhattan) 1783-
1898. With an introd. by John Ross Delafield. New
York, 1954. 96 p.

An annotated guide to all types of records and
primary sources (death records, birth, marriage,
maps, street records, court and church documents,
archives, etc.) for the period 1783-1855 with a supplement for the period 1855 to 1898. Includes bibliographies of secondary sources.

580. Furer, Howard B. New York: a chronological & documentary history, 1524-1970. Dobbs Ferry, New
York: Oceana, 1974. 153 p. (American cities
chronology series). Bibliography: p. 135-149.

An effort to summarize the history of New York
City in chronological form (pp. 1-55) with an addition
of primary documents and contemporary writings
(pp. 57-133).

581. Still, B. Mirror for Gotham: New York as seen by
contemporaries from Dutch days to the present. New
York: University Press, 1956. 417 p. Bibliography:
373-399.

Excerpts from some sixty-nine contemporary descriptions (articles, letters, diaries, or books) by

actual observers who represent a very wide range
of literary skill, nationality, and occupations provide
the basis of this compilation. Time span: 1626 to
post-war Manhattan. Each one is provided with in-
terpretive narrative supplemented by excellent illustrations and reproductions.

582. Longstreet, S. City on two rivers: profiles of New
      York--yesterday and today ... illustrated with the
      author's drawings and with old photos. New York:
      Hawthorn Books, 1975. 305 p. Bibliography: p.
      291-293; index: p. 295-305.
         Utilizing commission reports, court records, let-
      ters, newspapers, and periodicals, this is an account
      of the people who are the myriad cities that are gen-
      erally known as one--New York City. Spans the
      period 1524 to 1974, using the biographical approach.

Colonial Period
(chronological)

583. New York (City). Minutes of the executive boards of
      the Burgomasters of New Amsterdam. Berthold
      Fernow, editor. New York: Arno Press, 1970.
      197 p. (The rise of urban America).
         A chronological record (1661-1664) of the daily
      concerns of the administration of New Amsterdam--
      fortifications to be constructed, discipline of the
      night watch, petition of widows, standardization of
      weights and measures, etc.

584. Richmond, John F. New York and its institutions,
      1609-1873. The Bright side of New York. A library
      of information, pertaining to the great metropolis,
      past and present, with historic sketches of its
      churches, school, public buildings, parks and cem-
      eteries, of its police, fire, health, and quarantine
      departments, of its prisons, hospitals, homes, asy-
      lums, dispensaries, and morgue and all municipal
      and private charitable institutions. New York: E.B.
      Treat, 1872. 608 p. Front., illus., plates.
         Purpose of this book was to present a history of
      New York, the development of the city, and the ori-
      gins and objectives of some of its 200 institutions.

585. Singleton, E. Social New York under the Georges,
      1714-1776: houses, streets and country homes, with

chapters on fashions, furniture, china, plate and
manners. New York: B. Blom, 1968. 407 p.
Illus. First published in 1902.
Based upon journals, diaries, newspapers, merchants' advertisements, will, and other primary
sources; detailed emphasis is upon the social conditions and life styles of New York City's colonial
prosperous class.

586. Peterson, Arthur E. New York as an eighteenth-
century municipality prior to 1731. New York, 1917.
211 p. Columbia University Ph. D. thesis, 1917.
(Studies in history, economics and public law, ed.
by the Faculty of political science of Columbia University, Vol. 75, no. 1; whole number 177).
Carefully written, detailed and systematic coverage
of the various activities and functions necessary to
the City. Chapters devoted to government, regulation
of trade and industry, regulation of land and streets,
the dock, the ferries, the watch, fire, charities,
and corrections.

587/91. Edwards, George W. New York as an eighteenth-
century municipality, 1731-1776. New York: AMS,
1968. 205 p. (Studies in history, economics and
public law, v. 75, no. 2, whole no. 178). Reprint
of 1917 edition.
The Montgomerie Charter, secured in 1731, remained in force for over a century and at the same
time the Corporation of New York instituted policies
that were to influence the development of American
municipalities--levying of direct taxes, securing
fire engines, etc. This history reviews the powers
and duties of office holders, the political scene,
aspects of trade and industry (freemen, markets,
regulation of trade), charities and corrections, the
police, street illumination, fire protection, regulation
and administration of docks, streets, bridges, road-
ways, public lands, ferries, and the financial mech-
anisms (lotteries, direct taxes, bonds) of the city.

Revolutionary Period

592. Gerlach, Larry R. The American Revolution: New
York as a case study. Belmont, Calif: Wadsworth
Pub., 1972. 188 p. (The American history research
series). Bibliography: p. 183-188.

A selection of documents with an emphasis on
those that reflect an opposition to independence and
the federal constitution. Minimum chronology and
background information is provided. The Revolution
in New York was as complex and confusing an
event as a result of local circumstances, a major
urban port connected with an agrarian hinterland,
landed estates, unstable frontier, largest slave
population north of Maryland, and a political system dominated by two powerful families, etc.
This particular volume serves the series objectives
very well: to express the thinking process of particular groups, to examine the part as a way of
understanding the whole, and to allow the students
to act the historian with unabridged texts of documents that express contending ideas.

593. Dawson, Henry B. The Sons of Liberty in New York;
      a paper read before the New York Historical Society,
      May 3rd, 1859. New York: Arno, 1969. 118 p.
      (Mass Violence in America).
          Explores the fundamental differences, historical
      and accidental, that made New York unique as an
      English colony; factors resulted in that state's being
      particularly suited to lead the struggle against the
      Crown.

594. Schaukirk, Ewald G. Occupation of New York City by
      the British. New York: New York Times, 1969.
      28 p. (Eyewitness accounts of the American Revo-
      lution). Reprinted from the Pennsylvania Magazine
      of History and Biography, January, 1887.
          Excerpts from a diary, kept by the pastor of the
      New York Moravian congregation, for the period
      1775 to 1783. The manuscript for 1778 is missing
      so that year is excepted.

595. Scott, K. Rivington's New York newspaper; excerpts
      from a loyalist press, 1773-1783. New York: New
      York Historical Society, 1973. 470 p. Ports. (The
      John Watts DePeyster publications fund series, 84).
          Chronologically arranged, these excerpts, about
      people and events in New York City, were selected
      as having a particular value and interest related to
      the metropolitan life of the period. As a New York
      City directory did not exist for those years, this is
      a very useful substitute.

SEE ALSO 216.

1775 - 1865

596.   Ernst, R.   Immigrant life in New York City, 1825-
       1863.   Port Washington, New York: I.J. Friedman,
       1965, c. 1940.   331 p.   Illus.   (Empire State his-
       torical publications, 37).   Bibliography: p. 297-319.
       Extensive history with detailed data about immi-
       grant life; aspects of daily life, work, schools,
       church, culture, newspapers, politics, and the
       Americanization process.   Appendices--statistical
       tables on crime, health, population, occupations,
       land owners, etc.

597.   Svejda, George J.   Castle garden as an immigrant
       depot, 1855-1890.   Washington: Division of History,
       Office of Archeology and Historic Preservation, 1968.
       167 p.   Bibliography: p. 160-167.
       History of the first permanent landing depot for
       immigrants; established August 3, 1855, by the New
       York State Commission on Immigration, in an at-
       tempt to provide the new arrivals with an honest and
       decent reception.   In a situation too often character-
       ized by crime and theft this was an effort to help
       the immigrant purchase tickets, change his money,
       and find friends and relatives without being cheated
       or robbed.

598.   Albion, Robert G. and Jennie B. Pope.   The rise of
       New York port 1815-1860.   New York, London: C.
       Scribner's sons, 1939.   405 p.   Illus.   Bibliography:
       p. 423-470.
       Objectives of this history are to explain the oper-
       ation of the waterfront and business section, illumi-
       nate New York port's contribution to and place in
       American maritime life and examine the factors of
       its successful competition with other American ports.
       The arrangement is topical; thirty-six appendices
       contain extensive statistical data--tonnage, exports,
       imports, shipbuilding, port expenses of particular
       ships, nativity of residents of leading seaports, etc.
       Other valuable studies are:

       Pomerantz, Sidney I.   New York, an American city,
       1783-1803; a study of urban life.   2nd ed.   Port

Washington, New York: I. J. Friedman, 1965. 531
p. (Empire State Historical Publications, 17). First
edition, 1938. Bibliography: p. 505-519. A study
of the economic revival, expanded municipal services
(fire, streets, police, welfare, etc.), cultural progress (press, books, religion, education), city finance, politics, and the amenities of city life (theatre, music, societies, clubs, and the arts), and that
combination of factors that placed New York City
first in population, the foremost commercial center,
and the ranking center of cultural life in America.

Haswell, Charles H. Reminiscences of New York by
   an octogenarian (1816 to 1860). New York: Harper
   & brothers, c. 1896. 581 p. A chronological narrative of personal knowledge and memory, arranged
   by mayoral term of office, but the range of subjects
   includes: architecture, shipping, street changes,
   Roman Catholics, railroads, business, newspapers,
   entertainments, the police, etc. A treasure trove
   of detail.

Horlick, Allan S. Country boys and merchant princes;
   the social control of young men in New York. Lewis-
   burg, Pa.: Bucknell University, 1975. 278 p. Bibliography: p. 267-273. A study of the New York
   City business community in the 1860's and 1880's
   when it was the most powerful and wealthiest in the
   county; its merchants shifting capital into banking,
   insurance, railroads, and real estate, thus requiring
   greater numbers of employees just when many rural
   young men were seeking work in the cities. Custom
   and convention, for the smaller numbers, had
   replaced the apprentice system and had been adequate
   for the inculcations of traditions and social mores,
   thus protecting the profits and value system of the
   commercial community, but the influx of large numbers of young men were viewed as a potential danger
   to the status and prestige of business. This is an
   analysis of the mercantile class response to these
   social changes as reflected in the writings of the
   period (diaries, novels, newspapers) and its new
   institutions.

Grund, Francis J. Aristocracy in America, from the
   sketch-book of a German nobleman. With an introd.
   by George E. Probst. New York: Harper, 1959.

302 p. The author, European by birth, American
by choice, is a shrewd, astute observer of the social scene. Using his journalistic skills he highlights the increasing difficulties of the "aristocracy"
in Jacksonian America. About one half of this book
is concerned with the "bloods" of New York City.

Civil War

599. Freeman, Andrew A. Abraham Lincoln goes to New
York. New York: Coward-McCann, 1960. 160 p.
"Sources and Notes": p. 145-153.
A recreation of Lincoln's visit to New York City,
based upon contemporary accounts. During that time
Lincoln made his famous Cooper Union address--the
most important speech of his career, according to
some historians.

600. McCague, J. The second rebellion; the story of the
New York City draft riots of 1863. New York: Dial,
1968. 210 p. Bibliography: p. 203-205.
Interested by the parallel events and conditions
of our time with those of 100 years ago, the author
has written, in chronological format, a detailed account of the violence of 1863.

601. Foner, Philip S. Business & slavery; the New York
merchants & the irrepressible conflict. Chapel Hill:
University of North Carolina, 1941. 356 p. Bibliography: p. 323-336.
A detailed history of New York business men's
political activities and their objectives: maintaining
their economic ties with the South, preserving peace,
and finally preserving the Union.

LIBRARIES
(general to specific)

602. Columbia University. School of Library Service. Libraries in New York City. New York, 1971. 214
p. Bibliography: p. 171-174.
A description of some ninety libraries; followed
by "Notes on Subject Areas," which is arranged topically (art, children and young people, economics,
etc.) with references to 400 additional libraries. The

section on bookstores, arranged by geographic location, has brief descriptive notes.

603.   Dain, P. The New York Public Library; a history of
       its founding and early years. New York: New York
       Public Library, 1972. 466 p. Bibliography: p.
       423-449.
           Covers the period from the early 1890's to 1913,
       with a focus on library policies, practices, and tra-
       ditions examined within and related to the political
       systems, social values, library philosophy, education-
       al objectives, technology, and the intellectual trends
       of that time.
           Related publications:

       New York (City). Public Library. Beyond the lions;
       a guide to the libraries of the New York Public Li-
       brary. New York, 1973. 95 p. Map. An alpha-
       betic listing of entries describing book collection,
       installations, programs, and services--administrative
       office to young adult services. A subject index with
       references both to sections of this guide and to spe-
       cific libraries is very useful and is supplemented by
       a directory of the libraries of the New York Public
       Library system.

       New York. Public Library. The Library & Museum
       of the Performing Arts at Lincoln Center. Text by
       Rosine Raoul. New York, 1965. 52 p. Brief de-
       scription of the architecture, administration, and
       organization of the Library, supplemented by com-
       mentary on its research collections of music theatre
       and music.

SEE ALSO 89, 90.

                          LITERATURE
                 (chronological, then by format:
           stories, poems, and personal observations)

604.   Callow, James T. Kindred spirits; Knickerbocker writ-
       ers and American artists, 1807-1855. Chapel Hill:
       University of North Carolina, 1967. 287 p. Bib-
       liography: p. 253-273.
           Focusing on the lives of several dozen writers
       between 1807-1855, the author relates them to

contemporary artists and their areas to interaction--
clubs, academies, etc. He presents details of their
friendships, points out how the writers educated the
public about native landscape painting and how the
literary magazines provided publicity for the artists
underscoring the theme of writer/artist reciprocity
and affinities. Final chapter is concerned with the
place of art, landscape gardening, and city planning
in Knickerbocker literature. The Appendix lists the
authors and the names of their acquaintances and
friends with the documentation of those relationships.

605. Hemstreet, C. Literary New York; its landmarks and
      associations. With sixty-five illustrations. New
      York: G. P. Putnam's sons, 1903. 271 p.
          "Literary" includes poets, novelists, editors, re-
      porters, and magazine writers. Covers the period
      from the 1500's to the end of the 19th century. Bio-
      graphical material, references to published works
      are all skillfully included with social history, archi-
      tectural comments, and details about New York City
      life. Particularly interesting for the intellectual
      affinities noted.

606. Edmiston, S. and Linda D. Cirino. Literary New
      York: a history and guide/ maps by John V. Morris.
      Boston: Houghton Mifflin, 1976. 409 p.
          Tried to include those writers who were "estab-
      lished" by the 1950's. Attempts to retrace the ac-
      tivities of major authors, recreate their social and
      literary environment, and indicates landmarks--homes,
      gathering places, settings of their works, etc. The
      arrangement is by geographic area (Midtown, Bronx,
      Queens, etc.). Literary, social, and biographical
      material presented about the writer who lived/worked
      there. Each area has one or more tours where spe-
      cific landmarks/points of interest are located on a
      good map.

607. Maurice, Arthur B. New York in fiction. With a new
      introd. by Donnal V. Smith. Port Washington, New
      York: I. J. Friedman, 1969. 231 p. Illus. (Em-
      pire State historical publications series, no. 61).
          Concerned with writers (many of them acquaint-
      ances or personal friends of the author) and their
      associations with various aspects of New York City
      or their use of the City's locals in their writings.

Arranged, essentially, by geographic location--square,
neighborhoods, and suburbs. This literary history
also provides considerable evidence of the social life
of the times.

608.   Maurice, Arthur B.   The New York of the novelists.
       New York: Dodd, Mead, 1916.   366 p.
       Identifies those streets, buildings, businesses,
       landmarks, etc. that have either been incorporated
       by an author into his work or were important in his
       own life.   Scope: from Irving and Cooper to Porter,
       Rupert Hughes, and Edith Wharton.

609.   Gordon, J. and L. Rust Hills.   New York, New York;
       the city as seen by masters of art and literature.
       New York: Shorecrest, 1965.   408 p.
       A collection of short stories and poems encom-
       passing American literature from Washington Irving
       to James Baldwin, selected for their excellence,
       reflecting the discrepancy of the dream represented
       by New York City--freedom, opportunity, success,
       and the reality of indifference, loneliness, change,
       pointless activity.   Complemented by quality selec-
       tions from the work of such artists, ranging in time
       from the colonial period up to R. Marsh, Feininger,
       Jack Levine, Jacob Lawrence.   All schools of art
       are represented depicting the various moods and
       personalities of the city.

610.   McCullough, Esther M.   As I pass, O Manhattan; an
       anthology of life in New York.   North Bennington,
       Vt.: Coley Taylor, 1956.   1236 p.   Illus.
       Chronological (from discovery to the 20th century)
       within each of its three sections: short stories, po-
       etry, and historic events.   The latter section depends
       extensively upon newspapers, diaries, and magazine
       articles.

611.   Mitchell, J.   The bottom of the harbor.   Boston: Lit-
       tle, Brown, 1959.   243 p.
       These stories, about people connected with the
       waterfront of New York City, first appeared in the
       New Yorker.

612.   Miller, H.   Aller retour New York.   Printed for pri-
       vate circulation only, 1945.   88 p.
       An account of a voyage to and from New York

City, providing various views and opinions of New
York City life and its inhabitants, some of them not
particularly flattering.

613. Gor Kii, Maksim. The city of the yellow devil; pam-
      phlets, articles, and letters about America (by)
      Maxim Gorky. Moscow: Progress Publishers, 1972.
      138 p.
         A famous Russian writer's views on "capitalist
      and bourgeois" New York City and its "enslaved" cit-
      izens. While the articles and essays are polemic,
      his fourteen letters to friends are more revealing of
      the political and social climate of that city at the
      turn of the century.

614. Whitman, W. Walt Whitman's New York; from Man-
      hattan to Montauk. Edited by Henry M. Christman.
      Freeport, New York: Macmillan, 1963. 188 p.
         A collection of unsigned articles written by Whit-
      man for the newspaper, the Brooklyn Standard. Es-
      sentially regional history (Manhattan, Brooklyn, and
      Long Island) in content, Whitman wrote both of the
      contemporary scene and historical events--British
      prison ships, Indian money, old churches, etc., all
      presenting a portrait of the area in the early nine-
      teenth century.

SEE ALSO 323, 581, 694.

Poetry

615. Conrad, E. Battle New York; mural of the metropolis.
      San Francisco: West-Lewis Pub., 1969. 111 p.
         Free verse focused upon the negative aspects of
      the City--its dehumanization depicted with anger, rid-
      icule, and fury that betrays the poet's anguished loss.

616. García Lorca, Federico. Poet in New York. Com-
      plete Spanish text with a new translation by Ben
      Belitt. Intro. by Angel del Rio. New York: Grove,
      1955. 192 p.
         While he walked many parts of the city and did
      visit the Catskills, García Lorca stayed only a year
      in America--remaining within the circle of his Span-
      ish-speaking friends. This book of poetry has been
      characterized as an indictment of modern civilization

rather than a personal and particular response to
New York City.

617. Kramer, A. The tune of the calliope; poems and draw-
      ings of New York. Drawings by Theodore Fried (and
      others). Introd. by Saul Lishinsky. New York: T.
      Yoseloff, 1958. 107 p. Illus.
      The work of one poet paired with the drawings
      and paintings of fourteen artists combining to present
      a multidimensional view of the City.

618. Lewis, R. The Park. Photos by Helen Buttfield. New
      York: Simon & Schuster, 1968. 1 v.
      A poet's concept of Central Park; word images,
      supplemented, line by line, with photographs.

619. Benton, P. Manhattan mosaic; New York in poems and
      pictures. New York: F. Fell, 1964.
      The photographs, in black and white, present some
      unusual views of the city.

620. MacLeish, A. and O. Tamburi. New York. Milano:
      All'insegna del pesce d'oro, 1958. 55 p. ("All'in-
      segna del pesce d'oro." Serie illustrata n. 61).
      Bilingual presentation of "The Trees"; ... &
      Forty-Second Street; Geography of this Time; Music
      and Drum, with twenty-five drawings of New York
      scenes by Orfeo Tamburi.

621. Holden, Arthur C. Sonnets for my city; an essay on
      the kinship of art & finance as factors in the devel-
      opment of the city and the moulding of man's envi-
      ronment. New York: Schulte Pub., 1965. 231 p.
      Bibliography: p. 223-227.
      Use of sonnets to describe the city, its changes,
      problems, people, and potential. An architect and
      city planner, the author utilizes the poetic form to
      make his arguments about economics, government,
      institutions, city dwellers, and other aspects of
      metropolitan life. Prose essays restate the ideas
      expressed in the sonnet form. The bibliography is
      a list of the author's publications about housing, fi-
      nance, and city planning.

622. Voices of Brooklyn, an anthology. Edited by Sol
      Yurick. Sponsored by Brooklyn Public Library. Chi-
      cago: American Library Association, 1973. 278 p.

The Brooklyn Public Library created a project that had as one of its objectives the introduction of the various racial and ethnic groups of the borough to the diverse humanistic tradition that exists in Brooklyn. The program consisted of two parts: a public presentation--two series of five presentations; music, readings, dance, theatre, etc. The anthology phase was the second part of project--poems, short stories, essays, all written by Brooklyn residents that had not been published before. Much written is about Brooklyn with a great deal also about the world beyond.

SEE ALSO 326.

MEDICINE

General Works
(general to specific)

623. Directory of New York City health agencies and their library resources. New York City health agencies, library resources interface. 1976. 98 p.
    Lists, alphabetically, some 500 health care organizations that use or need library services. Entries include legal name of the agency, address, administrator's name, name of librarian, and a code symbol indicating the type of agency. Part two lists these agencies geographically by borough.

624. New York (State). Commission of Investigation concerning New York City's Municipal Hospitals and the Affiliation Program. Recommendations. New York, 1968. 75 ℓ.
    From 1961 to June, 1967 the City of New York, under affiliation contracts, paid to voluntary nonprofit hospitals $225,000,000 to staff and operate the professional services of city hospitals. The Commission's fourteen-month investigation uncovered fiscal abuses, serious deficiencies, and problems resulting in poor patient care. Recommendations of the Commission can be divided into two sections: 1) those to be implemented within the Department of Hospitals; and 2) those concerned with "A New Hospital System, " providing for extensive reorganizational changes and evaluation of methods and procedures.

625. Ginzberg, E.   Urban health services; the care of New
      York ... and the Conservation of Human Resources
      staff of Columbia University.   New York: Columbia
      University, 1971.   250 p.   Bibliography: p. 237-
      240.
         With forty to fifty percent of the city's population
      eligible for Medicaid, the sharp rise in medical
      costs, public dissatisfaction with the quality of mu-
      nicipal health and medical services creates many
      questions of medical economics.   The problems are
      explored by individual writers in separate chapters.

626. La Mar, E.   Health security by union action; a report
      on the Sidney Hillman Health Center of New York.
      New York: New York Joint Board, Amalgamated
      Clothing Workers of America, 1952.   62 p.
         Created by the Joint Board of The Amalgamated
      Clothing Workers of America, the Center opened its
      doors April 16, 1951.   This narrative provides a
      brief explanation of the center, the facilities it offers,
      how it is administered, and how it exemplifies the
      factors of health and health care in trade union social
      policy.

627. Van Ingen, P.   The New York Academy of Medicine;
      its first hundred years.   New York: Columbia Uni-
      versity, 1949.   573 p.   Illus.   (The History of
      Medicine series, no. 8).   Index: p. 545-573.
         The author achieved his goal of being informative.
      Chronological in format, it also uses the biographical
      technique (usually presidents of the Academy) for the
      presentation of materials.

Hospitals
(general to specific, then
alphabetical by institution)

628. Federational of Jewish Philanthropies of New York.
      Planning for better hospital care: report on the hos-
      pitals and health agencies of the Federation of Jewish
      Philanthropies of New York by Eli Ginzberg and Peter
      Rogatz.   New York: King's Crown, 1961.   131 p.
      Map, tables.
         In 1958, a study committee was established to
      evaluate the Federation; a Sub-committee on Hospitals
      and Health Agencies was created to review hospital

operation and to develop guidelines for support of
those institutions by the Federation, in the 1960's.
Such factors as financial trends, demographics, education and research, Federation hospitals' relationships with other Federation agencies and other hospital systems were part of the study.

629.   Levitan, Tina N.   Islands of compassion, a history of
       the Jewish hospitals of New York.   New York:
       Twayne, 1964.   304 p.   Illus., ports.   Bibliography:
       p. 283-293.
       A chronological history (1852-1960's) of thirteen
       voluntary Jewish hospitals of New York City, their
       origins, growth, activities, and contributions to the
       community and the evolution of medicine and medical
       education.

630.   Klarman, Herbert E.   Hospital care in New York City;
       the roles of voluntary and municipal hospitals.   New
       York: Columbia University, 1963.   573 p.   "Notes":
       p. 529-556.
       Summary of hospital care practices during the
       1940's, a review of and discussion of issues of hos-
       pital care in the 1950's and early 1960's and, because
       of the techniques and the analysis of the extensive
       collected data, provides a factual basis for hospital
       care planning; emphasis of this study has been on
       staffing, finances, programs of care, and organiza-
       tion.   One objective was to determine if the changes
       in medical care, finances, medical education, etc.
       had modified the possibilities of continued and effec-
       tive cooperation between voluntary and municipal hos-
       pitals.

631.   Yeshiva University, New York.   Albert Einstein College
       of Medicine.   The first decade: a progress report.
       New York, 1965.   160 p.   Illus.
       Brief, historical, and contemporary description
       of hospital activities, its research and medical edu-
       cation programs as well as its community services.

632.   Starr, J.   Hospital city.   New York: Crown, 1957.
       282 p.
       Another Bellevue Hospital history, readable but
       with extensive quotations and excerpts from letters,
       reports, newspapers, etc.
       Additional histories include:

184   New York City

Cooper, P. The Bellevue story. New York: Crowell,
1948. 277 p. Index: p. 271-277. A popular history of the hospital from its beginnings to the 1950's;
based upon primary sources.

Tjomsland, A. Bellevue in France; anecdotal history
of Base Hospital no. 1 ... New York: Froben,
1941. 251 p. Illus. Beginning with a short history
of Bellevue hospital, from 1736 to 1935, the emphasis is upon the human aspects of the operation of a
military hospital in France during World War I
(1916-1919). Appendices list officers, nurses, and
enlisted men.

633. Gallagher, T. The doctors' story. New York: Harcourt, Brace & World, 1967. 234 p. Bibliography:
p. 223-230. (In commemoration of the two-hundredth
anniversary of the Columbia University College of
Physicians and Surgeons).
Limited to the first hundred years of the history
of the Medical school that would become the College
of Physicians and Surgeons; its growth, internal conflicts, and development are set against the background
of a war-torn filthy New York City, a seaport town
where yellow fever and influenza were not less vio-
lent than the disputes between medical school faculty,
and the faculty and trustees about medical theories.

634. Gibney, R. Gibney of the Ruptured and crippled.
Edited by Alfred R. Shands, Jr. New York: Appleton-Century-Crofts, 1969. 152 p. "Bibliography of
Virgil Pendleton Gibney, 1876 to 1920": p. 145-152.
A biography of a leader and pioneer in orthopedic
surgery; a man that transformed the Home for Crippled Children into a modern hospital destined to
become one of the outstanding hospitals in the nation.

635. Hinshaw, D. Take up thy bed and walk. New York:
G. P. Putnam's Sons, 1948. 262 p. Bibliography:
p. 235-240.
A history of the Institute for the Crippled and
Disabled and its pioneering efforts in rehabilitation.

636. Hirsh, J. and B. Doherty. First hundred years of the
Mount Sinai Hospital of New York, 1852-1952. New
York: Random House, 1952. 364 p.
A carefully detailed account of the growth and
operation of a complex medical institution. The

appendices include: a chronology, lists of officers
and trustees, lists of standing committees, legacies,
bequests, and endowments.

637. Pool, James L. The Neurological Institute of New
York, 1909-1974: with personal anecdotes. Lake-
ville, Conn.: Pocket Knife, 1975. 154 p. Illus.
Bibliography: p. 147-150.
Continues Dr. Elsberg's The story of a hospital
for the period of 1939 to 1973 and chronicles the
development of investigative research and the high
standard of patient care, teaching, and training in
one of the largest hospitals for neurological disor-
ders. Appendices list directors, chiefs of services,
residents, fellows, etc.

638. Conway, H. and Richard B. Stark. Plastic surgery at
the New York Hospital one hundred years ago, with
biographical notes on Gurdon Buck. Forewords by
John Hay Whitney, Stanhope Bayne-Jones and Frank
Glenn. New York: P.B. Hoeber, 1953. 110 p.
Illus. Bibliography: p. 107-110.
Actually a volume devoted to the career of Gurdon
Buck, Jr., a distinguished surgeon who made many
contributions to surgery, the most outstanding of
these in the development of reparative and plastic
surgery, a medical specialty that had been forgotten.
The biography is also a history of the New York
Hospital, medicine in the nineteenth century, the
New York Academy of Medicine and other New York
City medical institutions.

639. Larrabee, E. The benevolent and necessary; the New
York Hospital, 1771-1971. Garden City, New York:
Doubleday, 1971. 346 p. Bibliography: p. 329-339.
The title is not quite accurate; there is little in
the history written for the "common reader" that includes the last twenty years. The emphasis is on
this hospital's eighteenth-century ideals, the near
abandonment of those ideals in the nineteenth century,
and the twentieth-century effort to recapture them.
A related history is:

Pool, Eugene H. and Frank J. McGowan. Surgery at
the New York Hospital one hundred years ago. New
York: P.B. Hoeber, 1930. 188 p. "References":
p. 176-182; index of personal names: p. 183-184;
index of subjects: p. 185-188. A chronicle of a

hospital closely identified with the history and development of surgery; based upon selections from a Surgical Register of the hospital covering the period 1808 to 1833. Each chapter is concerned with a particular disease or surgical need.

640.   Zisowitz, Milton L.   One patient at a time; a medical center at work.   New York: Random House, 1961. 287 p.
        An account, using case histories, of the multiple objectives of the hospital-university medical centers --healing, teaching, and research as demonstrated by the history, and accomplishments of the New York Hospital-Cornell Medical Center.

Medical Education
(general to specific, then alphabetical by institution)

641.   Wershub, Leonard P.   One hundred years of medical progress; a history of the New York Medical College, Flower and Fifth Avenue Hospitals.   Springfield, Ill.: Charles C. Thomas, 1967.   259 p.   Illus., ports. Bibliography: p. 225-232.
        Provides a sound account of the history of these institutions with reference to socio-economic, philosophic, and scientific factors as they influenced medical thought during the period 1860 to 1964.

642.   New York (State).   Downstate Medical Center, New York.   Medical education in Brooklyn, the first hundred years, 1860-1960.   Highlights in the development of medical education in Brooklyn on the occasion of the centennial celebration of the State University of New York Downstate Medical Center and its predecessors, the Long Island College of Medicine and the college division of the Long Island College Hospital (by Evelyn Goodwin, public relations director). Brooklyn, 1960.   61 p.   Illus., ports, map, facsims.
        The Long Island College Hospital establishment of a hospital and medical school as one unit inaugurated the college-hospital system of medical education. This centennial history highlights the development of medical education in New York State, the men who had the vision and set the standards.   List includes presidents, deans, department/division heads from 1860 to 1960.

643.   Nelson, Russell A. The governance of voluntary teach-
        ing hospitals in New York City: a study. New York:
        Josia Macy Jr. Foundation, 1974. 71 p.
        An examination of the role of trusteeship in a vol-
        untary teaching hospital; including a review of the
        organization of each institution (legal and manage-
        ment), nature and organization of trustee boards,
        and the relationships of such institutions to affiliated
        medical schools and other health-related institutions.

644.   Heaton, Claude E. The first one-hundred twenty-five
        years of the New York University School of Medicine
        consisting of a historical sketch of the first one hun-
        dred years by Claude Edwin Heaton and an account
        of the years between 1941 and 1966 by Allan Eliot
        Dumont. New York: New York University, School
        of Medicine, 1966. 41 p. Illus., ports.
        Brief, concise, and specific--dates, names, lists
        of faculty. Has a biographical section about famous
        alumni.

645.   Lamb, Albert R. The Presbyterian Hospital and the
        Columbia-Presbyterian Medical Center, 1868-1943;
        a history of a great medical adventure. New York:
        Columbia University, 1955. 495 p. Illus.
        A chronological presentation, based upon records,
        memoirs, reminiscences, anecdotes delineating the
        advances in medical sciences and education that also
        shaped the traditions and principles that created a
        great hospital. The sections on the hospital units
        participating in the First and Second World Wars
        are particularly interesting. Appendices include:
        lists of officers, trustees, and directors; summary
        of reports; reviews of programs, structure of com-
        mittees, etc.
        A biographical approach is provided by:

        Delavan, David B. Early days of the Presbyterian
        Hospital in the city of New York ... with thirty-nine
        full-page illustrations. East Orange, N.J.: Pub.
        priv., 1926. 191 p. Front., illus. "References":
        p. 190-191. A brief essay as to the origins of the
        hospital, but the burden of the record is placed upon
        the biographical sketches of the men and women
        associated with the institution--James Lenox, Robert
        Lenox, Willard Parker, John Jacob Crane, Anna
        Caroline Maxwell, etc.

646.   Marr, James P. Pioneer surgeons of the Woman's
       Hospital; the lives of Sims, Emmet, Peaslee, and
       Thomas. Philadelphia: F.A. Davis, 1957. 148 p.
       Illus.
           Four essays about James Marion Sims, Thomas
       Addis Emmet, Edmund Randolph Peaslee, and Theo-
       dore Gaillard Thomas that constitute a history of
       modern gynecology as it evolved in the Woman's
       Hospital, the first American institution of its type.
       Lists of surgeons, staff, and residents--1855 to
       1957.

SEE ALSO 251.

Nursing

647.   Lee, E. Neighbors, 1892-1967; a history of the De-
       partment of Nursing, Faculty of Medicine, Columbia
       University, 1937-1967 and its predecessor, the
       School of Nursing of the Presbyterian Hospital, New
       York, 1892-1937. New York: Columbia University-
       Presbyterian Hospital, School of Nursing Alumnae
       Association, 1967. 335 p. Illus., ports.
           The nine appendices include: lists of graduation
       speakers, editors of the Quarterly Magazine, pres-
       idents of the Alumnae Assn. and an explanation of
       the Presbyterian Cap. Also includes the play "With-
       out Regard to Race, Creed or Color" presented at
       the fiftieth anniversary of the Alumnae Association.

SEE ALSO 254-256.

Public Health

648.   New York (City). Commission on the Delivery of Per-
       sonal Health Services. Community health services
       for New York City; report and staff studies. New
       York: Praeger, c. 1969. 675 p. (Praeger special
       studies in the U.S. economic and social development).
       Bibliography: p. 595-632.
           Includes the report of the commission and its
       recommendations. Surveys the hospital system, the
       issues of medical manpower, impact and flow of
       public funds, the role of the Department of Health
       and similar organizations. States the problems,
       identifies the causes and possible solutions.

649. New York Hospital-Cornell Welfare Medical Care Project. Welfare medical care; an experiment (a report by) Charles Goodrich, Margaret C. Olenski (and) George G. Reader, Associate editors, J. R. Buchanan (et al.). Cambridge, Mass.: Harvard University, 1970. 343 p. Charts, tables.
A project of medical care for welfare families for the purposes of comparison between existing systems and the experimental one on the basis of unit costs, quality of care, patient satisfaction, utilization.

SEE ALSO 443.

MUSEUMS

650. McDarrah, Fred W. Museums in New York; a descriptive guide to seventy-nine fine arts museums, specialized museums, natural history and science museums, libraries, botanical and zoological parks, commercial collections and historic houses and mansions open to the public within the five boroughs of New York City. Foreword by Thomas P. F. Hoving. New York: Dutton, 1967. 319 p.
For each institution entry includes: address, schedule, and admission data (may be out of date now), transportation information for bus, subway, or auto. Additional remarks concerning gift shops, restaurants, special features, tours, etc., followed by a descriptive essay, supplemented with extensive photographs about the history, function of the museum, gallery, or historic site.

American Museum of Natural History

651. Saunders, John R. The world of natural history, as revealed in the American Museum of Natural History. New York: Sheridan House, 1952. 321 p. Illus.
Highlights of the first eighty-three years of the American Museum of Natural History plus a narrative of the museum's major exhibitions, its most important expeditions and research projects. The reader is also given "behind the scenes" experiences--how exhibits are created, the sources of Museum information etc.

Metropolitan Museum of Art

652. New York (City). Metropolitan Museum of Art. Guide
      to the Metropolitan Museum of Art. New York, 1972.
      320 p. Illus., diagrams, plans.
          Museum floor plans, departments/gallery floor
      plans, numerical and color keys provide easy access
      to collections and exhibits. Major works are dis-
      cussed in chronological order. Many photographs
      and reproductions.

653. Hess, John L. The grand acquisitors. Boston:
      Houghton Mifflin, 1974. 174 p. Illus.
          An expose of the administration of the Metropol-
      itan Museum of Art during a period of secret sales,
      peculiar arrangements with selected art dealers and
      other scandals that required the question: should
      tax-supported institutions function without public
      supervision? Well written, explores all the relation-
      ships--obvious and otherwise. Very informative
      about an esoteric topic.

654. Howe, Winifred E. A history of the Metropolitan Mu-
      seum of Art, with a chapter on the early institutions
      of art in New York. New York, 1913-1946. 2 v.
      Illus., plates, ports., maps, plans, facsims.
          Vol. 1: Based on the minutes of meetings and
      other documents, the conception and organization of
      the Museum is chronicled from 1869 to 1912. One
      third of this volume is devoted to previous attempts
      to establish similar institutions in New York. Has
      list of Museum officers for the period indicated.
      Index: p. 329-358.
          Vol. 2: Concerned with the events of 1905 to
      1941 and presents them topically: administrators,
      growth of collections, temporary actions, interpre-
      tations of collections, special facilities for students,
      museum extension. Appendices: list benefactors
      (1870-1945), trustees and officers (1879-1945), staff
      (1905-1945), "One hundred important purchases"
      (1905-1945).

655. Lerman, L. The Museum: one hundred years and
      the Metropolitan Museum of Art. Introd. by Thomas
      P. F. Hoving. New York: Viking, 1969. 400 p.
      Illus.
          Chronological in format, the lavish illustrations
      and photographs of paintings, objects of art,

furniture, lace, and the other acquisitions of the
period (1866-1970) dominate the text. Some colored
plates.

656. Tomkins, C. Merchants and masterpieces: the story
of the Metropolitan Museum of Art. New York:
E. P. Dutton, 1970. 383 p. Illus.
Covers the period from its creation to the ap-
pointment of Thomas P. F. Hoving as director.

657. New York (City). Metropolitan Museum of Art. Publications of the Metropolitan Museum of Art, 1870-
1964, a bibliography compiled by Albert TenEyck
Gardner, associate curator of American paintings
and sculpture. New York, 1965. 72 p. Index of
authors: p. 70-72.
Lists all books, catalogues, and pamphlets published by the MMA between 1870-1964. A chronological arrangement within category: catalogues of
special exhibitions, departmental publications, general guides, serials, miscellaneous publications (history, business, and legal documents, ephemera).

658. New York. Metropolitan Museum of Art. Art treasures of the Metropolitan; a selection from the European and Asiatic Collections of the Metropolitan
Museum of Art, presented by the curatorial staff.
New York: H. N. Abrams, 1952. 240 p. (Library
of Great Museums).
Arranged into categories: Ancient art, Medieval
art, Drawings and paintings, Prints, Decorative
arts, Oriental art, has "Notes on the paintings and
objects of art."

The Cloisters

659. New York (City). Metropolitan Museum of Art. The
Cloisters. Medieval monuments at the Cloisters as
they were and as they are. By James Rorimer.
Rev. ed. by Katherine Serrell Rorimer. New York:
Metropolitan Museum of Art, 1972. 81 p. Illus.
"Monuments" are defined as those "elements that
incorporate or support or enclose, as distinct from
elements that can be readily moved." This is an
account of how the buildings, doors, tombs, windows,
etc. were incorporated into the structure known as The
Cloisters which allowed them to "speak for themselves."

Museum of Modern Art

660. Lynes, R. Good old Modern; an intimate portrait of
      the Museum of Modern Art. New York: Atheneum,
      1973. 490 p.
            The author has the advantage of a long personal
      association with the Museum and friendships with
      many of the people connected, in various ways, with
      that institution--thus presenting an insider's view-
      point. Based upon interviews with museum person-
      nel, artists, former/retired employees, collectors,
      friends and enemies of the Museum, this history
      (1929-1972) also utilizes Museum documents and other
      secondary sources. The preface, in part, is a bib-
      liographic essay concerning publications about the
      MMA. The brief chronology includes a list of ex-
      hibitions (1929-1972).

Museum of Primitive Art

661. New York. Museum of Primitive Art. Masterpieces
      in the Museum of Primitive Art: Africa, Oceania,
      North America, Mexico, Central to South America,
      Peru. New York, 1965. 1 v. Maps, plates.
            "Primitive" as used by the Museum simply means
      underdeveloped in government, institutions, and tech-
      nological processes at the time of contact with West-
      ern culture.

Museum of the American Indian

662. New York. Museum of the American Indian, Heye
      Foundation. The History of the museum. New York:
      1956, 27 p. Front. (Its Indian notes and mono-
      graphs. Miscellaneous series no. 55).
            Brief description of the origins of the museum,
      its buildings, collections, relationship with other in-
      stitutions, important acquisitions, and lists of pub-
      lications.

Solomon R. Guggenheim Museum

662a. The Solomon R. Guggenheim Museum. New York.
       The Guggenheim Museum Collection. New York:

The Solomon R. Guggenheim Foundation, 1976.
Vol. --
The intent is to catalog the complete collection,
however, volumes 1 and 2 are limited to paintings
of the period 1880 to 1945, of one of the outstanding
collections of modern art. The catalog, intended for
students and scholars, incorporates for each item all
the relevant factual data available.

South Street Seaport Museum

663. Rosebrock, Ellen F. Walking around in South Street;
     discoveries in New York's old shipping district. New
     York: South Street Seaport Museum, 1974. 62 p.
     Illus., maps.
     Arranged according to eight street maps in the
     South Street area. Each structure on the street is
     described with the building's history, function, and
     biographical information about its owners. Repro-
     ductions, photographs, and architectural details en-
     hance the text. There is also a section describing
     the history of the ships and piers that are part of
     the South Street Seaport Museum.

664. Bixby, W. South Street; New York Seaport Museum.
     New York: D. McKay Co., 1972. 114 p.
     A history of the port of New York, the ships,
     cargoes, merchants, and shopkeepers (along with
     geography) that made New York City the major har-
     bor on the East coast. Chapters devoted to South
     Street in its 19th-century prime, shipbuilding, the
     merchants, immigration tides, and descriptions of
     individual ships owned by the South Street Museum.

SEE ALSO 167-171.

NATURAL HISTORY

Botany

665. Barlow, E. The forests and wetlands of New York
     City. Boston: Little, Brown, 1971. 160 p. Illus.,
     maps. Bibliography: p. 151-153.
     Beginning with the geologic forces that created
     the geophysical New York City area, the narrative

continues, describing the development of forests, wetlands, and vegetation that supported life. Only fragments of that "nature" are left in the area. Using the examples of Inwood Hill, Pelham Bay Park, Staten Island, Jamaica Bay Wildlife Refuge and Welfare Island, the author tells how they survived and why.

666. Schuberth, Christopher J. The geology of New York City and environs. Garden City, New York: Published for the American Museum of Natural History by Natural History Press, 1968. 304 p. Bibliography: p. 279-286.

Describes, for a radius of 100 miles from midtown Manhattan, the present day terrain, reviews the geologic primordial beginning of the northeastern continent and then presents in chronological order the events that shaped and modified the New York City landscape into an "unrivaled variety of geologic features." The eight one-day field trips have the objectives of emphasizing the rock types, general physical environment of Metropolitan New York and to point out structural relationships. Points of interest are noted and carefully explained.

667. Wyckoff, J. Rock scenery of the Hudson Highlands and Palisades; a geological guide. Glens Falls, New York: Adirondack Mountain Club, 1971. 95 p. Illus. Bibliography: p. 91.

A basic introduction to the variety of rock scenery available in and around metropolitan New York--the Palisades, Hudson Highlands, the Ramapos, and the Hudson Gorge. Many photographs of each type or sample of rock formation or geologic process with brief, less than one page, explanations. There are only general references to areas where the examples discussed can be seen.

Zoology

668. Paulmier, Frederick C. Higher crustacea of New York City. Albany: New York State education department, 1905. 189 p. Illus. (New York State museum ... bulletin 91. Zoology 12).

Only the most salient characteristics have been included in these descriptions. Extensive illustrations and line drawings aid in assisting the nonspecialists with the task of identification.

669.   Jacobson, Morris K. and William K. Emerson. Shells
        of the New York City area; a handbook of the land,
        fresh water and marine mollusks ranging from Cape
        Cod to Cape May. With original drawing by Anthony
        D'Attilio. Larchmont, New York: Argonaut Books,
        1961. 142 p. Bibliography: p. 139-140.
            Over 140 species of land, fresh-water, or marine
        shells can be found within a fifty-mile radius of
        Times Square. Arranged by type of mollusk, gen-
        erally one-half to one-page descriptions of the mol-
        lusk, type of environment in which it is found, and
        specific localities are named where they can be col-
        lected. Each description is illustrated. The Bib-
        liography contains sixteen references to journal ar-
        ticles devoted to the mollusks of a specific area in
        or around New York City.

670.   Arbib, Robert S. Enjoying birds around New York
        City: an aid to recognizing, watching, finding, and
        attracting birds in New York City, Long Island, the
        Upstate counties of Westchester, Putnam, Dutchess,
        Rockland, and Orange, and nearby points in New
        Jersey and Connecticut by.... Olin Sewall Petingill,
        Jr. and Sally Hoyt Spofford for the Laboratory of
        Ornithology, Cornell University, Ithaca, New York.
        Illustrated. Boston: Houghton Mifflin, 1966. 171
        p. Maps, illus. "Sources of Information on Birds":
        p. 156-158.
            There are some 400 species of birds located in
        and around New York City. Assuming that the reader
        is a beginner at bird watching, part of this book
        identifies some of the more familiar birds of the
        area, has a geographic section on where to find types
        of birds, a calendar indicating seasons or months
        that certain species can be seen, and final section
        on how to attract birds.

671.   Nichols, John T. Fishes of the vicinity of New York,
        with an introduction by William K. Gregory. New
        York: Printed at the Museum, 1918. 118 p. Illus.,
        col. front. (The American Museum of natural his-
        tory. Handbook series no. 7).
            Prefaced by brief articles on the structure, study,
        and classification of fish, the review of local fishes
        (a paragraph to a page of description with illustra-
        tions) comprise the major part of the text. The
        final section is "A List of the Fishes (247) Known to
        Have Occurred Within Fifty Miles of New York City. "

SEE ALSO 121, 430-441.

NEIGHBORHOODS
(general to specific; alphabetical by
street or area, with a subsection for
the famous Bowery and Turtle Bay)

672. Hemp, William H. New York enclaves. New York:
      C. N. Potter, distributed by Crown Publishers, 1975.
      One-page line drawings with one page of text de-
      scribe and recreate the atmosphere of each of the
      twenty-six enclaves--pockets of history, ethnicity, or
      life styles, that has its own attraction, such as:
      South Street Seaport, Washington-Harrison Street
      Houses, Mott Street, Orchard Street, SoHo, St.
      Luke's Place, Grove Court, Ale Place, Trendwell
      Farm, Striver's Row, Junel Terrace, etc.

673. Baral, R. Turn west on 23rd; a toast to New York's
      old Chelsea. New York: Fleet Pub., c. 1965. 128
      p.
      The most fashionable district of the late 19th cen-
      tury and early 20th century (1880-1920) which was
      the epitome--of art, entertainment, society, and
      wealth. This brief history covers chorus girls, mov-
      ies, millionaires, murders, opera, philanthropies,
      and ferry boats, among other aspects of New York.

674. Gruen, J. The New Bohemia; the combine generation.
      Photos by Fred W. McDarrah. New York: Shore-
      crest, 1966. 180 p.
      The East Village (Third Avenue to the East River,
      Houston Street to 14th) replaced Greenwich Village as
      it became the locus of the Combine Generation with
      its emphasis on Movement, Openness, and Irration-
      ality. The author attempts to define/explain/describe
      what the East Village represents in its life styles,
      art, poetry, plays, underground movies.

675. Ware, Caroline F. Greenwich Village, 1920-1930; a
      comment on American civilization in the post-war
      years. New York: Harper & Row, 1965. 496 p.
      Illus., maps.
      A study of the older American-born children of
      those immigrants that came to the United States at
      a rate of one million per year before World War I.

Their trauma of joblessness, rejection, and the war,
with the resultant social processes that created social problems enduring long after the original causes
have passed. This analysis reviews the failure of
education, the intervention of real estate interests,
the indistinct lines between justice and legality, political pragmatism, ethnic problems, new demands
on institutions. The most dated and perhaps the
interesting section is the one on the Village Bohe-
mians. Appendices include statistical data on social/
welfare problems, education, business, and real
estate factors.

676. Landesman, Alter F. A history of New Lots, Brooklyn
to 1887 including the villages of East New York,
Cypress Hills, and Brownsville. Port Washington,
New York: Kennikat, 1977. 258 p. Illus., maps.
(Empire State Historical Publications Series).
"Notes": p. 243-253.
Detailed account of the development of rural villages into these well-known sections of Cypress Hills,
East New York, New Lots, and Brownsville. It
begins with New Lots, its Dutch settlers, their way
of life, their role in the Revolutionary War, continuing to the establishment of East New York in 1835
as an attempted rival to New York City. New Lots
separated from Flatbush in 1852, its growth resulting in the additional communities of Cypress Hills
and Brownsville. New Lots merged with Brooklyn
in 1886, Brooklyn in turn merging with New York
City in the next decade. At that time, large numbers of Jews moved into these communities.

677. Lyford, Joseph P. The airtight cage; a study of New
York's West Side. New York: Harper & Row,
1966. 356 p.
A study of one of the world's most densely pop-
ulated areas--an average of over 1,000 persons per
block, that delineates: 1) effective connections between society and the urban poor have been broken;
2) the antihuman aspects of the system; and 3) the
basic inability of society to accurately "read" the
condition of the Area's residents (the poor)--by politicians, social reformers, and the churches, as
well as government. This analysis is based upon
personal observations, extensive interviews, and
documentation.

678. Zettler, Michael D. The Bowery. New York: Drake,
      1975. 150 p. Illus.
      The realities of an existence without hope, dreams,
      or illusions--a profile of Bowery inhabitants.

679. Bendiner, E. The Bowery man. New York: Nelson,
      1961. 187 p. Illus.
      A composite profile of the very individualistic
      men that inhabit the Bowery--some of the reasons
      they are there, the ways they survive, the people
      who care for them, and the mores and conventions
      of the Bowery itself.

680. Detmold, Mabel A. The Brownstones of Turtle Bay
      Gardens. New York: East 49th Street Association,
      1964. 77 p.
      Brief narrative of how and why this enclave (be-
      tween 48th and 49th Streets, 3rd and 2nd Avenues)
      of brownstones was created with their common gar-
      dens. The history of each house, its owners and
      tenants, is included--many famous and influential
      people from the worlds of art, literature, law, en-
      tertainment, etc.

681. Delaney, Edmund T. New York's Turtle Bay, old
      and new. Barre, Mass.: Barre Publishers, 1965.
      85 p. Bibliography: p. 83.
      The various periods of decay and regeneration
      that characterized the history of the Turtle Bay area,
      from colonial days to the present--are recorded by
      text, extensive drawings, illustrations, and photo-
      graphs (exterior and interior views). To a degree
      it is also a chronicle of the City.

SEE ALSO 543.

                          PARKS
                   (general to specific,
                     then alphabetical)

682. Heckscher, A. Alive in the city: memoir of an ex-
      commissioner. New York: Scribner, 1974. 294 p.
      Illus.
      Parks and politics. A review of office by a parks
      commissioner under Mayor John Lindsay. Details
      the accomplishments and triumphs as well as the

failures and frustrations. By indirection, provides
some insight into municipal administration.

683. Gilder, R. The Battery; the story of the adventurers,
artists, statesmen, grafters, songsters, mariners,
pirates, guzzlers, Indians, thieves, stuffed-shirts,
turn-coats, millionaires, inventors, poets, heroes,
soldiers, harlots, bootlicks, nobles, nonentities,
burghers, martyrs, and murderers who played their
parts during full four centuries on Manhattan Island's
tip. Boston: Houghton Mifflin, 1936. 304 p. Illus.
Spans the period 1524 to 1936 with brief sketches,
filled with details and facts, of people, events, and
activities that seem to recreate the life of the time
and place.

684. Johnston, N. Central Park country, a tune within us;
photos by Nancy and Retta Johnston. Introd. by
Marianne Moore. Text by Mireille Johnston. Edited
with a foreword by David Brower. San Francisco:
Sierra Club, 1968. 151 p. Col. illus.
A beautiful book--in concept and illustration.
Lavish color photographs present different facets of
the Park around four themes: Central Park, prov-
ince of dream, Nature and Central Park, Games and
Parade. Excerpts from the professional papers of
F. L. Olmsted are included with appropriate texts
for the colored plates.

685. Reed, Henry H. and S. Duckworth. Central Park; a
history and a guide. Rev. ed. New York: C. N.
Potter; Distributed by Crown, 1972. 166 p. Illus.,
maps. Bibliography: p. 164-166.
A brief history with detailed walking tours of the
Southern section and the Northern section of Central
Park. Appendices list: 1) points of interest; 2)
recreation and other events offered in the Park; 3)
birds of the Park; 4) Monuments, tablets, and
plaques; 5) Central Park statistics; 6) approximate
dates of leafing, budding, blossoming, and fruiting
of plants; 7) acreage of major urban parks of the
world.

686. Olmsted, Frederick L. Landscape in Cityscape, Frederick Law Olmsted's plans for a greater New York
City. Edited with an introductory essay and notes by
Albert Fein. Ithaca, New York: Cornell University,
c. 1967. 490 p. Illus., plans, front.

Of these twelve documents, nine are reports by
Olmsted to governmental agencies concerning public
works for what was to become Greater New York.
The others are: (doc. 1) autobiographical--Olmsted's
analysis of how he was appointed Superintendent responsible for construction of Central Park; (doc. 6)
is a survey of Rockaway Point as a summer resort
possibility; and (doc. 11) Olmsted's pamphlet, "Spoils
of the Park," defending the original intent of Central
Park against politicians and promoters.

687.   Olmsted, Frederick L.   Public parks and the enlarge-
       ment of towns.   New York: Arno Press & The New
       York Times, 1970.   (The Rise of urban America).
       Reprint of the 1870 edition.   Read before the Amer-
       ican Social Science Association, Lowell Institute,
       Boston, February 25th, 1870.
           Fascinating account of a contemporary analysis of
       the development and consequence of urban and sub-
       urban areas with effective arguments as to the need
       for and adequate support of public parks for the con-
       tinued "health" of cities; made by the creator of
       Central Park and other New York City parks.

688.   Lancaster, C.   Prospect Park handbook.   With a fore-
       word by Marianne Moore.   New York: W. H. Rawls,
       1967.   128 p.   Illus., maps, plans.
           A very comprehensive history of the park's first
       hundred years; its builders, buildings, plants, paths,
       trees, vandals, and victories.

                          PICTORIAL WORKS
                         (general to specific)

689.   Stokes, Isaac N. P.   The iconography of Manhattan
       Island, 1498-1909 compiled from original sources and
       illustrated by photo-intaglio reproductions of impor-
       tant maps, plans, views, and documents in public
       and private collections.   New York: Arno, 1967.
       6 v.   Illus., (part col.), facsims, maps.   Bibliog-
       raphy: vol. VI, p. 179-281.   Reprint of the 1922
       edition.
           A history emphasizing the topographical features
       of Manhattan and the City's physical growth.   Cov-
       ering the period 1498 to 1909, maps, views, plans,
       documents located in the principal libraries and

private collections of the U.S. and Europe are arranged in chronological order with appropriate text
about the period illustrated. The descriptions of
the plates are extensive--medium used, dates depicted, date issued, author or artist, provenance,
copies, etc. and information--historical, topographi-
cal, or antiquarian--concerning the sites or buildings
depicted. A Reference Key to the Landmark Map--
subject categories by types of buildings provide easy
access. The entries in this index include a brief
description or comment about the buildings and sites,
references to articles, and books about them. Also
includes a checklist of early newspapers (1725-1811),
with bibliography and reproductions. Volumes IV
and V are a chronology.

690.   King, M. King's handbook of New York City, 1893.
       First planned, edited & published by Moses King,
       Boston, 1893. 2d enl. ed., with 1029 illus., 1020
       pages and new introduction by A. E. Santaniello.
       New York: B. Blom, 1972. 1008 p. Illus.
          Over 1,000 photographs, maps, with thirty chap-
       ters that provide a concise history and description
       of various aspects of the city, notables, public insti-
       tutions, and particularly interesting features--water-
       ways, transportation, government, literary culture,
       shrines of worship, reformatories, amusements,
       insurance, architectural features, manufacturers,
       retailers, and wholesalers, etc.

691.   Kouwenhoven, John A. The Columbia historical por-
       trait of New York; an essay in graphic history. New
       York: Harper & Row, 1973. 550 p. Bibliography:
       p. 147-150.
          A survey of available illustrations of New York
       City from the earliest maps, views, and plans to
       current paintings, prints, and photographs--some 900
       pictures, each with commentary and historical data
       in individual captions. A brief essay provides the
       framework for the seven successive groupings of
       pictures--roughly chronological but actually selected
       and arranged to highlight the dominant interests and
       attitudes of the period. Both the choice land arrange-
       ments of material have the objectives of creating an
       awareness of the perceptions, blind spots, and values
       of another time; how people viewed their city and
       themselves, indicating their illusions and viewpoints
       by what is presented.

692. New York Historical Society. Old New York in early
      photographs, 1853-1901. Mary Black: curator of
      painting and sculpture. New York: Dover, 1973.
      228 p.
           These 196 prints, arranged by twelve geographic
      areas in Manhattan, were selected on the basis of
      being the most significant of those placed on exhibi-
      tion--Eye on the City--by the New York Historical
      Society, October 1970 to March 1971. While human
      events are not excluded (Lincoln's funeral cortege at
      City Hall, 1965), views of buildings seem to dominate
      this collection.

693. Byron, J. and C. Lancaster. New York interiors at
      the turn of the century: in 131 photographs by
      Joseph Byron from the Byron Collection of the Mu-
      seum of the City of New York. New York: Dover,
      1976. 154 p. Illus. Notes to the plates: p. 133-
      154.
           Covers the range of the social spectrum of New
      York City (1880-1910) with about one-third of the
      photographs devoted to institutions, banks, places of
      entertainment, offices, etc. The remainder are of
      domestic scenes.

694. Manhattan seascape: waterside views around New York
      (compiled by) Robert Gamber. New York: Hastings
      House, 1975. 256 p. Illus.
           Photographs emphasizing New York's shoreline,
      docks, bridges, boats, park and water views, sup-
      plemented by poetry and prose of such authors as
      Whitman, Thomas Wolfe, Hart Crane, Le Corbusier,
      O. Nash, Charles Dickens, W. H. Auden, and H. G.
      Wells.

695. Kertsez, A. Of New York ...; edited by Nicholas
      Ducrot, 1st ed. New York: Knopf, 1976. 191 p.
           No preface, introduction, text, or even titles,
      just the statement that "Photography must be realis-
      tic" supported by almost 200 photographs of New York
      City--in every season, time of night and day and
      circumstance--the ornate street light contrasted with
      the geometry of skyscrapers, the charity of a dwarf
      putting a coin in the cup of a blind street musician,
      the competition of religious sculpture and bill board
      advertising. Some are dramatic sequences, the
      sudden illness at a sidewalk art show, others are

simply beautiful: lines, patterns, and moods created
by trees, snow, buildings, water, stone, wires, or
an architectural detail.

SEE ALSO 124.

POLICE AND FIREMEN
(general to specific, then
chronologically retrospective)

696. Astor, G. The New York cops; an informal history.
      New York: Scribner, 1971. 249 p. Bibliography:
      p. 241-243.
          From its antecedents and birth (1844) to the
      1970's, a knowledgeable and detailed profile of the
      NYPD and its efforts, with shifting moralities and
      mores, in the conflicts between the criminals, the
      law abiders, and the law enforcers.

697. Alex, N. New York cops talk back; a study of a be-
      leaguered minority. New York: Wiley, 1976. 225
      p.
          Based upon taped interviews with forty-two white
      New York City policemen, this study seeks to pro-
      vide comparable data to that presented in the author's
      Black in Blue; an analysis of the personal and pro-
      fessional problems of black policemen. The time
      difference between the studies is reflected in the
      attitudinal changes of the concerned groups. This
      account deals with the occupational crises of New
      York City policemen, the factors eroding their au-
      thority, autonomy, codes, methods, and standards
      and the resultant discords and discontents.

698. Halper, A. and R. Ku. New York City Police Depart-
      ment, Street Crime Unit/ with the assistance of the
      New York City Police Department Street Crime Unit.
      Washington: National Institute of Law Enforcement
      and Criminal Justice, 1975. 165 p.
          This specialized police unit has two objectives:
      1) quality arrests (high percentage of convictions) and
      2) deterring would-be violent street criminals. The
      latter is accomplished by the police working in street
      clothes in high crime areas offering themselves as
      decoy victims. The result--to the criminal, every
      potential victim also may be a highly trained

policeman. This manual covers: the problem, organization, personnel, tactics, arrest procedures,
equipment, special legal considerations, costs, and
evaluation routines.

699. Bouza, Anthony V. Police intelligence: the operations
of an investigative unit. New York: AMS, 1976.
192 p. Bibliography: p. 179-184.
By describing the operations of the intelligence
organization of the New York Police Department
(Bureau of Special Services and Information) the
author seeks to examine the dilemma of society's
distaste for "spying" organizations and its need to
use them in combating police and political corruption
as well as organized crime and political terrorism.
The description of this unit's activities, its relationship to other police units, and New York City politics
and press provide an unusual perspective.

700. Morton, Dora V. New York Police Centre; a short
history, with tales bringing out the unity and fun
among the workers at the Police Centre. Cornwall-
ville, New York: Hope Farm, 1972. 86 p.
Very informal style with many photographs and
stories of the buildings, people, and pets associated
with this rest and recreational home for the New
York Police and their families.

701. Viteritti, Joseph P. Police, politics, and pluralism
in New York City: a comparative case study. Beverly Hills, Calif.: Sage, 1973. 72 p. (In Sage
Professional papers in administrative and policy
studies). Bibliography: p. 68-71.
Analysis of two issues concerning the Police
Department: 1) Mayor Lindsay's attempt to create
a civilian complaint review board (1966) and 2) his
efforts to eliminate the state law that limited the
authority of local police administrators at their own
discretion to deploy manpower. While the focus is
on the police department as these two situations are
used to evaluate New York City government's response
to the needs and demands of its nonwhite population,
in fact the total system is on trial.

702. Ruchelman, Leonard I. Police politics: a comparative
study of three cities. Cambridge, Mass.: Ballinger,
1974. 118 p.

The focus of this study is not the political pres-
sure exerted upon the police, but rather it is upon
the police power bloc effects on the community's
political structure and their assertions concerning
social policy. Three cities--New York, Philadelphia,
and Chicago--were used for comparisons and research.

703. Chevigny, P. Cops and rebels; a study of provocation.
       New York: Pantheon, 1972. 332 p. Bibliography:
       p. 329-332.
            The arrest and court trial of members of the
       Black Panther Party as a result of the efforts of
       provocateurs directed by the New York Police De-
       partment is examined from several viewpoints: the
       historical use made of provocateurs, the process by
       which individuals become radicals or revolutionaries,
       and the ideological aspects of police organizations.

704. Chevigny, P. Police power: police abuses in New
       York City. New York: Pantheon, 1968. 298 p.
       Bibliography: p. 296-298.
            Police abuses and the reasons why they exist and
       continue, a study of what was wrong with street law
       enforcement in New York City during 1966 and 1967
       and some of the remedies devised. Based upon
       actual cases taken to the courts or police depart-
       mental reviews.

705. Limpus, Lowell M. Honest cop, Lewis J. Valentine;
       being a chronicle of the commissioner's thirty-six
       years in the New York police department. New
       York: E. P. Dutton, 1939. 291 p. Illus.
            Biography of L. J. Valentine, who began as a
       probationary patrolman in 1903, up to and including
       his first five years as New York City's Police Com-
       missioner.

706. New York (City). Board of Aldermen. Police in New
       York City; an investigation. New York: Arno Press
       and the New York Times, 1971. 1 v. (Police in
       America).
            A collection of seventeen reports on various as-
       pects of the police department (school for recruits,
       policemen in court, surgical bureau, condition of
       station houses, etc.) and the report of the Citizens'
       Committee (1912); and the Board of Aldermen's report

of the special committee (1913). Many charts and
graphs. These primary source documents were
compiled by the Bureau of Municipal Research.

707. McAdoo, W. Guarding a great city. New York: Arno
Press and the New York Times, 1971. 350 p. (Police in America). Reprint of the 1906 edition.
A surprisingly candid and "modern account of
the police (New York City), their problems and activities, by the author, who was Police Commissioner between 1904-1906.

708. New York. Chamber of Commerce of the State of
New York. Committee on the Police Problem. Papers and proceedings of Committee on the police
problem. New York: Arno Press and the New York
Times, 1971. 723 p. Charts. (Police in America).
Reprint of the 1905 edition.
A Committee of Nine, established in 1905, "...
to inquire into the organization, discipline and administration of the police ... the present state of
the laws ... to ascertain to what degree improve-
ment in existing conditions must depend upon new
legislation ... to promote such measures of a legislative or other character...." The testimony,
interviews, and the other forms of investigation concerning standards, functions, and effectiveness of
the New York City police make this a primary source
document.

709. Walling, George W. Recollections of a New York chief
of police. New York: Caxton, c. 1887. 608 p.
A very detailed portrayal of crime and police
activities in nineteenth-century New York City. Good
if brief introduction to schemes, frauds, and crim-
inal activities that were characteristic of the times.
Also some of the colorful people outside the law--
Four-fingered Jack, Mother Mandelbaum, Queen of
Fences, Red Leary, etc. Final chapters on police
force, comparisons of New York City force with
London, the dangerous combination of Police and
Politics and some observations on the causes of
crime.

710. New York (City). Board of Aldermen. Special Committee to Investigate the Police Department. Report
of the special committee of the New York City Board

of Aldermen on the New York City Police Department, New York City Common council. New York:
Arno Press & the New York Times, 1971. 688-
1065 p. Illus., maps, lists. Reprint of the 1844
edition.

This report of the Special Committee established
in 1843, consists of three sections: a) a statement
of the condition of the New York City Police Department, a list of crimes and punishments as defined
by law and the Police Department's relationship with
other departments, i.e., the Judiciary; b) the defects
of the current system and the practices that have
resulted from them; c) recommendations of measures
and laws to correct the situation. These documents
plus the statistics included therein (convictions, prisoners, sentences, etc.) are primary source materials.

711.   Christian, C. A brief treatise on the police of the
        City of New York. New York: Arno, 1970. 32 p.
        (The Rise of urban America). Reprint of the 1812
        edition.

        Addressed to the mayor, the author offers sug-
        gestions, recommendations, and advice concerning:
        police department matters, state prison convicts,
        pardons, the city prison (Bridewell), prison reform,
        "women of the town," gambling, taverns, pawnbro-
        kers, and public baths as he observes, "... that
        bodily cleanliness has a favorable effect on moral
        purity." Presents an interesting picture of some
        aspects of early nineteenth-century life.

SEE ALSO 851, 852.

Firemen

712.   Smith, D. Report from Engine Co. 82. New York:
        McCall Books, 1972. 215 p.
        An account of the life of firemen in the South
        Bronx--their attitudes, activities, and the dangers
        they face. Well written, perceptive of both the men
        and the people they protect and contend with.

POLITICS AND GOVERNMENT
(general to specific)

713. Smith, Thelma E. Guide to the municipal government
      of the City of New York. 10th ed. New York:
      Meilen Press (distributed by Law-Arts Publishers),
      1973. 360 p.
         Divided into four parts: Legislative branch, Ex-
      ecutive branch, the Judiciary, and a section on the
      County and State. Provides historical data plus a
      detailed explanation of the organization and functions
      for each department or agency within those segments
      of city government.

Charters

714. New York (State). State Charter Revision Commission
      for New York City. Final report of the State Charter
      Commission for New York City. New York: The
      Commission, 1975. 35 p.
         Recognizing that New York City has problems in
      part due to a city government inadequately organized
      and structured, the Commission--by extensive inter-
      views, studies, and reviews of alternatives and pro-
      posals--offered the voters nine propositions to con-
      sider. Comparisons are made with current and pro-
      posed charter provisions. Appendices list the com-
      missioners, their staffs, and their reports and stud-
      ies.

715. City Club of New York. The New York City charter
      bill; text of difference between bill as proposed by
      the Charter Revision Commission and bill as passed
      by legislature, 5th April, 1901. 2nd edition. New
      York: City Club of New York, 1901. 104 p.

Investigations and Corruption

716. Seidman, H. Investigating municipal administration; a
      study of the New York City Department of Investi-
      gation. New York: Institute of Public Administra-
      tion, Columbia University, 1941. 215 p. Bibliog-
      raphy: p. 197-200.
         A history of the Department since its creation
      after the Tweed Ring scandals in 1873. It has had

many forms and functions, but in 1940 its purpose
was the application of scientific reform to problems
of public administration.

717. New York (State). Temporary State Commission of
      Investigation. Government for sale; a glimpse at
      waste and corruption in the City of New York. Fi-
      nal report of the Special Unit, New York State Com-
      mission of Investigation. New York, 1961. 37 ℓ.
         The corruption, irresponsibility, and misfeasance
      resulting from a one-party situation: payoffs to
      electrical inspectors, building plan examiners, real
      estate employees, comptroller's inspectors; waste
      maintenance contract extravagance, and municipal
      officials compliance. Also examines the question--
      is corruption necessary?

718. Amen, John H. Report of Kings County Investigation,
      1938-1942. New York, 1942. 247 p.
         This investigation included a review of: the jury
      system, fur swindles, bribery of police and district
      attorney office personnel, an abortion racket, a
      paving and gambling operation, reports on the courts
      and the department of correction as well as the
      specific prosecution of known criminals.

719. Northrop, William B. and John B. Northrop. The
      insolence of office; the story of the Seabury investi-
      gations. New York, London: G. P. Putnam's sons,
      1932. 306 p.
         A detailed and factual account of Judge Seabury's
      activities as reference (investigations of the Man-
      hattan and Bronx Magistrates Courts, 1930); as Com-
      missioner (investigation of Thomas C. T. Cain, Dis-
      trict Attorney of N. Y. County, 1931) and Counsel
      (investigations of the Legislature into the government
      of New York City, 1931). Judge Seabury's task was
      to obtain facts--facts when the Mayor, all five bor-
      ough District Attorneys, and all municipal officers,
      except one Alderman, were Tammany men!! A
      careful delineation of the conspiracy of silence and
      loyalty to a corrupt political organization.

720. Mitgang, H. The man who rode the tiger; the life and
      times of Judge Samuel Seabury. Philadelphia: Lip-
      pincott, 1963. 380 p. Illus. "Publications of
      Samuel Seabury": p. 367-368. "Books about Samuel
      Seabury": p. 369.

The tiger was the corrupt Tammany Hall of New
York City and this is the biography of a man, outstanding lawyer, judge, and investigator, that successfully opposed and defeated the Tiger. It is
based upon documents, court and legislative reports
of investigating committees, newspaper accounts,
books, Seabury family diaries and papers, supplemented by interviews with members of the Seabury
family, public officials, legal associates, and every
member of Seabury's investigative staff.

721. Hershkowitz, L. Tweed's New York: another look.
Garden City, New York: Anchor/Doubleday, 1977.
409 p. Bibliography: p. 381-391.
If not a vindication of "Boss" Tweed, this biography presents a very different perspective, chal-
lenging the myths, ignorance, legends, half truths,
and fictions that are perpetuated as historical fact
and common knowledge. A detailed account that will
help to balance the general concept of New York City
politics and politicians as corruption personified.

722. Myers, Gustavus. The history of Tammany Hall.
With a new introd. by Alexander B. Callow, Jr.
2d ed., rev. and enl. New York: Dover, 1971.
414 p. Reprint of the 1917 edition.
A classic study of this politically corrupt institution (1789-1917) of New York democracy, its greed
and deceptions illuminated by evidence, facts, and
details. A technique effective but in contrast to
the author's mudraking contemporaries who were
more inclined toward rhetoric and thundering indig-
nation.

723. Lewis, Alfred H. Richard Croker. New York: Life,
1901. 372 p. Front., plates, ports.
Biography of the successor of John Kelly as leader of Tammany Hall between 1886 and 1894. As
such he was one of the most powerful figures in
the political structure of a great city in an influential state of a country that was becoming a world
power.

Mayor's Office
(general to specific)

724. Westerhof, Caroline S. The executive connection:
     mayors and press secretaries, the New York experi-
     ence. New York: Dunellen, 1974. 191 p.
       A study of the mechanisms of the office of press
     secretary, how it functions, what its objectives should
     be, its influence on policy, planning, and decision
     making. Based upon interviews of press secretaries,
     printed sources, papers of past New York mayors
     and publications of Mayor Lindsay.

725. Caraley, D. New York City's deputy mayor-city ad-
     ministrator; accomplishments, problems, and poten-
     tialities. New York: Citizens Budget Commission,
     1966. 96 p.
       An evaluation of this office indicates that it is an
     asset to the Mayor, but is underpowered and perhaps,
     for that reason, it may be under utilized. Professor
     Caraley makes several recommendations for increas-
     ing the effectiveness of this staffing device.

726. Twentieth Century Fund. Task Force on Prospects and
     Priorities of New York City. A nice place to live;
     report. New York: Twentieth Century Fund, 1973.
     72 p.
       An examination of the power and influence of the
     mayor of New York and those critical problems that
     will most likely benefit from the attention of this
     office but also require most of the mayor's efforts
     and the resources of the city: collective bargaining,
     criminal justice, health, transportation, and economic
     development.

727. Lewinson, Edwin R. John Purroy Mitchel, the boy
     mayor of New York. New York: Astra Books, 1965.
     299 p. Bibliography: p. 279-295.
       A study of those factors that result in the failure
     of reform mayors and good government groups--pro-
     grams that fail to appeal to the poorer peoples, an
     indifference to the need for a voter rapport and per-
     haps an over-emphasis on economy and efficiency at
     the expense of compassion. Mitchell won his elec-
     tion (1913) by the largest plurality since the creation
     of the Greater City in 1897. He lost the next one
     by even a larger one.

728.   La Guardia, Fiorello H.   The making of an insurgent,
       an autobiography, 1882-1919.   Introduction by H. M.
       Christman and M. R. Werner.   New York: Capri-
       corn, 1961.   222 p.
            Covers his early activities in New York and Ari-
       zona, his political campaigns, freshman years in
       Congress, the Immigration Service, his World War
       I service in Italy and his concerns as Congressman
       with post-world war problems.

729.   Mann, A.   La Guardia comes to power: 1933.   Phil-
       adelphia: Lippincott, 1965.   199 p.   Maps.   "Notes":
       p. 176-192.
            The second installment in the author's attempt to
       tell the La Guardia story.   He tries to answer the
       question of how La Guardia came to power, by what
       process do the American people change the political
       guard, and why did La Guardia win the mayorality
       in 1933?   This is a sequel to A Fighter Against His
       Times, a biography of the "Little Flower" from 1882
       to 1932.

730.   Garrett, C.   The La Guardia years, machine and re-
       form politics in New York City.   New Brunswick,
       N.J.:   Rutgers University, 1961.   423 p.   Illus.
       Biographical Notes: p. 403-405.
            Basically a history of Fiorello H. La Guardia's
       mayorality from 1934 to 1945, a Funsion administra-
       tion that was to rehabilitate the administration, fi-
       nances, social and moral aspects of New York City.
       His contributions and his impact on government and
       politics are analyzed and evaluated within the Amer-
       ican traditions of machine rule and a reform govern-
       ment.

731.   Sayre, Wallace S. and H. Kaufman.   Governing New
       York; politics in the metropolis.   New York: Norton,
       1965.   777 p.   Charts, illus.   Includes bibliographies.
            The process by which the city is governed is the
       primary consideration: what is New York politics
       about, who participates and why, what are the re-
       wards and how are they acquired?   Describes the
       setting and background of the processes (the city),
       defines the stakes, and reviews the rules of the
       game.   Additional section delineates strategies and
       concludes with studies of the major categories of the
       participants: administrators, agencies, courts, the

political parties, etc. Appendices list autobiographies, biographies, and memoirs of prominent New Yorkers and lists sources of information about New York City.

732. Buckley, William F., Jr. The unmaking of a mayor. New York: Viking, 1966. 341 p. Illus., ports. Index: p. 337-341.
     Detailed and intimate analysis of the New York City mayoral elections of 1965 involving John Vliet Lindsay, Abraham Beame, and William F. Buckley, Jr.

Political Processes
(general to specific, then
chronologically retrospective)

733. Rogers, D. The management of big cities; interest groups and social change strategies. With a foreword by Amitai Etzioni. Beverly Hills, Calif.: Sage, 1971. 191 p. Bibliography: p. 177-182.
     A cross-city study--New York, Philadelphia, and Cleveland--analyzing municipal capacities, fragmented and weakened by interest group political in-fighting, to implement institutional change strategies and innovated programs. New York was particularly selected because of its size, its leadership in new programs, the range of its urban problems, and that it had a very flexible mayor in John Lindsay. His reforms and social strategies--successes or failures --have and had an impact on other urban centers.

734. Adler, N. and Blanche D. Blank. Political clubs in New York. Foreword by Roy V. Peel. New York: Praeger, 1975. 275 p. (Praeger special studies in U.S. economic, social, and political issues).
     An update of Peel's Political Clubs of New York that presents data on the social, economic, environmental, moral, and psychological behavior related to clubs and political club membership. Political clubs, while remaining outside legal state and local regulations, dominate the legally/formal forms of political organization; that is their importance and significance. The authors examine what is a club, who leads, who joins, what are the quarters like, who pays, how, the history of club activities, and the role clubs play in reform. Appendices list New York political clubs.

735. Peel, Roy V. The political clubs of New York City.
      Port Washington, New York: I.J. Friedman, 1968.
      360 p. (Empire state historical publications series
      no. 48). Reprint of the 1935 ed. Bibliography: p.
      336-347.
           The definitive book on the subject of local urban
      political clubs; this study covers the period 1927-
      1932. The social, civic, welfare, educational, and
      anti-social activities of political clubs are chronicled
      as well as their organization, leadership, history,
      and objectives. Author points out the existence of
      the variety of political clubs; nationality, minor party,
      suburban clubs, independent and revolt clubs.

736. Lowi, Theodore J. At the pleasure of the mayor;
      patronage and power in New York City, 1898-1958.
      New York: Free Press, 1964. 272 p. Bibliography:
      p. 253-264.
           The author considers this book to be an extension
      of Professors Sayre and Kaufman's Governing New
      York. Essentially embodies three different approach-
      es to the collected data: 1) it is a historical de-
      scriptive study; 2) a study of recruitment--socioeco-
      nomic changes in backgrounds of decision makers,
      sources of recruits, and who the recruits are; 3)
      an analysis of community power relations. Broad
      topical areas included appointments, political change
      and power, reform cycles, community power, plural-
      ism, and parties.

737. Breen, Matthew P. Thirty years of New York politics
      up-to-date ... New York: The author, 1899. 843 p.
      Front., plates, ports.
           Based upon public records, other sources of in-
      formation, and the author's personal involvement
      with city and state government, this is a history of
      New York City politics during the last three decades
      of the 19th century. Primarily concerned with Tweed
      and Tammany corruption. Many interesting obser-
      vations and sidelights presented about people; those
      principally involved in "Bossism."

738. Gardner, Gerald C. Robert Kennedy in New York.
      New York: Random House, 1965. 202 p.
           An insider's reconstruction of Robert Kennedy's
      New York senatorial campaign; interesting sidelights
      about New York political life, its entertainment world,
      and the City in general.

Protests and Proposals
(general to specific)

739. New York (State). State Study Commission for New
      York City. Task Force on Jurisdiction and Struc-
      ture. Restructuring the government of New York
      City; report of the Scott Commission Task Force on
      Jurisdiction and Structure (by) Edward N. Costikyan
      (and) Maxwell Lehman. New York: Praeger, 1972.
      128 p. (Praeger special studies in U.S. economic,
      social, and political issues).
          A proposal and plan to decentralize the bureaucra-
      cy of New York City, create local communities where
      resident participation is meaningful, all within the
      context of a strong central city government while
      avoiding the evils and problems of fragmentation.

740. Decentralizing city government: an evaluation of the
      New York City district manager experiment/ Allen
      Barton ... (et al.). Lexington, Mass.: Lexington
      Books, 1977. 279 p.
          The Office of Neighborhood Government was an
      experiment; an attempt to encourage citizen partici-
      pation and alleviate feelings of helplessness and re-
      moteness concerning the individual's control over
      the quality of urban life. It failed--for a variety of
      reasons including: inadequate funding, politics, and
      city official resistance. It also failed for other and
      less obvious reasons. Each chapter is concerned
      with a particular aspect of this experiment, each one
      written by different authors.

741. Governing the city; challenges and options for New York.
      Edited by Robert H. Connery and Demetrios Caraley.
      New York: Published for the Academy of Political
      Science by Praeger, 1969. 230 p. Bibliography:
      p. 224-227.
          Eighteen brief papers about New York City govern-
      ment, organization, and problems: education, crime,
      finance, housing, politics, etc. Good introduction to
      the problems of all urban centers and some of the
      possible resolutions to those problems.

742. Farr, Walter G. Decentralizing city government: a
      practical study of a radical proposal for New York
      City (by) Walter G. Farr, Jr., Lance Liebman (and)
      Jeffrey S. Wood. New York: Praeger, 1972. 242 p.

(Praeger special studies in U.S. economic, social,
and political issues).   Bibliography: p. 241-242.
The belief that decentralized government would,
at lower costs, meet the citizens' demand for municipal services is the basis for this study--one that
reviews the various alternatives of decentralization
and the consequences in terms of quality of service
and the costs of these choices.

743.   Lipsky, M.   Protest in city politics; rent strikes,
       housing and the power of the poor.   Chicago: Rand
       McNally, 1969, 1970.   214 p.
       All based upon his research in New York City
       situations, the author attempts to investigate the pol-
       itics and techniques of protest, the responsiveness
       of the political system (city government) to protest
       and to develop some generalizations concerning
       protest and its place in political activity.

Structure
(general to specific)

744.   Shaw, F.   The history of the New York City Legisla-
       ture.   New York: AMS, 1968.   300 p.   Tables.
       Reprint of the 1954 edition.   Bibliography: p. 265-
       284.
       A comparison of the City Council with the now
       defunct Board of Aldermen placed within a narrative
       of the city's political history from 1851 to 1953.

745.   Isaacs, Edith S.   Love affair with a city; the story of
       Stanley M. Isaacs.   New York: Random House,
       1967.   167 p.   Illus., ports.
       Biography of Stanley M. Isaacs (1882-1962), Mi-
       nority Leader of the (New York) City Council.   For
       his services to the City and its people the Herald
       Tribune called him Mr. New York and the Times
       labelled him Warrior for the People.

746.   American Institute of Architects.   New York Chapter.
       Committee on Housing.   The significance of the work
       of the New York City Housing Authority.   New York,
       1949.   129 p.   Illus., plans, diags.
       The work of the Housing Authority, its standards
       (livability, land use, construction costs, recreation,
       social needs, etc.), its methods of operation (staff,

administration, records, reports, etc.), cooperation
with governmental agencies, and its relationship to
housing in general. Appendix: summary of twelve
reports on public housing and lists of architects involved in design projects for New York City Housing
Authority.

747. Stanley, David T. and William C. Kroeger. Profes-
      sional personnel for the City of New York; report of
      the study of professional, technical, and managerial
      manpower needs of the City of New York. Washing-
      ton: Brookings Institution, 1963. 461 p.
        A national survey of the personnel needs of local
      government indicated: 1) a scarcity of administra-
      tive and professional talent combined with metropol-
      itan growth increasing the demands upon local gov-
      ernment; 2) effective and dramatic efforts will be
      required to attract, retain, and develop adequate
      members of skilled public personnel. This study
      is a counterpart to the national one; examining New
      York City's personnel system, focusing upon the
      30,000 appointed employees in categories considered
      "professional, technical, and managerial"--physicians,
      attorneys, accountants, social case workers, chem-
      ists, engineers, etc. A personnel crisis was identi-
      fied, its origins and nature delineated and recom-
      mendations were offered.

748. Jump, B. Financing public employee retirement pro-
      grams in New York City: trends since 1965 and
      projections to 1980. Syracuse, New York: Metro-
      politan Studies Program, Maxwell School of Citizen-
      ship and Public Affairs, 1975. 68 p. (Occasional
      paper--Metropolitan Studies Program. Syracuse Uni-
      versity; no. 16).
        Retirement systems costs for New York City and
      their projections provided some indicators for the
      fiscal difficulties of that municipality. The histori-
      cal analysis places the problem in context.

749. Brecher, C. Where have all the dollars gone? Public
      expenditures for human resource development in New
      York City, 1961-71. Foreword by Eli Ginzberg.
      New York: Praeger, 1974. 103 p. (Conservation
      of human resources studies; Praeger special studies
      in U.S. economic, social, and political issues).
      Chapter notes.

An examination of the factors (increased unit
costs and inflation) that account for the increase
in New York City's budget from 2.5 billion (1960's)
to 10 billion (1970's). A third factor (25 percent)
was municipal employees--their upgrading, higher
wages, and increased benefits. Allocations for
human development (health, education, welfare, and
family services) represented the major share of the budget; consequently they are the focal point of this study.

Urban Renewal

750. Caro, Robert A. The power broker: Robert Moses
      and the fall of New York. New York: Knopf, 1974.
      1246 p. Illus., maps. "Notes on Sources"; p.
      (1167)-1169. "Selected Interviews": p. (1170)-1172.
      "Selected Bibliography": p. (1173)-1177. "Note":
      p. (1178)-1246; index: p. (i)-xxxiv.
      A study of a city and the man who shaped it for
      forty-four years, physically, socially, and econom-
      ically, and perhaps even disasterly. The man had
      tremendous impact upon urban renewal nationally,
      was a great builder, an innovator in the area of
      public works, but who was also the center of a per-
      sonal empire of power and influence.

751. Moses, R. Public works: a dangerous trade. New
      York: McGraw-Hill, 1970. 952 p. Illus.
      A selection of correspondences, reports, talks,
      and writings from 1919 to 1969 with relevant expla-
      nations. Chapters are topical: museums and parks,
      the parkway system, bridges, tunnels, and other
      works, transportation, power, planning, World's
      Fair, City Trust investigation, government and pub-
      lic works, foreign and domestic surveys. The final
      chapter is composed of biographical sketches of
      outstanding state and national public figures.
      Background is provided by:

      Regional Plan Association, New York. From plan to
      reality: a third report of progress, 1929-1941, on
      the development of the New York-New Jersey-Con-
      necticut metropolitan region including details for the
      period starting 1937 and a program of proposals for
      post-war public works. The Association, 1942.
      Various paging.

The Regional Plan Association stimulated planning, keeps the Plan up to date and workable for a metropolitan area composed of parts of three states, twenty-two counties, and 495 autonomous municipal units. This volume covers parks and parkways, highways, transportation and public services, zoning, and planning.

SEE ALSO 586, 587, 682, 705, 707.

PORT
(general to specific)

752. Port of New York Authority. Public Affairs Dept. A Chronology of the Port of New York Authority, 1921-1967. New York, 1967. 21 p.
      The "Port Authority" is a self-supporting agency created in 1921 by the states of New York and New Jersey to: improve and protect the commerce of the Port of New York, plan, develop, and operate terminals and transportation facilities. As of 1967 the Port Authority operated a regional system of four airports, two heliports, six marine terminals, two motor truck terminals, a truck terminal for railroad freight, bus terminal, and six interstate tunnels and bridges plus the Hudson Tubes through its subsidiary--the Port Authority Trans-Hudson Corporation. The chronology with brief entries, notes, appointments of commissioners, legislation passed, the opening of facilities, court cases, etc.

753. Writers' program. New York. A maritime history of New York. Introduction by the Honorable Fiorello H. La Guardia. Compiled by workers of the Writers program of the Work Projects Administration for the City of New York. Sponsored by the Mayor of the City of New York. Garden City, New York: Doubleday, Doran, 1941. 341 p. Bibliography: p. 321-326.
      Emphasized the importance of the role of the port of New York in the growth of the city, state, and nation. This history of a seaport town becoming a world metropolis, from sail to steam, is chronological from its geologic past to 1941; an account filled with figures from a forceful and colorful past.

754. Russell, Charles E. From Sandy Hook to 62°: being
      some account of the adventures, exploits, and ser-
      vices of the old New York pilot-boat. New York,
      London: The Century Co., 1929. 400 p.
           Histories of events and incidents that have, by
      their drama or human interest, contributed to the
      folklore and maritime history of New York City.
      Based upon the records and archives of the United
      New York and New Jersey Sandy Hook Pilots' Asso-
      ciation and interviews with members of the associa-
      tion. The "account" begins with the War of 1812
      and continues up to the 20th century.

755. Burchard, P. Harbor tug, photos by Rollie McKenna.
      New York: Putnam, 1975. 62 p. Illus.
           Brief narrative of the types of tug boats used
      in the New York City Harbor, their various functions
      and a description of the activities and life styles of
      the men who operate them.

756. Braynard, Frank O. A tugman's sketchbook; pen and
      ink impression of New York harbor and the ships
      that use it, big and small. Tuckahoe, New York:
      de Graff, 1965. 143 p.
           A series of sketches (136), by an employee of the
      Moran Towing & Transportation Co., detailing an
      event or ship--a docking, a rescue, the atmosphere
      aboard a liner. A monochromatic presentation of
      one artist's perceptions of a particular aspect of
      New York Harbor. Brief text explains the situation
      or the action depicted.

757. McKay, Richard C. South street; a maritime history
      of New York. New York: G. P. Putnam's sons,
      c. 1934. 460 p.
           A standard history of the subject that includes
      data about ship yards, ship builders, life on the
      docks, laws, legislation, the influence of politicians,
      the effects of war, the prizes. Poetry, biography,
      and statistics also. Period covered: 1783-1914.

SEE ALSO 598, 611, 663, 664.

PRISONS

758. Macdonald, A. Prison secrets; things seen, suffered,
      and recorded during seven years in Ludlow Street
      jail. New York: Arno Press, 1969. 363 p. (Mass
      violence in America). Reprint of the 1893 edition.
      Firsthand account of 19th-century penal conditions;
      based upon 9,000 pages of notes taken during his
      imprisonment, the author, by exposing the waste,
      corruption, and horrors of debtor's prison, seeks to
      arouse public opinion for prison reforms.

759. Sutton, C. The New York Tombs: its secrets and its
      mysteries. Edited by James B. Mix and Samuel A.
      MacKeever. Reprinted with the addition of a new
      introd. by Thomas M. Dade. Montclair, N.J.:
      Patterson Smith, 1973. 668 p. Reprint of the 1874
      edition with a new introduction.
      A collection of cases and accounts of crime that
      reflects the spectrum of violence in 19th-century
      New York City and that society's reaction to it. Un-
      fortunately, the warder/author, at the expense of
      informing us of the more ordinary aspects of prison
      life and administration, emphasizes the dramatic
      incidents and colorful personalities. Consequently,
      we meet river thieves, pirates, slavers, murderers,
      ghosts, "Ned Buntline," Henry Ward Beecher, and
      learn about escapes from the Tombs, details, and
      ritual of public executions, the privileges of wealthy
      prisoners, and the history of the construction of the
      Tombs.

760. Harris, S. Hellhole; the shocking story of the inmates
      and life in the New York City House of Detention for
      Women. New York: Dutton, 1967. 288 p.
      With the collaboration of former inmates and her
      personal experience as a social worker in that insti-
      tution, supplemented by additional research, the
      author portrays the life of prisoners in an infamous
      women's prison; variously described as a "house of
      ill-repute," "a blight upon our civilization," "a hell-
      hole and present-day snake pit," by government offi-
      cials and reformers.

761. Harris, Mary B. I knew them in prison. New York:
      Viking, New York, 1936. 407 p.
      Administrator for a number of women's prisons,
      the author began her career as a penologist as a

"temporary" superintendent of the Women's Work-
house, Blackwell's Island, New York City, a position
she filled between July 1, 1914 to January 7, 1918.

SEE ALSO 446, 448-452, 718.

RECREATION AND SPORTS

762. Jenkins, Shirley. Comparative recreation needs and
     services in New York neighborhoods. New York:
     Research Dept. Community Council of Greater New
     York, 1963. 244 p. Maps, tables.
         This study asserts that the recreation services
     and distribution of group work do not meet the ex-
     isting needs--lack of wide distribution of outdoor
     facilities, part-time leadership, five-day week pro-
     grams, lack of coordination between agencies, etc.
     Over five hundred directors and supervisors of
     agencies and programs contributed data to this study.
     Extensive comparative statistical figures on all five
     boroughs and their neighborhoods.

Arenas

763. Hollander, Z. Madison Square Garden; a century of
     sport and spectacle on the world's most versatile
     stage. New York: Hawthorn, 1973. 187 p.
         Brief history of the "four gardens" with separate
     chapters devoted to basketball, boxing, hockey, track
     and field, the dog show and the National Horse Show
     as these activities and events were associated with
     the "Garden." Many photographs and reproductions
     of posters of the great, the talented, and the spec-
     tacular.

764. Durso, J. Yankee Stadium; fifty years of drama.
     Boston: Houghton Mifflin, 1972. 155 p.
         The scene of sport triumphs (Louis-Schmeling
     fights, Pele, the soccer star, the Giants-Colts 1958
     play off, Babe Ruth's sixtieth home run), the stad-
     ium's history is also a social one including poets,
     presidents and pope, lords, preachers, and comedi-
     ans. Over 150 photographs provide highlights.

Basketball

765. Curran, J. New York City high school basketball.
      West Nyack: Parker, 1972. 207 p. Illus., dia-
      grams.
          Assuming a knowledge of fundamentals, this hand-
      book concentrates on the skills, techniques, and
      strategies that characterized New York City basket-
      ball as played on its street corners and in its high
      schools--the fast break, man-on-man, and zone
      attacks, the Molloy zone, etc. Emphasis is upon
      plays, drills, and development of players.

Bicycling

766. Macia, R. The New York bicycler (with twenty-seven
      tours in and around New York City). Maps and
      illus. by Barbara Holloway. New York: Simon &
      Schuster, 1972. 123 p. Maps, illus.
          Tour descriptions include map, approximate dis-
      tance, minimum time, description of route with num-
      bered points of interest located on a map and spe-
      cific directions detailing street numbers and the re-
      quired turns. Supplementary sections: history of
      the bicycle, types of bikes, information on bike
      parts, comments on accessories, tools, repairs,
      maintenance, rules for biking in the City, bike club
      addresses, and bike shops.

767. Fund for the City of New York. The bicyclist's guide
      for Manhattan. New York: Quadrangle Books, 1972.
      48 p. Maps.
          Location of bicycle racks and shops, tours of Wall
      Street, Brooklyn Heights, Greenwich Village, art
      tours, etc., bikeway maps, advice about biking,
      rules, regulations, and survival hints.

Tennis

768. Minton, R. Forest Hills: an illustrated history.
      Philadelphia: Lippincott, 1975. 240 p.
          A history of tennis, the West Side Tennis Club,
      and the sixty-one years of national championships
      and international matches that have been played in
      this section of Queens Borough, New York City.

Covers the period from 1874 to 1975 with extensive
photographs, many of them in color.   Details about
players, promoters, and the many others that contribute to this tennis event.

SEE ALSO 115.

RELIGION
(general to specific, then
alphabetical by denomination)

769.   Miller, Kenneth D. and E. Prince.   The people are
       the city; 150 years of social and religious concern
       in New York.   New York: Macmillan, 1962.   258
       p.   Illus.
          A history of the New York Mission Society, its
       pioneering religious and social work, its nondenom-
       inational character, its emphasis on people and their
       needs, and its impact on the life of the City.

770.   The old brewery, and the new mission house at the
       Five Points.   By the ladies of the mission ... New
       York: Stringer & Townsend, 1854.   304 p.   Re-
       printed 1970.
          "Five Points," an area of New York City that
       contained the "most degraded portion of the popula-
       tion."   This is the story of the New York Ladies'
       Home Missionary Society of the Methodist Episcopal
       Church's successful invasion and defeat of the filth,
       crime, illness, decay, ignorance, and despair that
       pervaded that part of the city.   They established
       schools, cared for the sick, built churches, and
       cleaned tenement houses, and in general raised the
       quality of life.   First hand account of early social
       work, reform, and missionary zeal--with the gloves
       off--in the 19th century.

771.   Rosenberg, Carroll S.   Religion and the rise of the
       American city; the New York City mission move-
       ment, 1812-1870.   Ithaca, New York: Cornell Uni-
       versity, 1971.   300 p.   Bibliography: p. 283-293.
          Originally the function of the 19th-century mission
       was to purvey the truths of revealed religion and its
       hopes of salvation to all.   By midcentury it had be-
       come, for the respectable New Yorker, his principle
       device for dealing with social problems.   This study

is divided into two sections: 1) the period between
1812 and 1830, and 2) 1837 through the Civil War.
Each contains a description of the City's social conditions, evaluations of the largest and most influential city missions of the period and an analysis of
the modes of thought represented by their supporters
and workers.

772. Bonner, A. Jerry McAuley and his mission. Neptune,
      N.J.: Loizeaux Bros., 1967. 123 p. Bibliography:
      p. 120.
      Biography of one of New York City's 19th-century
      religious leaders and social reformers--a converted
      convict, thief and drunk, he instituted the innovation
      of rescue missions and havens for prostitutes, etc.
      This account also contains graphic descriptions of
      prison life, prison punishments, life on skid row,
      crime, vice, and social conditions of the poor.

773. Coffin, Henry S. A half century of Union Theological
      Seminary, 1896-1945; an informal history. New
      York: Scribner, 1954, 261 p. Illus.
      Written by the "President of the Faculty," the
      author's association with the Seminary as student,
      teacher, and administrator spans the period of this
      history. The format is essentially biographical
      sketches and appraisals of the faculty. Particularly
      interesting are those sections about Paul Johannes
      Tillich and Reinhold Niebuhr. About one-half of the
      book is devoted to student concerns, the libraries,
      the School of Sacred Music, and the Seminary's con-
      tribution to the Ecumenical movement and world serv-
      ice.

Anglican Church--Sources

774. Historical records survey. New York (City). Inven-
      tory of the church archives of New York City.
      Protestant Episcopal Church in the United States of
      America, diocese of New York, Manhattan, Bronx,
      Richmond ... Prepared by the Historical records
      survey, Division of professional and service proj-
      ects, Work Projects Administration. New York,
      1940. Bibliography: p. 130-135.
      Historical sketch of Church of England, explana-
      tion of organization of the Protestant Episcopal

Church. Each church citation, in chronological order
of organization includes: entry number, popular
name, full corporate title, address; brief sketch of
church, names of first and present clergyman; bibliography of items relevant to the church or institution; references to church records, registers, etc.
This survey of archives is not only concerned with
churches but also includes entries for church-related
schools, hospitals, the Seamen's Institute, social
service agencies, lay organizations, mission societies, etc.

775. Historical records survey. New York (City). Inven-
      tory of the church archives of New York City. Prot-
      estant episcopal church diocese of Long Island ...
      Prepared by the Historical records survey, Division
      of professional and service projects. Work Projects
      Administration. New York: The New York City
      Historical records survey, 1940. 2 v. Bibliogra-
      phy: p. 56.
          Limited to Brooklyn and Queens. Explanation of
      organization of Protestant Episcopal Church. Entries
      for churches and church-related organizations include:
      entry number, name, organization date, address,
      brief historical sketch, name of first and present
      clergymen, references to published materials, and
      citations to church records and registers.

Anglicanism

776. Dawley, Powel M. The story of the General Theolog-
      ical Seminary; a sesquicentennial history, 1817-
      1967. New York: Oxford University, 1969. 390 p.
      Index: p. 375-390.
          Based upon primary sources--diaries, letters,
      journals, reports, bulletins, official records, etc.,
      the emphasis is on the problem of education of the
      clergy and establishment of the first and official
      seminary of the Episcopal Church, the background
      and events that resulted in Seminary customs and
      traditions, highlights, and explanations of student
      and faculty life at different periods, and the biograph-
      ical vignettes detailing the continuity of Seminary
      life--students, teachers, priests, and candidates.

Churches

777. Anstice, H. History of St. George's Church in the
     City of New York, 1752-1811-1911. New York:
     Harper, 1911. 508 p.
          This history has several functions: record note-
     worthy events, sketch the careers of several rectors,
     wardens, vestrymen, and assistant ministers, and
     preserve and make accessible letters and documents
     of value. Appendices list wardens, vestrymen,
     treasurers, organists, sextons, communicants in
     1832, 1845, and 1868, parishioners in 1846, sub-
     scribers to the Chapel fund, 1911, etc.

778. Hall, Edward H. A guide to the Cathedral Church of
     Saint John the Divine in the City of New York. 17th
     ed. New York: The Dean and Chapter of the Cathe-
     dral Church, 1965. 231 p. Illus., port., plans.
          Brief history followed by descriptions, details,
     and interpretations of architectural features, windows,
     bays, tapestries, the choir, the organ, chapels,
     Sanctuary, presbytery, and ambulatory. The exhibit
     hall, garden, and other buildings are also included.
     Appendices list: bishops, deans, present dimensions,
     and comparative data of principal Christian edifices.
     Many photographs.

778a. Kennedy, James W. The unknown worshipper. New
     York: Morehouse-Barlow Co. for the Church of the
     Ascension, 1964. 202 p. Illus., facsim., plan.,
     ports.
          History (1827-1964) of the Episcopal Church of the
     Ascension (10th and 5th Avenue), a church famous
     for its "open doors" and its impact upon the City
     with its support of intellectual freedom, hospitality,
     and spirit of brotherhood. Includes lists of wardens,
     and descriptions and details of various art works--
     paintings, windows, the chapels, and the parish
     house.

779. Russell, Charles H. The Church of the Epiphany,
     1833-1958. New York: Published for the Church of
     Epiphany by Morehouse-Gorhan Co., 1956. 71 p.
     Illus.
          The first three chapters are a reprint of a history
     published on the occasion of this church's seventy-
     fifth anniversary. This account continued the record
     up to 1958.

780. Carmer, Carl L. <u>The years of Grace, 1808-1958.</u>
New York: Grace Church, 1958. 46 p. Illus.
A delightful history of Grace Church, established
by that "mother of all churches," Trinity, one that
emphasizes its social, liberal, and human values.
The narrative stresses the peppery rectors, witty
sextons, controversies, and parishioners such as the
Mad Poet of Broadway rather than programs and
architecture, although these aspects are not neglect-
ed. The author is a well-known historian of New
York State.

781. Stuart, Suzett G. <u>Illustrated guide book with historical
sketch of the Little Church Around the Corner, New
York City.</u> New ed., rev. and reset. New York:
Church of the Transfiguration, 1963. 32 p. Illus.,
ports.
Brief history of the Little Church with some highlights of its service that has made it a national
shrine. Most of the publication is devoted to a description of the architecture of the buildings, its
windows, and other art treasures.
These histories highlight other aspects of this
famous church:

Ray, R. <u>My Little Church Around the Corner.</u> In
collaboration with Villa Stiles. New York: Simon
and Schuster, 1957. 365 p. Illus. This history
includes an account of that thirty years Dr. Ray
served as the third rector of the Little Church
Around the Corner. In that capacity he established
the Episcopal Actors' Guild and as a consequence
his narrative contains many vignettes of the famous
of stage and screen.

Ross, I. <u>Through the lich-gate; a biography of the
Little Church around the Corner; sixteen illustrations
from dry points by Ralph L. Boyer.</u> New York:
W. F. Payson, 1931. 164 p. Front., plates, ports.
Part of the New York City mystique, this church,
which opened in 1848, is famous for its marriages
and its associations with entertainers when actors
were not always socially acceptable.

782. Ehle, J. <u>Shepherd of the streets; the story of the
Reverend James A. Gusweller and his crusade on
the New York West Side.</u> Forward by Harry Golden.
New York: Sloane, 1960. 239 p. Illus.

An account of Reverend Gusweller, Episcopal
priest of the Church of St. Matthew and St. Timothy
and his Puerto Rican parish.

783. DeMille, George E. Saint Thomas Church in the City
and County of New York, 1823-1954. Austin, Texas:
Church Historical Society, 1958. 198 p. Illus.
(Church Historical Society. Publication no. 47).
Bibliography: p. 192.
A scholarly and detailed history that includes the
most famous of society weddings (Miss C. Vanderbilt and the Duke of Marlborough), the organ music
of Dr. Warren, and the witness of this Fifth Avenue
church. Many financial reports, letters, and other
documents are included. The appendices list: rectors, wardens, clerks, officers, etc. (1823-1960).

784. Morehouse, Clifford P. Trinity: mother of churches;
an informal history of Trinity Parish in the City of
New York. New York: Seabury, 1973. 338 p.
Illus. Bibliography: p. 325-327.
An apt title for a record of 275 years of establishing, aiding, or endowing some 1400 churches and
related institutions in this country. This Mother of
churches also has "children" in Britain, the Phil-
ippines, and other parts of the world. Originally
chartered in 1697 to found "The Church in New
York," it has been and continues to be a force in
the City, the state, and the whole Church by its
leadership, sense of mission, and example.

785. Dix, M. A history of the parish of Trinity Church in
the city of New York. Compiled by order of the
corporation and edited by Morgan Dix. New York:
Putnam, 1898. 6 pts.
Pt. 1: To the close of the rectorship of Dr.
Inglis, 1783. Pt. 2: To the close of the rectorship
of Dr. Moore, 1816. Pt. 3: To the close of the
rectorship of Dr. Hobart, 1816-1830. Pt. 4: To
the close of the rectorship of Dr. Hobart and the
rectorship of Dr. Berrian. Pt. 5: The rectorship
of Dr. Morgan Dix. Pt. 6: The rectorship of Dr.
William Thomas Manning, 1908-1921. Each part
has its own index and bibliography.

786. New York. Trinity Church. Churchyards of Trinity
Parish in the City of New York, 1697-1947.

Published in observance of the 250th anniversary of
the founding of Trinity Church. Enl. ed. New York,
1955. 85 p.

A catalog of the monuments and markers that may
be of interest to a visitor--the grave of Charles
Dickens' son, the tombstone with the cryptogram inscription, graves of Revolutionary War soldiers, the
Civil War dead, etc. Biographical data provided for
many of the entries. All three cemeteries--Trinity
Church, St. Paul's Churchyard, and Trinity Church
Cemetery--are now maintained and opened to the
public as parks. Final section: list, with portraits,
of former Trinity Church rectors, 1697-1966.

Baptists

787. De Plata, William R. Tell it from Calvary; the record
of a sustained Gospel witness from Calvary Baptist
Church of New York City since 1847. New York:
Calvary Baptist Church, 1972. 189 p. Illus., ports.

A history (1847-1971) of one church's evangelism
and missionary activities.

788. Schoonover, M. Making all things human; a church in
East Harlem. Foreword by William Stringfellow.
New York: Holt, Rinehart and Winston, 1969. 188
p.

An intimate and special view of urban problems
by a white crippled pastor of a Black Baptist church
between the late 1950's up to and including the riots
and civil rights movement of the 1960's.

Catholic Church (Roman)

789. Historical records survey. New York (City). Inventory of the church archives in New York City. Roman Catholic Church, archdiocese of New York....
Prepared by the New York City WPA, Historical
records Survey, Division of community service projects. New York City, 1941. Vol. 2. Bibliography:
p. 152-158.

Entries (219) for churches include: entry number,
popular name, full corporate name, organization
date, brief sketch of church history, name of first

and present pastor, name of parochial school,
address, organization date, number of students
(by sex), and name of religious order providing
teachers. Also bibliography of related items.
Excellent historical presentation of the establishment of Catholic faith and institutions in New
York State; also good explanation of the Uniate
churches in the U.S. and New York. Very
useful outline of the role, function of the different
offices in the organization of the Roman Catholic
hierarchy.
N.B.: Volume one of this inventory was never
completed.

790. Smith, John T. The Catholic Church in New York;
a history of the New York diocese from its establishment in 1808 to the present time ... with introduction by the Right Reverend Joseph F. Mooney,
v.g. New York and Boston: Hall & Locke company,
1908. 2 vol.
Includes details about the Church's organization,
its various bishops and outstanding priests, the establishment of monasteries and convents, Catholic
laity's political affiliations, newspapers and magazines, the development of a Catholic educational system, church-related social organizations and clubs,
conflicts within the Church, relations with Rome and
Europe--in a word--a social, religious, economic,
political profile of Catholics and the Roman Catholic
Church.

791. New York. Church of Our Lady of Esperanza. Our
Lady of Esperanza, New York: fiftieth anniversary.
New York: Prepared by Customboo, 1963. Unpaged.
Illus.
Separate sections are devoted to the art and his-
tory of the second "Spanhis" Roman church estab-
lished in the City; particularly interesting is its
associations with its principal benefactor, Mr.
Hungtington, a non-Catholic, scholar, poet, and
founder of the Hispanic Society of America.

792. Browne, Henry J. St. Ann's on East Twelfth Street,
New York City, 1852-1952. New York: Roman Cath-
olic Church of St. Ann, 1952. 65 p. Illus.
The growth, problems, and social history of New
York City are reflected and recorded in this

centennial parish history. Interviews and printed
sources combined with the goal of objectivity contribute to this document's value, as do the photographs
of the church's interior and the register of clergy.

793. Browne, Henry J. The Parish of St. Michael, 1857-
      1957; a century of grace on the West Side. New
      York: Church of St. Michael, 1957. 72 p.
      Based upon unpublished and archival sources,
      newspaper clippings, interviews, etc., this parish
      history provides unique insight into the life of Irish
      immigrants. Also has lists of assistants, trustees,
      lay teachers, priests, and religious.

794. Kelly, George A. The story of St. Monica's parish,
      New York City, 1870-1954. New York: Monica
      Press, 1954. 154 p.
      An account of this church's impact upon its York-
      ville parishioners; appendices list: the religious of
      the parish, presidents of the various parish socie-
      ties, chairmen of Catholic Charities, faculty of the
      school, etc.

795. Burton, Katherine (Kurz). The dream lives forever;
      the story of St. Patrick's Cathedral. Foreword by
      Francis Cardinal Spellman. New York: Longmans,
      Green, 1960. 238 p. Illus. Bibliography: p. 229-230.
      A detailed history (1858-1959) of a great church,
      its construction, influence, and its associations with
      priests, peoples, bishops, national, and world events.
      An earlier work:

      Farley, John Murphy, Cardinal, 1842-1918. History
      of St. Patrick's Cathedral. New York: Society for
      the propagation of the faith, Archdiocese of New
      York, 1908. 262 p. Front., plates, ports, plan.
      An extremely detailed chronicle of the circumstances
      preceding and involving the construction of this
      church; the social, economic, religious, and archi-
      tectural factors receive complete coverage. In many
      ways it is also a history of Roman Catholicism in
      New York City.

796. Makulee, Louis L. Church of St. Stanislaus Bishop
      and Martyr, on East Seventh Street in New York
      City, 1874-1954. New York: Roman Catholic Church
      of St. Stanislaus, B. M., 1954. 240 p. Bibliography:
      p. 238-239.

Based upon documents, parish registers, and interviews, the eighty-year history of this church is also an account of the economic, social, and religious problems of three generations of Polish immigrants and their adaption to their new country. A detailed table of contents compensates for the lack of an index. Of particular interest are the brief descriptions of the various Polish American religious organizations, charitable societies, mutual benefit associations, military groups and cultural societies and their connections with members of this parish.

Saints

797. Di Donato, Pietro. Immigrant saint; the life of Mother Cabrini. New York: McGraw-Hill, 1960. 246 p.
    A very readable biography of the Italian nun who came to New York, worked among the Italian immigrants--establishing schools, orphanages, classes in Christian doctrine, and Columbus Hospital. She extended her activities nationally and finally even to Europe and Latin America. The first American saint, she was canonized July 7, 1946.

798. Dirvin, Joseph I. Mrs. Seton, foundress of the American Sisters of Charity. New York: Farrar, Straus and Cudahy, 1962. 498 p. Illus. Bibliography: p. 465-469.
    Written prior to the canonization of this second American saint, this biography makes extensive use of quotations from her letters and papers, thus allowing her to present her own sanctity, character, and personality. A convert to Catholicism, she established hospitals, orphanages, and schools; but her close association with New York City and Columbia University did not diminish her impact upon the emerging nation. Canonized September 14, 1975.

Eastern Orthodox

799. Historical records survey. New York (City). Inventory of the church archives in New York City. Eastern orthodox churches and the Armenian church in America. Prepared by the Historical records

survey, Division of professional and service projects. Work projects administration. New York,
1940. 178 p. Bibliography: p. 153-160.
Historical background followed by explanation of
organizational structure and the relationships between
the different churches (Syrian, Greek, Ukrainian,
Rumanian, Bulgarian, Armenian, and Carpatho-Rus-
sian). Entries are chronological by synodical, di-
ocesan, or archdiocesan body; each entry for each
church includes: entry number, popular name, full
corporate name, sketch of church's history, name
of present and first clergymen, bibliography of relevant items with additional references to records
and registers of the church.

Evangelism

800. Mitchell, C. God in the Garden; the story of the Billy
Graham New York crusade. Garden City, New York:
Doubleday, 1957. 195 p. Illus.
Documents the largest and longest, to date (5/15-
9/1/57), series of evangelistic meetings--the thou-
sands that gathered in the Garden, Yankee Stadium,
and Times Square. Relates case histories, conver-
sions, as well as takes the reader behind the scenes
--the organization, the committees, the planning,
use of media, etc. Includes the sermons presented.

Friends

801. Historical records survey. New York (City). New
York City church archives. Religious society of
Friends. Catalogue. Records in possession of, or
relating to, the two New York yearly meetings of the
Religious society of Friends and their subordinate
meetings. Compiled by John Cox, Jr., Chairman,
Joint committee on records. Copied by the Historical records survey.... New York: The Historical
records survey, 1940. 224 num. ℓ.
Cites the Yearly Meeting (with committees and
miscellaneous affairs), the Quarterly Meetings, and
then the Monthly Meetings are listed with all known
records of each meeting down to the Separation of
1828. Since that date the records of the Fifteenth
Street Branch are followed by the records of the

Twentieth Street branch. This compilation gives the
name of every meeting that, at any time, was part
of either branch of the New York Yearly meeting:
with location in township and county, date of meeting
for worship, date of Discipline meeting established,
brief history, and descriptive list of its records.

Judaism

802. Monsky, J. Within the gates; a religious, social, and
     cultural history, 1837-1962. New York: Congrega-
     tion Shaare Zedek, 1964. 180 p.
        A chronological presentation of the events and
     activities of the first 125 years of Congregation
     Shaare Zedek, the third oldest Hebrew Congregation
     in New York City. Appendices list founders, presi-
     dents, spiritual leaders, cantors.

803. Pool, David de S. and Tamar de S. Pool. An old
     faith in the New World; portrait of Shearith Israel,
     1654-1954. New York: Columbia University, 1955.
     595 p. Bibliography: p. 555-562.
        Scholarly but very readable history of the popular-
     ly known Spanish and Portuguese Synagogue, a nar-
     rative of both a congregation and a synagogue and
     their contributions to America. Includes a reading
     list (547-553), glossary (537-545), and lists of the
     "Servants of the Congregation" (502-503).

Lutheranism

804. Historical records survey. New York (City). Inven-
     tory of the church archives in New York City. Lu-
     theran. New York City. Historical record survey,
     Division of professional and service projects. Work
     Projects Administration. 1940. 152 p. Bibliog-
     raphy: p. 128-131.
        Preceded by a historical sketch of Lutheranism
     in the U.S. and an explanation of its organizational
     structure, each entry for a church, in chronological
     order under the synods, includes: entry number,
     popular name, full corporate name, organizational
     date, address, brief profile of the church, names of
     first and present pastors, and a bibliography of
     items related to the church. References may also

be made to the registers and records of the specific
church. Also has "Index to Ministers": p. 135-
139; "Index to Churches and Organizations," p. 132-
134; "Chronological Index by Borough": p. 140-143;
and a "Street Location Index": p. 144-151.

Methodist Church

805. Historical records survey. New York (City). Inventory of the church archives of New York City. The
Methodist Church. Prepared by the Historical records survey, Division of professional and service
projects administration. Sponsored by the Mayor of
the City of New York, the Hon. Fiorello H. La
Guardia. New York: The Historical records survey,
1940. 216 numbered ℓ. Bibliography: p. 187-194.
    Historical sketch followed by explanatory notes
concerning the organizational structure. Each entry
is chronological under its administrative body and
includes: entry number, popular name (of church or
institution), full corporate title, organizational date,
brief historical sketch, name of first and present
clergymen, bibliography of items relevant to the
church or institution. Also references to records.
Under the various "conferences" there are citations,
not only to churches, but also to hospitals, homes
for the aged, boards of museums, seminaries, and
other church-related institutions. Several indexes
to ministers, churches, organizations, and additional
bibliographies, including the "Bibliography of annual
conferences, state, and regional histories": p. 168-
176.

Presbyterianism

806. Historical records survey. New York (City). Inventory of the church archives in New York City. Prepared by the Historical records survey, Division of
professional and service projects, Work Projects
Administration. Presbyterian Church in the United
States of America. New York: The Historical records survey, 1940. 160 p. Bibliography: p. 133-
140.
    Lists every Presbyterian congregation in the five
boroughs of Greater New York. Preceded by a

historical sketch and explanation of the organization
of congregations, each citation includes: entry number, corporate title, date of organization, address;
brief history of each church, date, names of first
and present pastor; clergymen; bibliography of items
relating to the particular church; and citations to
church records and registers.

807.   New York.   Fifth Avenue Presbyterian Church.   A
       noble landmark of New York; the Fifth Avenue Pres-
       byterian Church, 1808-1958.   New York, 1960.   174
       p.   Illus.
       A history (1808-1958) of this institution with
       separate sections on church music, church organi-
       zations, and lists of ministers, elders, trustees,
       deacons, etc.

808.   Van Norden, Warner M.   The fatness of Thy house,
       1807-1924.   New York, 1953.   242 p.   Illus., ports,
       maps.
       A very detailed, scholarly, and chronological his-
       tory of the Fifth Avenue Presbyterian Church (1807-
       1924), limited to the period represented by the first
       ten ministers.

Reformed Church of America

809.   Historical records survey.   New York (City).   Inven-
       tory of the church archives of New York City.   Pre-
       pared by the Historical records survey, Division of
       professional and service projects.   Work projects
       administration.   Reformed Church in America.   New
       York: The Historical records survey, 1939.   95 p.
       Bibliography: p. 79-86; Indexes for ministers, p.
       87-89; alphabetic, p. 90-92; and chronological index,
       p. 93-95.
       A historical sketch of the Dutch Reformed Church
       is preceded by an explanation of its organization and
       governance followed by entries for churches in the
       five boroughs and their church related organizations.
       Each entry includes: its number, popular name,
       corporate title, organization date, address, a brief
       sketch of the church (or organization), name of first
       and present clergymen, bibliography of relevant
       items, and citations to church records.

Theosophy

810. Murphet, H. When daylight comes: a biography of
      Helena Pegrovna Blavatsky. Wheaton, Ill.: Theo-
      sophical Pub. House, 1975. 277 p. Bibliography:
      266-274.
         Based upon diaries, letters, journals, and other
      documentary sources, this portrayal includes living
      Mahatmas and psychic phenomena as some of the
      realities of H. P. B.'s life while steering a course
      between the two false legends: that she was a craf-
      ty, immoral charlatan and free lover and/or she
      was a saint, perfect and infallible.

Unitarianism

811. Kring, Walter D. Liberals among the orthodox: Uni-
      tarian beginnings in New York City, 1819-1839.
      Boston: Beacon, 1974. 278 p. Illus.
         Complete minutes of all meetings contribute to
      the thoroughness and detail of this narrative which
      is a record of remarkable ministers and laymen
      that created what is now known as the Unitarian
      Church of All Souls. Appendices list the signers of
      the Covenant, officers of the Church, and includes
      biographical sketches of laymen and laywomen who
      were prominent in the life of the church.

                    SOCIAL CONDITIONS
                    (general to specific)

812. Berenyi, J. The quality of life in urban America;
      New York City: a regional and national comparative
      analysis (using urban, economic, social, environ-
      mental, and general indicators and indices to meas-
      ure the quality of life). New York: City of New
      York, Office of Administration, 1971. 2 v. Illus.
         Initial effort was to develop a meaningful set of
      urban environmental, economic, and general indices
      and indicators for comparative measures of quality
      of life in New York City. Care has been taken to
      cite bibliographic sources. Final section primarily
      of statistical data: crime, environmental quality,
      revenue and budget, taxation, welfare and social
      services.

813.   First National City Bank. Economics Dept. Profile
       of a city. Prepared by members of the Economics
       Dept. Introd. by Nathan Glazer. New York: Mc-
       Graw Hill, 1972. 273 p. Illus.
          A series of studies on aspects of New York City
       life--poverty, education, housing, transportation,
       environment, city government--by economics that
       assess these urban problems, evaluate them, identi-
       fy alternatives, and suggest practical solutions.

814.   Jones, Thomas J. The sociology of a New York City
       block. New York: AMS Press, 1968. 136 p.
       (Studies in history, economics and public law, no.
       55). Reprint of the 1904 edition.
          An attempt "to study a New York City street
       according to a complete system of social principles."
       While the techniques and principles of 1904 require
       reader caution the information about the people,
       their life style, and urban living conditions in gen-
       eral remains valuable.

815.   De Forest, Robert W. and L. Veiffer, eds. The ten-
       ement house problem. New York: Arno, c. 1903.
       516 p. (The rise of urban America). Reprinted
       1970. Bibliography: p. 117-118.
          The report of the New York State Tenement House
       Commission of 1900 was adopted and became law in
       1901. This is an account of the results and progress
       made in tenement reform and a guide of what was
       yet needed. Detailed coverage of the financial as-
       pects of tenement house operations, sanitation, fire
       escapes, tuberculosis, fires, etc., all very dispas-
       sionately recorded. A comprehensive view of one
       aspect of living conditions at the turn of the century.
       Appendix IV: "A History of Tenement House Legis-
       lation in New York, 1850-1900."

816.   Riis, Jacob A. The battle with the slum. New York:
       Macmillan, 1902. 465 p. Illus., port.
          Written three years after "How the Other Half
       Lives," this is a review of the progress made to-
       ward the elimination of slums and slum way of life.
       Preceded by arguments concerning how slums affect
       and infect every citizen, Riis' accounts of slum peo-
       ple and their plight provide the human factor bal-
       ancing his logical rhetoric.
          A companion volume:

        . How the other half lives; studies among the
tenements of New York. Introd. by Donald N. Big-
elow. New York: Hill and Wang, 1962, c. 1957.
231 p. Originally published in 1890. A police re-
porter and colorful newspaperman, the author became
famous as a reformer concerned with housing and
slum conditions. This, his first of many books, had
the objective of creating an awareness of slum hor-
rors in the American people. The appendix has comparative and historical statistics.

817. Brace, Charles L. The dangerous classes of New
      York and twenty years' work among them. 3rd ed.
      with addenda. New York: Wynkoop & Hallebeck,
      1880. 468 p.
      An account of the condition of children in New
York City; causes of crime, various institutions,
reforms and projects to combat the circumstances
resulting in delinquency, the need for additional services to children and an exposition of the elements
resulting in and need for successful crime preven-
tion and social reform. Very detailed account.

818. Kapp, F. Immigration and the Commissioners of Em-
      igration. New York: Arno Press and the New York
      Times, 1969. 241 p. (The American immigration
      collection). Reprint of the 1870 ed.
      An attempt to establish the "facts" concerning
immigration despite American society's indifference
to this social force and its impact upon the nation.
Based upon documents--reports and minutes of the
Commissioners of Emigration, the Common Council
of New York City, comptrollers' reports, acts, and
papers of the U.S. Senate and the New York Legis-
lature--this study examines the attraction of the U.S.
for immigrants, the trials of the voyages, the aspects of arrival in New York, the function and objectives of the Board of the Commissioners of Emigration of the State of New York, the function, organization, and administration of Castle Garden and
Ward's Island. Appendix: statistical data.

819. Mohl, Raymond A. Poverty in New York, 1783-1825.
      New York: Oxford University, 1971. 318 p. (The
      Urban Life in America series).
      A study of New York City, a history of its social
welfare efforts, public, during a period of social,

economic, and political transition. Provides perspective on the problem and issues of poverty and
some attempted remedies.

SEE ALSO 678, 746, 772, 796, 797, 993.

Criminology and Juvenile Delinquency
(chronological by scope of work, then
by specific topic)

820.   Greenberg, D.   Crime and law enforcement in the Col-
       ony of New York, 1691-1776. Ithaca, New York:
       Cornell University, 1976. 259 p. Bibliography: p.
       237-252.
           The author uses a select sample of the popula-
       tion--defendants in colonial New York courts--to
       highlight the value system and issues of that colony's
       social history. He questions: who were these peo-
       ple and what happened to them as they were pro-
       cessed through the system of criminal justice? By
       finding the answers to these questions he hopes to
       illustrate colonial New York's world view.

821.   Pickett, R.   House of Refuge; origins of juvenile re-
       form in New York State, 1815-1856. Syracuse: Syr-
       acuse University, 1969. 217 p. Tables. (A New
       York State study).
           The House of Refuge closed its doors in 1935,
       but this history is limited to the origins and devel-
       opment of the Refuge idea before and including the
       period when it acquired a national acceptance. This
       is a chronicle of the activities, hopes, and fears of
       the small group of men who in the interest of moral
       reform created from informal discussions one of the
       world's largest institutions for juveniles.

822.   Kahn, Alfred J.   Police and children; a study of the
       Juvenile Aid Bureau of the New York City Police De-
       partment. New York: Citizen's Committee on Chil-
       dren of New York City, 1951. 83 p. Tables. Bib-
       liography: p. 83.
           The organization, structure, objectives, and func-
       tions of the Juvenile Aid Bureau with case histories.

823.   Furman, Sylvan S.   Reaching the unreached; fundamen-
       tal aspects of the program of the New York City

Youth Board. New York: New York City Youth
Board, 1952. 147 p. Illus.
    Established in 1947 in the Mayor's Office under
the auspices of the State Youth Board, this agency
coordinates other agencies' activities, makes studies, seeks to remove causes of juvenile delinquency,
provides information on juvenile delinquency, and
approves applications for funds for public and private agencies operating recreation and youth projects. However, its primary function and objective
is to "actively and aggressively go out to help parents and children when either are in or are approach-
ing some kind of trouble." Particularly those who
do not ordinarily seek help though they may need it.

824. Myers, Chauncie K. Light the dark streets. Green-
      wich, Conn.: Seabury, 1957. 156 p. Illus.
          Overcrowded, low incomes, poverty, crime, a
      variety of religious, ethnic, and cultural backgrounds
      all create conflicts and tensions in Manhattan's Low-
      er East Side. This is the story of the efforts of
      the clerical and lay staff of St. Augustine's Chapel
      to help the youth of that area, prevent delinquency,
      provide guidance and concern.

825. Pierce, Bradford K. A half-century with juvenile de-
      linquents; the New York House of Refuge and its
      times. With a new introd. by Sanford J. Fox.
      Montclair, N.J.: Patterson Smith, 1969. 384 p.
      Illus., ports. Reprint of the 1869 ed.
          Within the historical context of European and
      American prisons and prison reforms, this account
      of the House of Refuge is positive and detailed. The
      introduction by S. J. Fox must be read to properly
      appreciate and evaluate the social and moral reform-
      ers that created child welfare institutions during the
      19th century.

826. Kahn, Alfred J. A court for children; a study of the
      New York City Children's Court. New York: Col-
      umbia University, 1953. 359 p.
          An evaluation of the Court's goals, how well they
      are achieved, the deficiencies and defects with some
      recommendations concerning corrective measures
      and positive improvements. Provides another in-
      sight into the preventive aspect of juvenile delin-
      quency.

827.   Peck, Harris B. and J. Horowitz. A new pattern for
       mental health services in a children's court. Spring-
       field, Ill.: Charles C. Thomas, 1958. 82 p.
       Generated by the Court Intake Project conducted
       by the New York City Court of Domestic Relations
       the report seeks to enlist the support of all the
       Court's professional staff, the judges, and the pro-
       bation department personnel for more and intensive
       mental health services for the delinquent children.

828.   Tappan, Paul W. Delinquent girls in court, a study
       of the Wayward Minor Court of New York. New
       York: Columbia University, 1947. 265 p. Bib-
       liography: p. 243-251.
       An analysis of the administrative, judicial, and
       social processes of this juvenile court in an attempt
       to study the ends and means of that Court; the adap-
       tions and innovations used to attain the ascribed
       ends. The author also makes some recommenda-
       tions for the improvement of the Court's effective-
       ness. This is one of the few extensive studies of
       a lower court.

SEE ALSO 696-711.

Race Relations and Minorities

829.   Benjamin, G. Race relations and the New York City
       Commission on Human Rights. Ithaca, New York:
       Cornell University, 1972. 274 p. Bibliography: p.
       261-268. Originally the author's thesis, Columbia
       University, 1970.
       A thirty-year history that includes the circum-
       stances that created the Commission and an analysis
       of its operations: within the context of city politics,
       conflicts created by and among the minorities it
       sought to serve and the administrative errors (lack
       of legal powers, no precise definitions of functions,
       etc.) that it was required to operate within.

830.   Kantrowitz, N. Ethnic and racial segregation in the
       New York metropolis; residential patterns among
       white ethnic groups, Blacks, and Puerto Ricans.
       Foreword by Nathan Glazer. New York: Praeger,
       1973. 104 p. (Praeger special studies in U.S. eco-
       nomic, social, and political issues).

New York City

Separation and segregation of ethnic and racial
groups and economic classes within those groups are
a result of conservative factors, not very susceptible
to planned change--these are the findings of this
study. A wealth of statistical data.

831. Bellush, Jewel L. and Stephen M. David, eds. Race
and politics in New York City; five studies in policy-
making. New York: Praeger, 1971. 202 p.
Using issues of major concern to the black community in the 1960's (health, education, welfare,
housing, and police) the thesis of political scientists
(pluralists) claiming that urban political systems are
democratic and responsive to the needs/demands of
its citizens, is challenged.

832. Glazer, N. and Daniel P. Moynihan. Beyond the melt-
ing pot: the Negroes, Puerto Ricans, Jews, Italians,
and Irish of New York City. Cambridge, Mass.:
M.I.T., 1963. 360 p. Map. (Publication of the
Joint Center for Urban Studies of the Massachusetts
Institute of Technology and Harvard University).
Chapter notes: p. 325-247.
Rejecting the melting pot concept, discusses the
Negroes, Puerto Ricans, Jews, Italians, and the
Irish in terms of cultural and religious values as
well as political ones. Actually provides detailed
analysis of each group's unique qualities and problems.

Chinese

833. Chen, Julia I. The Chinese community in New York:
a study in their cultural adjustment, 1920-1940:
dissertation, American University, Washington, 1941.
San Francisco: R. and E. Research Associates,
1974. 127 p. Bibliography: p. 123-127.
Objectives of this study of the second largest U.S.
Chinese community includes an analysis of New
York's Chinatown: its social, political, and religious
institutions, its philosophy and behavior patterns, the
problems of its second generation, relationships with
China and its adopted country. Emphasizes the need
for improved recreational and social conditions and
to eliminate racial misunderstandings. N.B.: Study
was completed in 1941.

834. Kuo, Chia-ling. Social and political change in New
York's Chinatown: the role of voluntary associations.

New York: Praeger, 1977. 160 p. (Praeger special studies in U.S. economic, social, and political issues). Bibliography: p. 154-160.

Extensive historical background with an examination of Chinatown's voluntary associations as they evolved while assisting in the community's adaption, adjustment during increased social change and political maturity as that community interacted with the larger society.

SEE ALSO 514.

Dominicans

834a. Hendricks, G. The Dominican diaspora: from the Dominican Republic to New York City--villagers in transition. New York: Teachers College Press, Columbia University, 1974. 171 p. (Publications of the Center for Education in Latin America). Bibliography: p. 161-166.

An analysis, from a social anthropological viewpoint, of the Dominican migration describing the acculturation process within the context and perspective of the older ethnic and national groups. Appendices contain statistical data.

Finns

835. A history of Finnish American organizations in Greater New York, 1891-1976: a project of the Greater New York Finnish Bicentennial Planning Committee, inc. edited, translated and in part written by Katri Ekman, Corinne Olli, John B. Olli. New York: The Committee, 1976. 311 p.

Arranged by category: athletic clubs, churches, cooperative movement, kaleva lodges, labor, Masonic clubs, musical organizations, newspapers, and other diverse organizations, (each brief history 1-3 pages) usually includes photographs.

Irish

836. O'Brien, Michael J. In Old New York; the Irish dead in Trinity and St. Paul's churchyards ... New York: The American Irish historical society, 1928. 262 p. Front., plates, facsim.

A history of the considerable Irish contribution to the history of New York City from its early

settlement based upon the baptismal, burial, and
marriage records of Trinity House, tombstone inscriptions of Trinity Church and St. Paul's Chapel
plus additional data from official sources. Includes
many of these inscriptions, lists of marriages (con-
tracting parties, and date) from church records,
wills (testators, legatees, date and where recorded),
legatees, letters of administrators, deeds, and convey-
ances.

SEE ALSO 792, 793.

Italians

837. Cordasco, F. Italian Americans: a guide to informa-
      tion sources. Gale, 1972. 222 p.
          A classified, partially annotated bibliography of
      about 2,000 citations to reference sources: bibliog-
      raphies, directories, histories, and other works ar-
      ranged by topic--history, the social sciences, etc.,
      or by form.

838. Parenti, M. Ethnic and political attitudes: a depth
      study of Italian Americans. New York: Arno, 1975.
      344 p. (The Italian American experience). Bibliog-
      raphy: p. 336-344. Author's thesis, Yale, 1962.
          Three generations of Italo-American males, repre-
      senting six families, were interviewed on topics of
      ethnic, personal, and political importance in an at-
      tempt to identify the ways ethnic attitudes and expe-
      rience interacts and influences political opinion and
      values.
          Historical perspective is provided by:

      Italians in the city: health and related social needs.
      New York: Arno, 1975. 138 p. Illus. (The Ital-
      ian American experience). A collection of reprints:
      The Italian colonies of New York City by Natonio
      Mangano (M.A. thesis, 1903); The Effects of urban
      congestion on Italian women and children by Antonio
      Stella, published in 1908 by W. Wood; John C. Geb-
      hart's The Growth and development of Italian chil-
      dren in New York City, Publication no. 132 of the
      New York Association for Improving the Condition of
      the Poor; Some special health problems of Italians
      in New York City: a preliminary survey, first
      printed in the Quarterly Bulletin, New York City,
      Dept. of Health, vol. 2, no. 3, 1934.

Mariano, John H. The Italian contribution to American democracy. New York: Arno, 1975 (c. 1921). 317 p. Tables. Bibliography: p. 311-317. Originally author's thesis, New York University, 1920. Particularly valuable for the socio-economic data on: population, health, literacy, social organizations and clubs, etc. concerning Italians in New York City. The section on the Italian American contribution may suffer due to the hindsight provided by the half-century time lapse.

Miranda, Edward J. and Ino J. Rossi. New York City's Italians: census characteristics at a glance. New York: Italian-American Center for Urban Affairs, 1976. 173 p. Bibliography: p. 172-173. A study designed to accurately estimate the total numbers of Italians of all generations living in the five boroughs of the City of New York. It also examined this group's residential patterns, educational level, income, and poverty structure; by comparisons with the two larger ethnic groups--Blacks and Puerto Ricans and the all-white group, the Italian-Americans' status is profiled. Forty-three appendices of statistical data complement the forty-six tables of additional information.

SEE ALSO 844.

Jews
(chronological by
scope of work)

839. Birmingham, S. The Grandees; America's Sephardic elite. New York: Harper & Row, 1971. 368 p. Bibliography: p. 355-357.
      The story of some 200 American Jewish families that trace their origins back to 1654 and beyond to medieval Portugal and Spain where they, the Sephardim, were an elite, "the nobility of Jewry" as scientists, poets, jurists, bankers to kings, philosophers, etc. Similar contributions in government, commerce, literature, medicine, law, education, etc. were made during America's development. This narrative highlights some of those accomplishments while providing insights into and about the members of this Sephardic community and its values.

840. Birmingham, S. "Our Crowd"; the great Jewish fam-
      ilies of New York. New York: Harper & Row,
      1967. 404 p.
      "Our crowd" included hundreds of people; the au-
      thor focused upon those individuals that were in his
      opinion exceptional or most representative of their
      times. "Our crowd" refers to that group of German
      Jewish banking families, known nationally and inter-
      nationally for their banking and industrial expertise,
      government service, and patronage of the arts, edu-
      cation, and science. In the author's opinion, as a
      cohesive and recognizable part of New York society,
      they were the closest approximation to Aristocracy
      that the city and even the county had seen.

841. Pool, David de S. Portraits etched in stone; early
      Jewish settlers, 1682-1831. New York: Columbia
      University, 1952. 543 p. Illus., genealogical ta-
      bles. Bibliography: p. 513-517.
      A history of the Congregation Shearith Israel's
      burial ground--known as the New Bowery Cemetery,
      the Oliver Street Cemetery, or Chatham Square
      Cemetery. Beginning in 1682, this second oldest
      existing New York City cemetery reflects the his-
      tory of the Jewish community of New York for three
      centuries. Part of that history is indicated by the
      introductory essays devoted to early settlers, title
      deeds, threats to the cemetery, the monuments, the
      rights to burial, etc. The final half is devoted to
      178 biographies of individuals buried in the cemetery.
      The appendices include an alphabetical and chrono-
      logical register.

842. Grinstein, Hyman B. The rise of the Jewish com-
      munity of New York, 1654-1860. Philadelphia: Por-
      cupine, 1976. 645 p. (Perspectives in American
      history, no. 27). Bibliography: p. 597-607.
      Emphasis has been placed upon the second quarter
      of the 19th century to 1860 and is primarily con-
      cerned with the "interior" life of New York City
      Jews--their religion, culture, and the institutions
      and social activities that developed in the Jewish
      community. The cultural, economic, social, and
      political activities that they participated in with
      Christians has been excluded.

843. Howe, I. and K. Libo. World of our fathers. New
      York: Harcourt Brace Jovanovich, c. 1976. 714 p.
      Bibliography: p. 685-693.
      A social and cultural history of East European
      Jews in New York City; based upon English and
      Yiddish memoirs, writings, the Yiddish press, ma-
      terials from American newspapers, journals; other
      secondary sources; personal interviews, and to a
      degree, fiction relating to this facet of American
      life.

844. Kessner, T. The golden door: Italian and Jewish
      immigrant mobility in New York City, 1880-1915.
      New York: Oxford University, 1977. 224 p. Bib-
      liography: p. 214-216.
      An analysis of the upward mobility of these "New
      Immigrants"--poor, ill equipped--their successes or
      lack of them in their first thirty-five years in New
      York City contributes to our knowledge of social ad-
      vancement and urban life at the turn of the century.
      Comparisons of one group with the other, this urban
      history, using the new techniques of quantitative his-
      tory very carefully, provides new insight into the
      factors of Americanization as well as data about
      specific immigrant problems and attitudes.

845. Sanders, R. The Downtown Jews: portraits of an
      immigrant generation. New York: New American
      Library, 1977. 395 p. Illus. Bibliography: p.
      382-385.
      A review and history of the politics, newspapers,
      labor movements, literature, the Yiddish theatre,
      and all the other cultural and social factors that made
      the Lower East Side a famous Jewish neighborhood.

846. Weinstein, G. The ardent eighties. New York: Arno,
      c. 1928. 182 p. Illus. (The Modern Jewish ex-
      perience). Reprinted 1975.
      Autobiographical account of a Jewish immigrant
      in New York City, the living and working conditions
      of the 19th century, his involvement with unions and
      reform movements, and his introduction to new ideas
      and ideals. The second part of this book contains
      brief sketches of people prominent in social reforms
      --Father McGlynn, Josephine Shaw Lowell, Charles
      F. Wingate, etc. or compact essays on cultural or
      political aspects of New York--Cooper Union, The
      Liberal Club, the Astor Library, etc.

847.   Hassidic Corporation for Urban Concerns. The study
       of poverty in the Jewish community, City of New
       York. Prepared by Joel Rosenshein (and) Sol Rib-
       ner. Brooklyn, 1973. 91 p. Maps, tables.
            A preliminary study of the incidence of Jewish
       poverty and the outlines of a sociological profile of
       poverty among Jews that indicates some very real
       differences between the Jewish poor and the non-
       Jewish poor with particular reference to the kosher
       Jewish family and its food costs. Careful, detailed
       statistical data included.

848.   Rabinowitz, D. The other Jews; portraits in poverty.
       Introd. by Bertram H. Gold. New York: Institute
       of Human Relations Press, American Jewish Com-
       mittee, 1972. 63 p.
            Eight stories demonstrating different aspects and
       consequences of the "myth of universal Jewish afflu-
       ence." This deception includes the Jewish commu-
       nity and the objective of this small book is to
       awaken that community to several needs--better and
       more information about the Jewish poor, the special
       reasons, cultural factors, and circumstances result-
       ing in a poverty situation, the human consequences
       of the condition, and the role, present and projected,
       of Jewish organizations and agencies regarding the
       Jewish poor.

849.   American Jewish Congress. Commission on Urban
       Affairs. The Jewish poor and the anti-poverty pro-
       gram; a study of the Economic opportunity act, its
       failure to help the Jewish poor, and recommendations
       for its revision so that all of this nation's poor may
       share more equitably in its programs and assistance.
       New York, 1971. 45 ℓ.
            This study contrasts the traditional Jewish ap-
       proach to the poor with the prevailing American
       modern one. Includes a review of the Economic
       Opportunity Act and how its language deters Jewish
       participation, followed by a discussion of the pover-
       ty program in New York City, the number of Jewish
       poor and their participation in the New York City
       poverty program. Concludes with a series of rec-
       ommendations designed to increase that participation.

850.   Landesman, Alter F. Brownsville; the birth, devel-
       opment and passing of a Jewish community in New

York. 2nd ed. with a foreword by Louis Finkelstein.
New York: Bloch, 1971. 418 p. Bibliography: p.
376-380.
  A chronicle of the establishment, growth, contributions, and decline of the Jewish communities of
East New York and Brownsville, neighborhoods of
Brooklyn, New York. Based upon books, biographies, magazine articles, memoirs, newspapers,
novels, studies, other printed sources and interviews, this is "an historic record of a vital Jewish
center that has made a distinctive contribution to
the life of our great metropolis."

SEE ALSO 22, 29, 802, 803.

Negroes
(chronologically retrospective)

851. Shapiro, Fred C. and James W. Sullivan. Race riots,
      New York, 1964. New York: Crowell, 1964. 222
      p. Map.
        A day-by-day account of the riots in Harlem and
      Bedford-Stuyvesant area. Appendix: text of the re-
      port of the District Attorney of New York County.

852. Citizens' Protective League, New York. Story of the
      riot. New York: Arno, 1969. 79 p. (Mass vio-
      lence in America). Reprint of the 1900 edition.
        A statement about New York City police brutality
      during a night of riots against Negroes (August 16,
      1900). Official condonement, legal evasions, and
      mayoral indifference resulted in the creation of the
      Citizens' Protective League, September 3, 1900,
      which published this account of the riot and the sup-
      porting sworn affidavits.

853. Headley, Joel T. The great riots of New York, 1712
      to 1783; including a full and complete account of the
      four days' draft riot of 1863. With a new introd. by
      James McCague. New York: Dover, 1971. 335 p.
      Illus. Originally published in 1873.
        Accounts of riots either reconstructed from rec-
      ords and/or witnessed by the author. Analytical
      table of contents substitutes for an index. Major
      portion of this book is devoted to the draft riots of
      1863.

854. Horsmanden, D. The New York conspiracy. Edited
      with an introd. by Thomas J. Davis. Boston: Bea-
      con, 1971. 491 p.
          Actually the day-by-day record of the trial of over
      one hundred and fifty slaves and twenty white per-
      sons for plotting for purposes of theft and arson.
      Verdict resulted in thirteen Negroes burned at the
      stake, sixteen others and four whites being hung, and
      more than seventy other blacks and whites being ban-
      ished from North America. A primary document
      illuminating colonial New York's attitudes between
      rich and poor, black and white.

855. Andrews, Charles C. The history of the New York
      African free schools, from their establishment in
      1887 to the present time, embracing a period of
      more than forty years; also a brief account of the
      successful labors of the New York Manumission So-
      ciety, with an appendix.... New York: Negro Uni-
      versities, 1969. 148 p. Originally published in
      1830.
          A history of the school, including various legal
      documents as well as accounts of classroom activ-
      ities. The appendix contains "pieces spoken at
      public examinations," prose composition, and poetry
      of the students; attempts to support the "practicabil-
      ity of imparting the useful branches of education to
      the descendants of Africans...."

856. New York African Society for Mutual Relief. Histor-
      ical sketch of the New York African Society for Mu-
      tual Relief, organized in the City of New York, 1808,
      chartered by the Legislature of the State of New
      York, 1810, now existing under the General Law of
      the State, passed 1848, the oldest society of its kind
      in the United States. Compiled by John J. Zuille.
      1892. 55 p.
          Objectives were several: to provide support for
      those members due to illness or infirmity that were
      unable to work and care for their families, the re-
      lief of widows and orphans of deceased members.
      This brief history includes the constitution, original
      charter, certificate of incorporation, reports of the
      trustees, the reports of the treasurer, lists of mem-
      bers, and other primary documents of the Society.

Puerto Ricans
(general to specific)

857. Jaffe, Abram J. Puerto Rican population of New York
City. New York: Arno, 1975. 61 p. (The Puerto
Rican experience). Papers originally published in
1954.
A series of papers designed to dispel the myths
and half truths about the Puerto Rican immigrants/
population and to identify what is known with some
degree of certainty about them: demographics, labor
force characteristics, age, education, occupational
and employment distribution, vital statistics, social
and welfare data. Now this information is most
useful in terms of historical perspective.

858. Lewis, O. La Vida; a Puerto Rican family in the
culture of poverty--San Juan and New York. New
York: Random House, 1966. 669 p.
The tape-recorded story of a Puerto Rican family living in the slums of San Juan and New York
City--the culture of poverty presented without frills
but in a humanistic manner.

859. Lopez, A. The Puerto Rican papers; notes on the re-
emergence of a nation. Indianapolis: Bobbs-Merrill,
1973. 383 p.
A narrative of the development of (New York City)
Puerto Rican nationalism, political maturity, and the
evolution of the movement's leadership. Good presentation of the hardships, life, and conditions of
Puerto Ricans in New York City.

859a. Welfare Council of New York City. Committee on
Puerto Ricans in New York City. Puerto Ricans in
New York City: the report of the Committee....
New York: Arno, 1948. 60 p. Reprinted 1975.
A description of the problems resulting from an
examination of the spiritual, economic, educational,
health, and employment needs of the Puerto Ricans,
the resources and agencies available to meet those
needs and the identification of existing lacks and in-
adequacies in those services. The recommendations
recognize that the problem is a national one--over-
crowding of cities--requiring Federal aid and a special effort on the part of service agencies to meet
these needs, i.e., Spanish-speaking personnel, etc.

860.   Puerto Rican Forum. The Puerto Rican Community
       Development Project/ Puerto Rican Forum, inc.
       New York: Arno, c. 1964. 145 p. (The Puerto
       Rican experience).
            The plight of the New York City Puerto Rican
       results from a poverty cycle that community leaders
       and concerned citizens believed can be broken by
       self-help programs and projects effectively using the
       ethnic community to provide support and to foster
       acculturation. The statistical profile, pages 26-75,
       is particularly comprehensive but historical as it
       is twenty years old.

861/74. Wakefield, D. Island in the city: the world of Spanish
       Harlem. New York: Arno, 1975. 278 p. (The
       Puerto Rican experience). First published 1959.
            The author attempts to describe life in a slum--
       the terrible, sickening things and the beautiful ones
       that happen to and are the Puerto Rican people of
       East Harlem.

SEE ALSO 782, 791.

                  SOCIAL LIFE AND CUSTOMS
                     (general to specific)

875.   Churchill, A. The upper crust; an informal history of
       New York's highest society. Englewood Cliffs, N.J.:
       Prentice-Hall, 1970. 167 p. Bibliography: p. 277-
       278.
            A lavishly illustrated (over 200 photographs, re-
       productions, prints, etc.) chronicle of Society from
       colonial New York to its death throes in the recent
       present. Informative, insightful, fortunes and foibles
       are exposed, customs, conventions, fashionable re-
       sorts, architecture, fashion, and personalities from
       Hamilton Fish to Elsa Maxwell are depicted--not al-
       ways discreetly.

876.   Berger, M. Meyer Berger's New York. Foreword by
       Brooks Atkinson. New York: Random House, 1960.
       322 p.
            This is a compilation of columns written between
       1953 to 1959 by a Pulitzer Prize winner and Times
       reporter. Arranged chronologically, the writer pre-
       sents a varied, intimate, and knowledgeable--from
       art to wine--picture of life in Manhattan.

877. Batterberry, M. and A. Batterberry. On the Town in
      New York, from 1776 to the present. New York:
      Scribner, 1973. 354 p. Bibliography: p. 335-340.
      Chronologically arranged, covers all aspects of
      activities that occur in taverns, hotels, night clubs,
      restaurants, speakeasies, and other places where
      people gather to eat and drink. A wealth of detail
      about British soldiers, entertainers, writers, gang-
      sters, stars, political figures, and even ordinary
      people; all at board and bottle.

878. Britchky, S. Seymour Britchky's new, revised guide
      to the restaurants of New York: an irreverent ap-
      praisal of the best, most interesting, most famous,
      most underrated, or worst restaurants in New York
      City. New York: Random House, 1976. 325 p.
      Concerned with three categories of restaurants--
      the best, the best known, and worthwhile but little
      known. One-or two-page descriptions of each--type
      of food, service, and atmosphere--arranged into
      sections by ethnicity, areas, or lifestyles. Has a
      variety of indexes: by type of food, by rating, loca-
      tion, open on Sunday, outdoor dining, open late, etc.
      Includes notes on reservations, prices, credit cards
      accepted.

879. Canaday, John E. The New York Times guide to dining
      out in New York. New 1976 ed. New York: Athe-
      neum, 1975. 249 p.
      Some 250 restaurants are reviewed and assigned
      a star or stars signifying a rating that is an average
      of the factors of: quality of service and food, price,
      and ambiance. Arranged alphabetically, each entry
      includes: telephone numbers, address, credit card
      information, hours open, comments about the food,
      service, atmosphere, and specialties. Sub-directo-
      ries list establishments by geographic areas, ratings,
      and by type of food.

880. Yeadon, D. and R. Lewis. The New York book of
      bars, pubs and taverns. New York: Hawthorn, 1975.
      276 p. Illus.
      Arranged by areas or distinct neighborhoods, the
      intent is to highlight the less widely known establish-
      ments. A historical description of the area or dis-
      trict precedes the reviews of each bar, pub, or tav-
      ern. Each review includes address, hours, type of

food, credit cards accepted, dress requirements,
special features, and the "Liveliest Time" plus a
brief description of the bar, its clientele, and the
owner. The section "Pubs at a Glance" is an alphabetic listing of the bars combined with symbols for
characteristics, location, and page references to the
text.

881. New York Herald Tribune. New York Herald Tribune
      presents New York, New York by Tom Wolfe (and
      others). New York: Dial, 1964. 190 p.
            Insiders--Tom Wolfe, Walter Kerr, Judith Crist,
      Emily Genauer, Maurice Dolbier, Eugenia Sheppard,
      Red Smith, and Clementine Paddleford--and their
      world--New York (big league), psychology, drama,
      theatre, television, movies, art, books, publishing,
      fashion, sports, and restaurants.

882. Botkin, Benjamin A. New York City folklore: legends,
      tall tales, anecdotes, stories, sagas, heroes and
      characters, customs, traditions, and sayings; edited,
      with an introd. New York: Random House, 1956.
      492 p.
            A compendium of amusing information of the life,
      activities, and people primarily associated with the
      lower/older end of Manhattan from colonial times
      to the present. Arranged by categories--occupations,
      ethnic groups, politics, the wealthy, nightlife, etc.,
      the sources for these stories and folklore are diaries,
      journals, memoirs, newspapers, magazines, guide-
      books, histories, travel books, emphemera, etc.

883. Talese, G. New York: a serendipiter's journey. With
      photos by Marvin Lichtner. New York: Harper,
      1961. 141 p. Illus.
            A marvelous collection of facts and figures, sto-
      ries, and observations about the little noticed and
      unexpected occupations, activities, and life styles
      that are very much a part of the ethos of New York
      City.

884. Sardi, V. and R. Gehman. Sardi's, the story of a
      famous restaurant. New York: Holt, 1953. 244 p.
      Illus.
            Sardi's, the most famous of theatrical restaurants,
      is the creation of Vincent Sardi. This is his auto-
      biography and incidentally a history of New York

theatre and theatre people during the first fifty
years of the 20th century.

885.   Harriman, M.   Blessed are the debonair; illustrated
       by Mircea Vasiliu.   New York: Rinehart, 1956.
       254 p.
            Great fun and informative, this is the story of
       Frank Chase and his famous hotel, The Algonquin--
       a theatrical hotel, home for some, and rendezvous
       for many in the arts.   Starting around 1919, its
       Round Table, which included the best known artists,
       musicians, critics, writers, playwrights, and news-
       papermen, became an artistic locus.   This account,
       written by Chase's daughter, herself a staff writer
       for Vanity Fair and the New Yorker, allows the
       reader to share some of the excitement and drama
       and fun of the stage, publishing, and social life of
       the 1920's and 1930's.

886.   Spectorsky, Auguste C.   The exurbanites.   With draw-
       ings by Robert Osborn.   Philadelphia: Lippincott,
       1955.   278 p.
            Deceptively readable, but nevertheless very infor-
       mative about a unique species--"For the exurbanite
       is a displaced New Yorker"--how he lives, where
       he works, etc.   Amusing but also seriously provides
       a perspective on a very important facet of New York
       City life.

887.   Dreiser, T.   The color of a great city; illustrations by
       C. B. Falls.   New York: Liveright, c. 1926.   287
       p.
            Dreiser finds New York larger but duller- lacking
       zest, contrast, poetry, idealism, and the dramatic
       in comparison to the first fifteen years of the cen-
       tury.   Noting that the conditions, landmarks, neigh-
       borhoods, and even the city was changing, he decided
       to collect the sketches he had made and finish others
       he had started.   The titles of his prose pictures of
       the period are descriptive: Hell's Kitchen, Christ-
       mas in the Tenements, The Rivers of the Nameless
       Dead.

888.   Fairfield, Francis E.   The clubs of New York/ Francis
       Gerry Fairfield and Sorosis, its origin and history/
       Jane C. Croly.   New York: Arno, 1975.   349, 44 p.
       Reprint of the 1873 edition of the Clubs of New

York by F. G. Fairfield and the 1886 edition of
Sorosis by J. C. Croly.
    Prefaced by an interesting essay about club life
in general in New York City, the following chapters
are devoted to the origin, history, organization,
rules, lists of members, etc., of thirteen clubs.
Concludes, using the same format, with a separate
reprint about Sorosis, a women's club started by the
women members of the New York press but excluded
from the New York Press Club.

889. Dayton, Abram C. Last days of Knickerbocker life
      in New York. Illustrated ed. New York: G. P.
      Putnam's, 1897. 386 p.
          A description of the fading influence of the Dutch
      element--customs and habits--in New York City so-
      ciety. Comprehensive in scope this history considers
      various aspects of: business, churches, hotels, pol-
      itics, horse racing, spiritualism, holidays, customs,
      theatres and actors, etc. Specific and detailed in-
      formation about persons, places, and things of 19th-
      century New York City.

890. Child, Mrs. Lydia. Letters from New York. New
      York, Boston: C. S. Francis, J. Munroe, 1843.
      276 p.
          Forty "letters," dated from 1841 to 1843, of ob-
      servations, poetry, and commentary about such di-
      verse subjects as flowers, Long Island farms, cap-
      ital punishment, Indian sarcasm, Jews, and animal
      magnetism--in short, topics of interest of that day.
      Highlights the social conditions, customs, and mores
      of the time.

        STREETS, BUILDINGS AND MONUMENTS, SQUARES
                    (alphabetical by category)

Bridges

891. McCullough, David G. The great bridge. New York:
      Simon and Schuster, 1972. 636 p. Bibliography:
      p. 603-612.
          History of one of the most famous of American
      bridges, the Brooklyn Bridge--how it was built, the
      politics involved, its impact upon the ordinary cit-
      izen, the struggles and difficulties of its builders.

It is also very much a book about the Chief Engineer
of the bridge--Washington Roebling; the man he was
and perhaps why he was that way.

892. Trachtenberg, A. Brooklyn Bridge, fact and symbol.
      New York: Oxford University, 1965. 182 p.
      A study of this famous bridge as: 1) a major
      physical construction; and 2) a symbol of the feelings
      and values associated with America's transition from
      a rural society to one that is industrial and urban.
      Extensive footnotes compensate for the lack of bib-
      liography.

893. Young, Edward M. The great bridge; the Verrazano-
      Narrows Bridge. Drawings by Lili Rethi. New
      York: Ariel, 1965. 103 p.
      An informative account, in a very readable style,
      of the problems and techniques involved in the con-
      struction of this famous bridge. Drawings supple-
      ment the text which emphasizes facts and quantitative
      statistical data. The appendix cites comparative data
      for the six largest bridges in the U.S.

Buildings and Monuments

894. Noakes, A. Cleopatra's Needles. London: H. F. &
      G. Witherby, 1962. 128 p. Bibliography: p. 117-
      123.
      Detailed history of those Egyptian obelisks, raised
      by Thotmes III, the Napoleon of ancient Egypt, and
      their transfer to London and New York City's Central
      Park.

895. James, T. The Empire State Building. New York:
      Harper & Row, 1975. 180 p. Bibliography: p. 175.
      Completed in 1931, the Empire State Building was
      the world's tallest building; becoming a major tourist
      attraction and a symbol of New York City. This ac-
      count includes human interest stories related to the
      structure, details of construction and its operation,
      a history of the site back to pre-Revolutionary ori-
      gins, the filming of King Kong, and a report of the
      day an airplane hit the building.

896. Marshall, D. Grand Central. New York, London:
      Whittlesey House, McGraw-Hill, 1946. 280 p.
      Plates, ports.

Not the largest, or the busiest, but the most famous, Grand Central Station's story is presented in
terms of the people who work there, its famous
trains, the history of its construction and unique architectural decorations, the Kissing Gallery, the star
ceiling, the history of the men who created it and
the behind the scenes procedures involving a daily
average of 600 odd trains and 178,000 passengers.

897.   Grant Monument Association, N.Y. Handbook of the
       Grant Monument Association: charter and by-laws,
       list of officers and trustees, plans adopted for the
       completion of the monument. New York: The As-
       sociation, 1929. 56 p. Illus.
          Includes photographs of unfinished monument and
       ground plans.

898.   Loth, David G. The city within a city; the romance
       of Rockefeller Center. New York: W. Morrow,
       1966. 214 p.
          From the history of its site, this detailed nar-
       rative not only includes the facts of the physical
       structure and its construction but also the philoso-
       phy, attitudes, and incidents that make Rockefeller
       Center New York City's village green.

899.   Levine, B. and Isbelle F. Story. Statue of Liberty,
       national monument, Bedloe's Island, New York.
       Washington, 1952. 35 p. Illus. (National Park
       Service historical handbook series no. 11).
          History of the idea of France's gift to the U.S.,
       biographical sketches of the men involved, history
       of Bedloe's Island, physical dimensions and struc-
       tural aspects of the statue plus details and descrip-
       tions of related facets of this national monument.

Squares

900.   Congress for Jewish Culture. Peretz year and the
       New York Peretz Square; memorable events in Jewish
       cultural life in America. New York: Congress for
       Jewish Culture, 1954. 174, 50 p. Illus., group
       ports.
          Itschok Leibush Peretz, poet and literary figure,
       was a world-renowned advocate of secular Jewish-
       ness. A Peretz year (1951-1952) was proclaimed by

a coalition of Jewish organizations. The New York
City Council dedicated a square on the East Side in
Peretz' honor. The volume contains the various
speeches, proclamations, publications, and descrip-
tions of activities in various countries relating to the
Peretz Year. Also copies and statements from the
Mayor of New York, college and university presi-
dents, Norman Thomas, etc.

901.   Laas, W.   Crossroads of the world; the story of Times
       Square.   New York: Popular Library, 1965.   159 p.
       Illus., map.
       Comprehensive history, from colonial past to the
       1970's, of Times Square--its people, personalities,
       firsts, buildings, and events--written by a New York
       magazine editor and writer. Profusely illustrated
       with photographs and drawings.

902.   Paneth, P.   Times Square, crossroads of the world.
       With exclusive photos by Boris Erwitt.   New York:
       Living Books, 1965.   114 p.   Illus.   Bibliography:
       p. 115-116.
       Some history of the square, comments about the
       entertainment world, the people in the square--their
       attitudes, habits, and conventions with digressions
       into such topics as crime, the diamond market, so-
       cial conditions, etc. Many full-page photographs
       reinforce the "New York/Times Square" style of
       comment and observation.

903.   Rogers, William G. and M. Weston.   Carnival cross-
       roads: the story of Times Square.   Drawings by
       O. Soglow.   Garden City, New York: Doubleday,
       1960.   103 p.   Bibliography: p. 181-183.
       The history, legends, myths, and idiosyncracies
       of this famous square and the people that are a part
       of it.

904.   Kertesz, A.   Washington Square, with an appreciation
       by Brendan Gill.   New York: Grossman Publishers,
       1975.   96 p.   Illus.
       An internationally known photographer's views of
       Washington Square--its skyline, roof tops, side
       streets, in all seasons; a record of its inhabitants
       and buildings, flowers, and fences. Emphasis is on
       line, patterns, and texture. No text.

Streets

905. Honce, Charles. Murder on Beekman Place. New
      York, 1951.
      With a light touch, a resident recalls the various
      murders (six) that have occurred on or near the
      street; some interesting neighbors (Billy Rose, a
      call house that served caviar and champagne) and
      the changes that time has imposed upon these two
      blocks--favorite of artists, movie producers, and
      others looking for New York with trees, flowers,
      grass, and cobblestones.

906. Kerfoot, John B. Broadway, drawings by Lester G.
      Hornby. Boston and New York: Houghton Mifflin,
      1911. 188 p.
      Anecdotes and observations of and about life, pres-
      ent and past, along one of the world's most famous
      streets. Imaginative rather than factual.

907. Jenkins, S. The greatest street in the world: the
      story of Broadway, old and new, from the Bowling
      Green to Albany ... 160 illustrations and 6 maps.
      New York and London: G. P. Putnam's, 1911. 509
      p. Bibliography: p. 460-473.
      Broadway is used as a device for presenting a
      social history of New York City and the eastern part
      of the state by narrating the circumstances and events
      that occurred on or involving a particular segment
      of the street, i.e., The Fort and Bowling Green,
      Park and Canal Street, Union Square to 42nd Street,
      continuing right out of the city and upstate through
      Westchester, Putnam, Dutchess, Columbia, and
      Rensselaer counties.

908. Davidson, B. East 100th Street. Cambridge, Mass.:
      Harvard University, 1971. 129 p. Illus.
      Stark black and white photographs of East Harlem,
      depicting the ghetto, the home of some--a life style
      alien to most of us.

909. Fifth Avenue Association, New York. Fifty years on
      Fifth, 1907-1957. New York, 1957. 162 p. Illus.
      Bibliography: p. 160.
      A history of the Avenue, the people who work,
      live, and shop there, with comments about the
      churches, banks, libraries, museums, Grand Central,

the Rockefeller Center, and other features of New
York within sight of the Avenue. With many interesting facts and details about the Avenue itself, this
narrative also includes the organization, purpose,
and influence of the Fifth Avenue Association and how
it has preserved, protected, and enhanced one of the
greatest thoroughfares in the world.

910. Brown, Henry C. Fifth Avenue old and new, 1824-
      1924. Official publication of the Fifth Avenue As-
      sociation in commemoration of the one hundredth an-
      niversary of the founding of Fifth Avenue. New York,
      1924. 126 p. Illus., maps, front., col. plates.
          Attempts to present a comprehensive history of
      the industry, art, and romance of Fifth Avenue--
      tracing its development from a rural route to a na-
      tional symbol of quality. The Fifth Avenue Associa-
      tion was formed in 1917 and a summary of its ac-
      tivities is also included. Established to carry out
      an organized effort to protect the highest standards
      of the Avenue, the Assn. promoted architectural har-
      mony, had streets improved and widened, solved
      traffic problems, and in all ways supported commer-
      cial progress and land values within the context of
      good taste. The advertisements of Avenue merchants
      and businesses that conclude this centennial history,
      themselves now over fifty years old, provide addi-
      tional information about the Avenue beyond the orig-
      inal intent of the text.

911. Maurice, Arthur B. Fifth Avenue, drawings by Allan
      G. Cram. New York: Dodd, Mead, 1918. 331 p.
      Front., plates.
          A history of the lives and life of the avenue--
      Knickerbocker associations, clubs, literary figures,
      "society," commerce, draft riots, market gardens,
      churches, etc.

912. Schecter, E. Perry Street, then and now. Illustrated
      by Carol Creutzburg. New York, 1972. 66 p. Bib-
      liography: p. 64-66.
          A historic street in historic Greenwich Village is
      described by fact, fancy, folktale, and hearsay from
      Indian days and to the present, including its modern
      urban problems of crime, drugs, poverty, etc. A
      succinct history, full of charm, with a list of nota-
      bles that lived on the street.

913.   Binzen, B.   Tenth Street.   New York: Paragraphic
       Books, c. 1968.   95 p.   Map.
       From the Hudson River to the East River, Tenth
       Street bisects Manhattan at its widest point.   This
       is a photographic essay about those twenty-one blocks
       and the spectrum of humanity that inhabits them--
       middle-class home owners, ethnic groups, Bowery
       bums, academics, gays, artists, etc.   Patchen Place
       and Tompkins Park are also commented on.

914.   Walton, Frank L.   Tomahawks to textiles; the fabulous
       story of Worth Street.   New York: Appleton-Cen-
       tury-Crofts, 1953.   177 p.   Illus., maps, 19 maps.
       Worth Street is the main street of Worth Village,
       the business district in the heart of Manhattan that
       is the textile market of the world.   This history be-
       gins with an account of the Indian village of "Man-
       hattan" that became the site of Worth Street.   In-
       cludes brief sketches of the banks, firms, pioneers,
       and merchants of Worth Street.   Includes eighteen
       historical maps and a chronological review of the
       buildings and architecture of the district.

SEE ALSO 527.

                   THEATRE AND ENTERTAINMENT
                    (general and chronological)

915.   New York Theatre critics' reviews....   v. 1- May 27,
       1940-   New York, Critics' theatre reviews, 1940-
       Weekly.
       "Theatre reviews is a complete guide and record
       of the New York stage, reprinted from New York
       Sun, New York Times, New York Herald Tribune,
       New York Post, New York Daily News, New York
       World Telegram."   Today reviews are also included
       from such publications as Time, Women's Wear
       Daily, the Christian Science Monitor, Newsweek.
       Annual index provides access to authors, producers,
       directors, set designers, composers and lyricists,
       choreographers, costume designers, and members
       of the cast of each play reviewed.   Cumulative in-
       dexes for 1940-1960, 1961-1972.   Includes reviews
       of both Broadway and off-Broadway productions.

916.   The New York Times directory of the theater.   Introd.
       by Clive Barnes.   New York: Arno, 1973.   1009 p.

A title index and a separate personal name index for every Times notice and theater story from 1920 to 1970. Also has reprints of Times articles on theater awards and listings of the theater awards: Nobel Prizes, Pulitzer Prizes, New York Drama Critics Circle Awards, Antoinette Perry (Tony) Awards and Obie (Off-Broadway) Awards. This is a reprint of volumes 9 and 10 (Appendix and Index) of the 10-volume set of New York Times Theater Reviews (Arno Press), reprinting all reviews and stories, 1920-1970.

History

917.   Henderson, Mary C. The city and the theatre; New York playhouses from Bowling Green to Times Square. Clifton, N.J.: J. T. White, 1973. 323 p. Bibliography: p. 294-306.
        Limited to Manhattan and its historical theatrical districts, the author's premise is that the theatre has a particular place in that entity as the modern city, and the Theatre/theatrical district adapts, adopts, moves, and contracts as the city responds to its own pressures, needs, and demands. The shift of the New York theatrical district is traced during the city's urbanization. Each chapter has a dual focus: a section on the background of the city, followed by a discussion of theatres and theatrical districts of the time period being considered--pre 1798 to after 1900. Final chapter has photographs of Times Square theatres with name of architect, date and name of opening production, brief historical profiles.

918.   Odell, George C. D. Annals of the New York stage. New York: Columbia University, 1927. 14 v. Front., plates, ports., map, facsims.
        Utilizes primary sources, i.e., account books, autobiographies, diaries, letters, newspapers, pamphlets, and playbills to reconstruct the successive eras of theater life in the city. Theater is broadly defined to include the variety of entertainments from the circus and minstrels to opera and concerts. Covers the period from amusements in the colonies up to 1894. Each volume has its own index.

919.   Ireland, Joseph N.   Records of the New York stage
       from 1750 to 1860. New York: B. Blom, 1966. 2
       v. "First published New York, 1866."
          Very detailed chronicle of the performance (dra-
       mas, operas, etc.) presented at the various theaters
       --by year and day. Includes names of cast mem-
       bers, actors' biographical data, and comments and
       observations concerning audience reactions to the en-
       tertainments.

920.   Brown, Thomas A.   A history of New York stage from
       the first performance in 1732 to 1901. New York:
       B. Blom, 1964. 3 v.
          First published in 1903. This history begins
       eighteen years before Ireland's Records ... and ends
       forty-one years after they finished. Chronologically
       arranged, presents detailed accounts of performances,
       at the various theaters, audience reactions, circum-
       stances of presentation, biographical data, etc.

Theatres
(chronological)

921.   Steinberg, Mollie B.   The history of the Fourteenth
       Street Theatre.   New York: Dial, 1931. 105 p.
          Emphasis upon the plays and actors that made
       this theatre famous between 1866 and 1901. In 1926
       it was reopened by Eva le Gallienne as the Civic
       Repertory Theatre and this brief account concludes
       with a survey of its first five years. A chart lists
       all plays and number of performances for that peri-
       od of time.

922.   Le Gallienne, E.   At 33.   New York, Toronto: Long-
       mans, Green, 1934. 262 p.   Front., plates, ports.,
       facsims.
          Autobiography of the famous actress that created
       the Civic Repertory Theatre.

923.   Spitzer, M.   The Palace.   With an introd. by Brooks
       Atkinson.   New York: Atheneum, 1969. 267 p.
       Illus., ports.
          This theatre, at one time, represented the best
       of vaudeville, the pinnacle of success for such per-
       formers as Sarah Bernhardt, Ed Wynn, Sophie Tuck-
       er, Fanny Brice, Will Rogers, W. C. Fields, Ethel

Barrymore, Judy Garland, Jerry Lewis, and Harry
Belafonte, among others. This is an intimate history, sometimes eyewitness account, of this theatre's
beginnings in 1913, its international fame, the near
oblivion and its restoration to success in 1966. The
writer, once employed on the publicity staff of the
Palace and since then actively working as a screen-
writer, novelist, and script writer for radio and tel-
evision, is particularly qualified to write this story.

924. Crowley, Alice L. The neighborhood playhouse; leaves
from a theatre scrapbook. New York: Theatre Arts,
1959. 266 p. Illus. "Productions of the Neighborhood Playhouse." 1912-1926.
The Provincetown Theatre, the Washington Square
Players, and the Neighborhood Playhouse each contributed uniquely to the renaissance of the American
theatre at the start of the century. This history,
written by one of the founders of the latter, describes its beginnings, the development of its special contributions, and the reasons for its closing
in 1927, emphasizing not details of dates, people,
or places but the values that allowed all to partici-
pate in a "unified creative experience."

925. The living book of the Living Theatre. With an introductory essay by Richard Schechner. Greenwich,
Conn.: New York Graphic Society (1971). 1 v.
Brief history and explanation of the founding and
development of this avant-garde theatre group that
has evolved into an experiment in collaborative cre-
ativity and nomadic communal living--one that uses
theatre to express "radical" social, moral, and political positions. Photographs, of all aspects of this
group's life, constitute most of the book; with some
text of the Living Theatre's philosophy, some personal details, some poetry.
Additional information provided by:

Mantegna, G. We, the Living Theatre; a pictorial documentation by ... of the life and the pilgrimage of
the Living Theatre in Europe and in the U.S....
Introduced by a panel discussion on Theatre as revolution, co-ordinated by Aldo Rostagno with the participation of Julian Beck and Judith Malina. New
York: Ballantine, 1970. 240 p. Extensive photographs of scenes from Living Theatre productions,

group living, and political activity. Most illustrations have some text--usually an excerpt (unflatter-
ing) from a review. Includes an extensive statement
of Julian Beck and Judith Malina's artistic, economic,
political, and social philosophy.

Neff, R. The Living Theatre: USA. Indianapolis:
Bobbs-Merrill, 1970. 254 p. Bibliography: p. 245.
A chronology of the Living Theatre's American tour,
September, 1968-March, 1969. Considering this
group's unconventional collective life style and its
revolutionary political and social philosophies, this
presentation is reasonable and balanced.

Directors

926. Little, Stuart W. Enter Joseph Papp; in search of a
new American theater. New York: Coward, McCann
& Geoghegan, 1974. 320 p.
While not a biography, this is a very readable
explanation of how Papp--administratively, financially, and artistically--works and functions within and
for the New York Shakespeare Festival.

927. Strasberg, L. Strasberg at the Actors Studio: tape
recorded sessions. Edited by Robert H. Hetlman.
New York: Viking, 1965. 428 p.
Based upon taped sessions, made since 1956, at
the Actors Studio, the materials, with some exceptions, are taken from the Actors Unit and are arranged into three sections: 1) the nature, function
of the Studio, and the relationships of the actor to
it; 2) the actor's work on himself (his art, training,
will, discipline, problems, etc.); and 3) the actor
and other people--directors, audience, commercial
theatre, world theatre. Appendices list: life-time
members, projects presented, productions, materials used.

Dance

928. Reynolds, N. Repertory in review: 40 years of the
New York City Ballet ... with an introduction by
Lincoln Kirstein. New York: Dial, 1977. 358 p.
"Sources": p. 339-340; Notes: p. 341-349.

A chronicle of all works, in full company, performed by the New York City Ballet and its predecessor companies (1936-1976), listing creators in: choreography, music, costume, decor, lighting, with premier dates and significant subsequent castings followed by excerpts of reviews from newspapers and magazines. Includes a sampling of European reviews. Additional data and information obtained from interviews with choreographers and dancers.

929. Kirstein, L. The New York City Ballet. Photos. by George Platt-Lynes and Martha Swope. New York: Knopf, 1973. 261 p. Illus. "List of premiere performances": p. 248-256.
A history in "diary" form of the building of a company, school, and theatre for the period 1912 to 1973.

930. Owen, Walter E. Ballerinas of the New York City Ballet. With an introd. by Charles Boultenhouse. New York: Dance Mart, 1953. 38 p.
Photographs of Maria Tallchief, Nora Kaye, Janet Reed, Diana Adams, Patricia Wilde, Marie-Jeanne, Yvonne Mounsey in their various roles.

Radio

931. Sanger, Elliott M. Rebel in radio; the story of WQXR. New York: Hastings House, 1973. 190 p. Illus.
Written by one of the original owners, this is a chronicle of the creation of a unique radio station--one solely devoted to good music and tasteful commercials--its sale to the New York Times, the development of its network of stations across New York State from Poughkeepsie north to Ogdensburg and west to Niagara Falls.

932. Nobel, M. The Municipal Broadcasting System, its history, organization, and activities. New York: 1953. 76 ℓ. Thesis in Public Administration, City College of New York, School of Business and Civic Administration. Bibliography: p. 65-76.
History of the System (1934-1952), the impact of various mayors (Hylan, Walker, LaGuardia, O'Dwyer, and Impellitteri), structure and activities of the System and its influence.

SEE ALSO 152, 161-165, 781.

TRANSPORTATION
(general to specific)

933. Regional Plan Association, New York. Transportation
     and economic opportunity. A report to the Trans-
     portation Administration of the City of New York.
     New York, 1973. 206 p. "Selected Bibliography":
     p. 204-206.
        A region-wide transportation and economic analy-
     sis including a survey of 2,500 low-income house-
     holds focusing upon the impact of reduced bus fares,
     additional bus routes, free transfers, the need for
     new subways, and new policies concerning the auto-
     mobile needs of the low-income commuter.

934. Doig, Jameson W. Metropolitan transportation politics
     and the New York region. New York: Columbia Uni-
     versity, 1966. 327 p. Map. (Metropolitan politics
     series, no. 6).
        A study and analysis of metropolitan politics by
     focusing upon one major issue--transportation. It
     explores the actions, motives, and perspectives of
     the region's various private and public groups--local
     officials, federal agencies, private interests, regional
     authorities, etc. and the nature of political frag-
     mentation with its counter balance of political sub-
     systems. Review of New York City's regional trans-
     portation system is followed by an examination of the
     policies developed in the 1950's and some of the new
     approaches devised in the 1960's.

935. Chinitz, B. Freight and the metropolis; the impact of
     America's transport revolution on the New York re-
     gion. Cambridge: Harvard University, 1960. 211 p.
     (New York metropolitan region study 6).
        Concerned with two types of freight: 1) the kind
     that is transshipped in foreign trade and 2) the kind
     that is processed in the New York Metropolitan ar-
     ea's factories. Author seeks to estimate impact
     freight transportation will have on that area's growth
     and employment future by studying foreign trade
     freight and the condition of the region's freight trans-
     portation system as it affects the location and per-
     formance of other industries.

936. Cudahy, Brian J. Rails under the mighty Hudson: the story of the Hudson Tubes, the Pennsy tunnels and Manhattan Transfer. Brattleboro, Vt.: S. Greene, 1975. 78 p. (Shortline RR series).
Presents a century of specialized railroad history --a complex subject clearly written and supplemented by maps, plans, and many photographs. The economic, social, personal, and literary aspects of the projects are noted in relation to the technical and financial details of the achievement. The epilogue is devoted to the history and details of Penn Station.

937. Ornati, Oscar A. Transportation needs of the poor, a case study of New York City (by) Oscar A. Ornati, with assistance from James A. Whittaker and Richard Solomon. New York: Praeger, 1969. 127 p. Illus., maps. (Praeger Special studies in U.S. economic and social development). Bibliography: p. 127.
Part of a project to study the relationship between job markets and poverty in New York City, the factors of travel-to-work as barrier to employment were studied in depth. Due to the poor's patterns of job search and employment there was an awareness of the importance to reduce the large numbers of travel-to-work inconveniences. Chapters are devoted to how the poor travel to work, the use they make of the New York City transportation system; specific recommendations are made.

938. Fischler, S. Uptown, downtown: a trip through time on New York's subways; research editor, Dave Rubenstein; drawings by Ray Judd. New York: Hawthorn, 1976. 271 p. Illus. Index: p. 263-271.
A compendium of information: brief history of early subways and elevateds, the construction of New York City's systems, disasters, details of operations, profiles of subway employees, people associated with subways (antique dealers, historians, and others of less conventional bent), art, graffiti, movie making, etc. The appendices include: opening dates of subway lines, chronology of elevateds. Many excellent and historical photographs.

939. Walker, James B. Fifty years of rapid transit, 1864-1917. New York: Arno, 1970. 291 p. (The Rise of urban America). Reprint of the 1918 ed.

Includes the romance and drama of legislative bat-
tles, financial empires, and politic infighting concerning rapid transit in New York City. Considerable details about the conception and construction of
the surface transportation, the elevated railroad, the
subways, and the tunnel under Broadway. Also
about the people involved--those who dreamed, failed,
succeeded, died poor or rich.

940. McGinley, James J. Labor relations in the New York
rapid transit systems, 1904-1944. New York: King's
Crown Press, 1949. 635 p. Tables. "Selected
Bibliography": p. 603-623.
A detailed history of the employee-employer relationship, in this particular case, one characterized
by a lack of policy, labor discontent, and the failure
of government. This study is supported by over 100
pages of tables of data on all aspects of rapid transit operations--cars, employees, wages, earnings,
casualties, etc.

941. Daley, R. The world beneath the city. Philadelphia:
Lippincott, 1959. 223 p.
A delightful history of the overlapping systems of
electrical wires, sewers, waterlines, gas lines, and
subways that serve New York City and of the men
who created them, worked on them, and in other
ways involved their lives in these utilities.

WATER

942. New York (City). Board of Water Supply. 1,820,000,000
gallons per day; 50th anniversary of the Board of
Water Supply. New York, 1955. 38 p.
The Board was created in 1905; this account provided the details of the various projects that in 1955
supplied the City with 1,200,000,000 gallons of fresh
water daily.

943. New York (City). Board of Water Supply. The water
supply of the City of New York; a volume descriptive
of its sources, storage reservoirs, and transportation, with certain construction features of the Catskill, Delaware, and interconnected water supply systems. New York: 1950, 115 p.
Includes the history and organization of the Board
of Water Supply with an account of the planning and

construction of the Catskill and Delaware systems plus details of those projects--public relations, police protection, labor camps, etc.

944. Weidner, Charles H. Water for a city; a history of New York City's problem from the beginning to the Delaware River system. New Brunswick, N.J.: Rutgers University, 1974. 339 p. Illus. "References": p. 315-322.

A historical survey of New York City's problem of a water supply that is concluded by the narrative of the construction of the Delaware River system in the 1950's. Very detailed concerning all aspects of the problem: technical, political, and economic.

SEE ALSO 938, 941.

AUTHOR INDEX

(including editors, illustrators, corporate bodies, etc.)

SUBJECT INDEX